GEOFFREY CHAUCER
An Introduction to his Narrative Poetry

This book serves both as a lucid introduction to Chaucer's narrative poetry (*The Book of the Duchess, The Parliament of Fowls, The House of Fame, Troilus and Criseyde, The Legend of Good Women* and *The Canterbury Tales*) for those tackling it afresh and as an intelligent examination of the themes and techniques employed by Chaucer in these poems, taking comprehensive account of other critical readings and producing its own distinctive and highly readable interpretations, which will interest students who already have a sense of the difficulties the narratives pose.

Professor Mehl's starting-point is a consideration of Chaucer's real-life identity, and of the way in which it may or may not be of relevance to our reading of the poems. He points out the dangers of reading into Chaucer's narratives either too autobiographical or too detached an account of life, and this leads to discussions of the relationship between the author and narrator in general, and of that between the constraints of tradition and their enrichment by the poet's original and subtle imagination. He pays attention to another relationship – that of the author or narrator to the listener/reader – and shows how an ambiguous, teasing and occasionally provocative dialogue between the narrator and his audience lies at the heart of nearly all the narrative poems and discourages clear-cut or definite interpretation. This applies to the early love-visions as well as to *Troilus and Criseyde*, where the poet seems to rely more than ever on the intelligent and open-minded response of an attentive audience, and to *The Canterbury Tales*. Many traditional critical problems lose their urgency if this is recognized, and it seems more profitable for the critic to help the reader participate in the debate the poems want to provoke than to offer final pronouncements on the poet's intention.

Dieter Mehl's book first appeared in German in 1973. This is the author's own translation, and he has revised the text, updated the bibliography and added to his original version a chapter on *The Legend of Good Women*, a poem which he considers in the light of Chaucer's attitude to his own art and other critical perspectives. In English no less than in his native language, Professor Mehl's style combines to an unusual degree the discrimination, authority and accessibility which are the marks of a first-rate literary critic. The book should be indispensable to all students of Chaucer.

GEOFFREY CHAUCER

An Introduction to his Narrative Poetry

DIETER MEHL

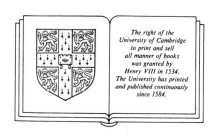

The right of the
University of Cambridge
to print and sell
all manner of books
was granted by
Henry VIII in 1534.
The University has printed
and published continuously
since 1584.

CAMBRIDGE UNIVERSITY PRESS

Cambridge
London   New York   New Rochelle
Melbourne   Sydney

Published by the Press Syndicate of the University of Cambridge
The Pitt Building, Trumpington Street, Cambridge CB2 1RP
32 East 57th Street, New York, NY 10022, USA
10 Stamford Road, Oakleigh, Melbourne 3166, Australia

Originally published in German as *Geoffrey Chaucer. Eine Einführung in seine erzählenden Dichtungen* by Erich Schmidt Verlag Gmbh, 1973 and ©Erich Schmidt Verlag Gmbh, 1973

English translation © Cambridge University Press 1986

First published in English by Cambridge University Press 1986 as
Geoffrey Chaucer. An Introduction to his Narrative Poetry

Printed in Great Britain at
the University Press, Cambridge

British Library cataloguing in publication data
Mehl, Dieter
Geoffrey Chaucer; an introduction to his
narrative poetry.
1. Chaucer, Geoffrey—Criticism and interpretation
I. Title   II. Geoffrey Chaucer. *English*
821'.1   PR1924

Library of Congress cataloguing in publication data
Mehl, Dieter.
Geoffrey Chaucer, an introduction to his narrative
poetry.
"A revised and expanded translation ... Geoffrey
Chaucer, ein Einführung in seine erzählenden Dichtungen,
which was published in 1973"—Pref.
Bibliography: p.
1. Chaucer, Geoffrey, d. 1400—Criticism and
interpretation. 2. Narrative poetry, English—History
and criticism. 3. Narration (Rhetoric) I. Title.
PR1933.N27M43   1986   821'.1   86–6794

ISBN 0 521 26839 7 hard covers
ISBN 0 521 31888 2 paperback

Contents

Preface

THIS BOOK IS A REVISED AND EXPANDED TRANSLATION OF MY
Geoffrey Chaucer. Eine Einführung in seine erzählenden Dichtungen,
which was published in 1973. I have tried to take note of the great
volume of Chaucer criticism that has appeared since then, but to discuss
it all and to modify my text accordingly would have meant rewriting the
book completely. I have added a chapter on *The Legend of Good
Women*, an inexcusable omission in the German version, noted by at
least one reviewer. In a way, however, this is still very much a book of the
early seventies, with its then perhaps more necessary insistence on the
role of the reader's cooperation and the conversational character of
Chaucer's poetry.

Although the book calls itself an introduction, it is not meant as a
complete guide to all the facts or as a full survey of all the poems and the
problems of interpretation. It is frankly selective in its approach, its aim
being above all to invite the reader to enter into a critical dialogue with
the text and thus to come to a fuller appreciation and enjoyment of
Chaucer's immensely versatile and rich narrative art. No critical
summary can possibly replace the personal encounter with the text, and
the book was chiefly written to encourage such an encounter and to give
some help towards it. I am fully aware that I have ignored many
important and rewarding aspects of Chaucer's art, but it seemed to me
more useful to single out some particularly characteristic points and
discuss them at length. In the notes I have provided enough material, I
hope, to restore the balance and to enable the reader to make use of the
full range of Chaucer criticism. The annotated bibliography at the end is
meant to serve the same purpose.

Most of the German text was written during a very happy and
stimulating sabbatical term at Cambridge (1971–2), where I enjoyed not
only the generous hospitality of Clare Hall as a visiting fellow, but above
all the invaluable company and invigorating conversation of many
colleagues who were free with their advice and (often unintentional)

scholarly contributions. I should like to single out with particular gratitude Ursula and Peter Dronke, Derek Brewer, Peter Johnson, Jill Mann and Michael Lapidge.

For the English version I have profited greatly from regular discussions with a group of medievalist colleagues. They helped me especially to a better understanding of *The Legend of Good Women* – particularly Dr Kurt Gamerschlag and Dr Götz Schmitz. The thorough and reliable assistance of several graduate students has made my work much easier: Burkhard W. Franke compiled a very useful working bibliography, Jochen Meibrink gave substantial help with translation, manuscript and index, and Christa Jansohn did a great deal of checking and correcting. None of them, of course, is in the least responsible for any of the book's weaknesses.

D.M.

Bonn 1985

1

Chaucer in his time

THERE ARE FEW POETS OF THE MIDDLE AGES WHOSE LIVES AND public careers are as copiously documented as Chaucer's. Even Shakespeare's biography, though much better attested than is often realized, is, by comparison, in many ways quite a shadowy affair. As for Chaucer, the remarkable fact is that we have some 500 different documents in which he is mentioned by name or which have some direct bearing on his career. The collection of *Life-Records*, published after many years of dedicated team-work, presents a wealth of facts that might well arouse the envy of biographers of less well-documented authors.[1] The documents in the collection cover a period of almost half a century, and they illuminate the wide range of aspects of a busy and publicly appreciated life. There is thus no doubt whatsoever about the identity of this poet.

Nevertheless, those interested in the personality behind Chaucer's poetry will not easily accept this impressive collection of historical records as particularly enlightening; in fact, the central question with regard to Chaucer's biography is how to bridge the gap between two separate individuals apparently existing side by side: there is the citizen, diplomat and court official restored to life by all the records, and there is the author and storyteller speaking to us from the text. Plenty of imagination and misdirected critical effort have been exhausted in the attempt to reconstruct the missing link between these two figures; but it remains more honest to admit that there is little or nothing to support such speculations. The danger in all such cases is of arguing in a circle, of discovering autobiographical traits in poetry by assuming a direct impact of personal experience on poetry. Any account of Chaucer's life has to start with the plain fact that of all the historical records virtually none refers in any way to Chaucer's literary activity, and that on the other hand his poetry offers very little reliable information about the manner in which he spent his life. This is by no means surprising: Chaucer's literary career had no direct bearing on his official duties, so that there was little reason why it should be mentioned in the documents; and whatever the poet himself discloses about his private life always depends on the context of the work in hand, which can thus hardly claim the authority and precision of a legal document. It is tempting, therefore, to interpret Chaucer's poetry disregarding the historically recorded person altogether, as is in fact the practice of many critical studies.

The *Life-Records*, however, do not only give us a particularly precise picture of the background to Chaucer's poetry and that of his contemporaries; they also raise the perennial but still fruitful question of the relationship between poetry and its creator, of the autobiographical significance of literature and its individual character. This explains the continuing interest in authors' biographies in spite of all variations and about-faces in critical method.

Chaucer's life is in many ways representative of the particular historical situation and the opportunities for gifted men during the second half of the fourteenth century. He came from a class that seems to have been increasingly influential in the economic and political life of the country, his father being a prosperous wine merchant and thus responsible for the distribution of the most important item in the list of imported goods. The wine trade with France was not only a very significant branch of the economy at that time, but was also of considerable political importance; its repercussions as well as its vulnerability were felt especially during the Hundred Years War. It appears from the documents that the Chaucers were quite a well-to-do family; they owned a sizeable house by the standards of the time, with a good wine cellar, in the City of London.

The wine trade must have brought Chaucer's father into frequent contact with the royal court. This explains why we meet Geoffrey Chaucer as page in the household of the Duke of Ulster, one of King Edward III's sons, when he was still quite young. The earliest documents specify presents to the young Chaucer as well as a contribution from the King towards a ransom to free him from French captivity. Chaucer, it appears, was an active participant in Edward's French campaigns around 1360. Later he undertook several diplomatic missions in the King's service, at first as a junior member of larger delegations, then in a more responsible position as one of the leaders of the negotiations. We do not know much about the nature of these missions; presumably they were mostly concerned with England's continental trade. It is not only these activities that suggest that Chaucer enjoyed the King's confidence and esteem; this is also confirmed by other favours, especially the promise of a regular life annuity for services rendered. Such annuities were not exceptional, but they were usually the reward for very long services and were rarely granted after so comparatively short a time.

2

What is even more remarkable than the mere promise of such financial benefits is the fact that they were actually paid out over a period of many years. As the documents from the period show, this was not at all the rule, which allows the conclusion that Chaucer must have employed diplomatic skill and, probably, an intimate knowledge of the royal bureaucracy to secure these regular payments; they are recorded with almost uninterrupted continuity from 1367 nearly up to the time of the poet's death (1400), and they were explicitly confirmed by Edward's successors, Richard II and Henry IV, at their respective accessions, whereas for many of Chaucer's contemporaries the change of government was far more disruptive.

Among Chaucer's missions abroad, his journey to Genoa and Florence (1372/3) has naturally attracted the particular interest of literary historians. It has been compared to Goethe's journey to Italy,[2] but the known historical facts give little evidence to justify such a comparison. It was most probably a rather mundane trip with a very practical economic purpose. What it may have meant for Chaucer's development as a writer, or what famous fellow-poets he may have met in Italy, will always remain matters of creative guesswork. Some of these guesses are more likely to have some support from actual fact than others, but there is always a danger of presupposing a too-simple relationship between a poet's biography and his literary production. There is no historical warrant for assuming that Chaucer saw an organic correspondence between his life and his poetry in the way Goethe or the Romantics did.

It is, however, certain from Chaucer's poetry that he was deeply impressed and influenced by the achievement of the three great Italian poets of the trecento, and his sojourn in Florence must have brought him into contact, if not with the poets themselves, at least with some of their admirers and with texts of their works, and it must have given him a very lively idea of their cultural impact. This is largely speculation, of course; what we do know is that Anglo-Italian relations in the late fourteenth century were varied and substantial. It is quite possible, and indeed very likely, that Chaucer met Italian tradesmen in London and learnt from them about their country and their language.[3]

Between 1367, when Chaucer was a member of the royal household, and the year of his death he never seems to have lost contact with the court, even though several of his appointments made him move about a great deal and repeatedly forced him to leave the immediate vicinity of London.

Another important and as yet rather mysterious chapter of Chaucer's biography concerns his relationship with John of Gaunt, one of the most powerful political figures of the second half of the fourteenth century.

From him, too, Chaucer received a life pension (1374). The relevant document in this context specifically refers to Chaucer's wife, who was in John of Gaunt's service at the time and continued as a member of his household for years after her marriage. Marks of the duke's favour towards her are documented until shortly before her death – probably about 1387. And there was yet another relationship between the two families. Chaucer's wife, Philippa, was in all probability the sister of Katharine Swynford, who was for many years John of Gaunt's mistress and later became his (third) wife. One is tempted to weave all these fragments of information into a colourful biographical novel,[4] but suffice it to observe that there were indeed close personal connections between Chaucer and the royal family. Apart from that it is surely not too speculative to conclude that through the Duke of Lancaster and his many connections as a military leader, administrator, politician and patron of the arts Chaucer must have been in a favourable position for meeting a fair number of interesting contemporaries from very different walks of life. We are on much less firm ground when we ask whether John of Gaunt was anything like a personal patron to Chaucer with a direct influence on his poetry. One of the clearest indications to that effect is the fact that, according to an old and by no means improbable tradition, Chaucer wrote the first of his longer poems, *The Book of the Duchess*, as a consolation for the Duke of Lancaster on the death of his wife Blanche in 1369. Such an act of personal homage would indicate a rather personal and friendly relationship, although there is no irrefutable proof that such a relationship existed and most allusions to John of Gaunt which scholars have from time to time discovered in Chaucer's writings are more or less inconclusive. Even this personal relationship does more to contribute to our knowledge of the general background of Chaucer's literary career than to make accessible a concrete aspect of his biography.

One of the most important among Chaucer's various public offices was that of Controller of Customs in the Port of London, a post which he held for twelve years, from 1374 to 1386. This mainly concerned the duties on the export of wool which were among the most significant royal revenues. These duties were fixed and listed on the basis of complicated calculations, so that Chaucer's almost continual presence was indispensable. It was only under exceptional circumstances, as when the King needed Chaucer for some other urgent business, that a substitute could be put in his place by special decree. The administration of the customs was obviously a very demanding job, requiring administrative skill and personal integrity. From all the available evidence it is clear that the office was given only to particularly respected citizens and for limited periods. It is surely proof of the amount of confidence Chaucer enjoyed that he was entrusted with this office for a longer period than anyone before or after him, between 1351 and 1391 (with one exception).

During his employment at the Port of London Chaucer occupied a house above one of the London city gates (Aldgate). Through this gate the rebel peasants entered the city in 1381; apart from that it was an extremely busy thoroughfare, guarded at times like a fortress. Again, it is tempting to speculate as to what opportunities the poet may have had to observe the life of his time at first hand.

Chaucer's subsequent employments, too, are proof of his being ranked as one of the most trusted members of his class. Thus, he held the office of Justice of the Peace from 1385 to 1389, a post habitually given only to substantial landowners, members of the gentry or lawyers. It is difficult to be sure which of his qualifications made him suitable for this office. Possibly it was his wide knowledge of places and people, acquired at the Port of London and during his missions abroad. And it was probably for similar reasons that he was elected into Parliament in 1386 as Knight of the Shire for Kent. This Parliament, during its stormy two-month session, engaged in several skirmishes with the King, on issues – such as life appointments for customs controllers – which must have concerned Chaucer personally.

Another job, as many-sided as it must have been wearing, was given to Chaucer in 1389 when he was appointed Clerk of the King's Works. It included responsibility for the preservation and restoration of a number of royal palaces, bridges and parks, later even of St George's Chapel in Windsor. Among his duties were the hiring, overseeing and paying of workmen, the provision and transport of building material, and the keeping of exact accounts. This office, too, was reserved for men who enjoyed the King's particular confidence; as a rule only members of the clergy were chosen. There is no document to tell us why Chaucer resigned this post after about two years. It may have something to do with the fact that once, when he was on his way to pay some workmen, he was waylaid and robbed. At least this seems to me more plausible than the suggestion, made by some earlier biographers, that he wanted to have more time for his literary activities.

Another alleged employment, that of Overseer of the King's Forests in Somerset during the 1390s, is less well documented; in fact there are no contemporary records to prove it, although it would be perfectly compatible with what we otherwise know about Chaucer.

There is a rather intriguing and at the same time mysterious document which concerns Chaucer's lease of a house in the immediate vicinity and possession of Westminster Abbey. It is difficult to decide whether this necessarily implies a direct connection between Chaucer and the monks of the Abbey. Other leaseholders about whom we know were mostly experienced servants of the court. The details of the contract, signed on 24 December 1399, have given rise to colourful speculations – especially the duration of the lease given as fifty-three years. It is unparalleled by any similar document of the period. What makes it particularly teasing is the fact that Chaucer occupied the house for less than a year – up to his death in 1400. We do not know the exact date of the poet's birth, which must be between 1340 and 1345, so that we cannot exclude the possibility that the number of fifty-three has something to do with Chaucer's age at the time of the signing of the contract. Against the theory that Chaucer indulged in a little joke, registering his reluctance to face the approach of death, I find it more convincing to assume that this contract was meant as a symbolic expression of a turning-point having been reached midway in the poet's life, of a pious hope for a second half to atone by seclusion for the first half spent in sinful dissipation. This would align the contract with the famous 'Retraction' at the end of *The Canterbury Tales*, and it would confirm the conviction of some earlier biographers that Chaucer, near the end of his life, experienced a kind of conversion to a more strictly religious attitude. Whether this meant that he actually entered the order it is impossible to say. Like many other details in our picture of the poet's life and personality, this last phase remains open to speculation.[5]

The same applies to all attempts to assemble, with the help of documented facts, a portrait of Geoffrey Chaucer the court official and his character. The number of offices he held and the apparent consistency of his friendly relations with the court allow us at least to infer that he had diplomatic skill, as well as a rich fund of experience and a knowledge of human affairs and of diverse trades, walks of life and environments. But beyond this rather general characterization, Chaucer the man is no longer within our historical grasp. This may leave our curiosity unsatisfied, but it need not deprive us of a closer understanding of his poetry. Often enough, information which the reader only too readily extracts from biographical facts turns out to be rather illusory and, in the last resort, of little substance.

Is it not illuminating enough to realize that this busy and trusted civil servant became at the same time the most original, the most influential and perhaps the most widely read poet of his age? This alone would suffice to demonstrate that the most vital literary impulses were no longer to be expected from the clergy or the nobility, but that there was a new and growing class of potential authors and readers whose economic importance was beginning to be balanced by its contributions to the arts and to letters. At the same time, Chaucer's social position may partly account for the characteristic attitude towards courtly conventions and values that we find again and again in his works – an attitude shaped by intimate familiarity, respect, detached irony and the modesty of the outsider. But this is already beyond the range of my introductory chapter, which was to have been confined to documentary evidence and solid biographical fact. It serves, however, to indicate that there is no such thing as the perfect separation of Chaucer the court official and Chaucer the poet. The correlation between these two personalities is certainly more complicated than some earlier critics, who simply took everything the poet said as autobiographical truth, would have it; on the other hand, it is possible to draw certain cautious conclusions regarding the poet's attitude towards his audience and the social climate in which poetry such as his could flourish and be appreciated.[6]

2

The narrator and his audience

THE DOCUMENTS REFERRING TO CHAUCER BY NAME GIVE US THE portrait of a man highly esteemed and trusted at the royal court, and busy in a variety of public affairs. His literary interests, however, are not mentioned at all.

The personality which the reader encounters in Chaucer's poetry is a completely different one, in many ways more substantial and individual. This is not just a matter of certain human qualities and opinions, such as we can gather indirectly from the poems – a somewhat dangerous undertaking, as in almost any period of literary history – but of Chaucer the narrator introducing himself, with a frankness and consistency rare in English medieval literature, as an author who is eager to establish a spontaneous contact with his audience, and at the same time bringing us face to face with a man of most impressive individuality. This aspect of Chaucer's authorship has sparked off a lengthy discussion among critics, sometimes rather unnecessary but often illuminating, and mainly concerned with the question of how far Chaucer reveals his true face in his poetry, or of how far he tries to disguise it. The question, of course, arises in all our reading of medieval literature; it is a question that cannot be evaded by anyone who wants to describe the effect of Chaucer's poetry on its readers with any claim to precision. At the same time, this is a problem which is more urgent to the professional critic, whose approach to the texts is complicated by his familiarity with theoretical concepts and techniques of analysis, than to the 'ordinary' reader, and which thus often seems more complicated in criticism than in the actual experience of most readers.

Both the 'layman' and the sophisticated reader will be at once impressed by the distinctly personal and immediate voice of the narrator in almost any Chaucerian poem. There is no doubt that Chaucer discovered and refined an artistic device, which we meet again and again in many different forms in narrative literature from the Middle Ages to the present and which seems above all to be an expression of the sociable nature of poetry and storytelling. We find this personal voice of the author in works as different from each other as *Paradise Lost, Tristram Shandy* and the *Pickwick Papers*; of all of them, as of Chaucer's poems, we may say, as Laurence Sterne says of his novel: 'Writing, when properly managed (as you may be sure I think mine is) is but a different name for conversation' (*Tristram Shandy*, II, 11).

When the partner in this kind of conversation turns out to be as lively and sociable a personality as Chaucer, it is only natural that we should form the impression of a very distinctive character, and it is well worth reading the poems with this aspect in mind.

Even at a first reading we will find certain highly individual traits recurring in all the major works and may sense very soon that they are all created and informed by the same personality; we recognize the same voice from one poem to the next. It is almost like meeting an old acquaintance and this is obviously one of the intended effects.

As early as in *The Book of the Duchess*, which may have been the first of Chaucer's more ambitious poems, the poet portrays himself as a man who views the conventions and the symptoms of courtly love with sympathetic detachment. He suffers with the knight, so deeply shaken by the loss of his beloved, who tells him the story of his woe in love. Yet the poet is anxious to avoid giving the impression that he himself has any personal experience or expertise in these matters. It is by the man's suffering alone that he is moved to compassion, but the more specific reasons behind it are beyond the limits of his experience, and he therefore does not presume to offer any opinion.

This particular form of modesty in the face of such an important subject recurs in the other early poems, but in *Troilus and Criseyde* it is most markedly pronounced. The whole poem is affected by this deliberately pointed discrepancy between the intensity of the lovers' experience and the inexperience, emphasized time and again, of the narrator, who therefore appeals to those members of his audience more versed in matters of courtly love, asking for their cooperation where his own knowledge fails him. From the very beginning Chaucer presents himself as a man whose diligent perusal of books has resulted in a kind of theoretical knowledge of the world, and yet when it comes to actual experience he can but keenly observe the emotions of the actors with distanced admiration and a certain amount of scepticism. There is no question about the impossibility of his actively serving in the cause of love, and this effects a perceptible detachment of the author with regard to his own poetry, from which, as it were, the more experienced listeners and readers may derive 'best sentence and most solas', at least more than the narrator himself is conscious of:

Geoffrey Chaucer

For I, that God of Loves servantz serve,
Ne dar to Love, for myn unliklynesse,
Preyen for speed, al sholde I therfore sterve,
So fer am I from his help in derknesse.
But natheles, if this may don gladnesse
To any lovere, and his cause availle,
Have he my thonk, and myn be this travaille!   (I. 15–21)

No less explicitly, though in a slightly different way, does the narrator of *The Canterbury Tales* display modesty along with keen observation. When he describes his fellow-pilgrims without encouraging simple definitions and evaluations, we have the impression of a poet taking in the whole spectacle of human life and all the manifestations of professional activity around him with inexhaustible attentiveness yet without ever gaining the experience necessary for a well-founded critical verdict. He asks the reader's pardon for possible inconsistencies as well as for any improprieties of style and describes the most atrocious abuse with the serenity of a man who is unworried by good or evil, or who at least does not feel called upon to act as a judge. Since the narrator abstains from any posturing and any claim to social or moral superiority, the reader feels himself to be in the company of a distinct human personality, one he can recognize in every new work by the same author.

While this seems to be obvious to most readers and must have been one of the most attractive aspects of Chaucerian narrative for centuries, modern literary criticism has turned it into a problem. This 'problem' could only arise because the novel of the last two or three centuries has introduced narrative techniques which would have been beyond all artistic consideration during the Middle Ages. At the same time, some naive forms of literary criticism, by tending to confuse autobiography and fiction and by mistaking the author for the narrator, have called for a reconsideration of the fictional character of all narrative literature. This has led to the use of the idea of an unreliable narrator as an instrument of literary analysis, and Chaucer's narrator, so clearly individualized, has been seen as a particularly striking example. While some of the older critics appear, without much reflection, to have equated the 'I' in Chaucer with the author himself, there is a tendency in many interpretations of the last two or three decades to separate the narrator completely from his creator, taking him to be a figure no less fictional than, and as pointedly individualized as, all the other characters.[1]

This new method has been applied to all of Chaucer's major poems with more or less subtlety and ingenuity, resulting in a number of rather controversial interpretations. E. T. Donaldson, for instance, in a particularly lively and influential study, distinguished between Geoffrey

Chaucer the poet and 'Chaucer the Pilgrim' in *The Canterbury Tales*. This pilgrim is a purely fictional persona, a character in his own right, just like all the other Canterbury pilgrims. Donaldson's point is that Chaucer's irony works by putting his descriptions into the mouth of a rather simple and undiscriminating observer, who hardly understands the implications of what he sees and faithfully reports. The reader, however, draws conclusions quite different from those of the naive narrator, who is continually deceived by the seemingly obvious, ultimately giving his audience a comfortable feeling of superiority. Keeping our knowing distance, we watch the uncritical, even gullible, narrator, and we perceive through him the omniscient author who tries to provoke us to an independent judgement through his narrative technique.[2]

At first sight, this interpretation looks convincing enough; the point, however, is whether such a rigid distinction between author and narrator does not mislead the reader by ignoring the fact that 'narrator' is a concept, an abstraction, invented by modern theorists of the novel, which should be used with some discretion. It hardly needs arguing that any verbal utterance, once it has lost its immediate connection with the speaker, can be analysed in that way – by tracing the implied narrator – and that the persona thus abstracted is by its very nature different from the actual speaker, even though they may have many opinions or personal traits in common. Every reader of modern fiction knows, too, that it is a very common device to put a first-person narrative into the mouth of a character whose mentality, temperament and convictions are totally unlike those of the author. Accordingly, some of these narrators appear to reproduce a state of mind suggested in Macbeth's cry of despair, employed by Faulkner as a motto to his novel *The Sound and the Fury*:

> Life's but a walking shadow, a poor player,
> That struts and frets his hour upon the stage,
> And then is heard no more; it is a tale
> Told by an idiot, full of sound and fury,
> Signifying nothing.   (*Macbeth*, v. 5. 24–8)

It seems to me, however, that for various reasons it is hardly imaginable that Chaucer's narrative should be based on this principle with anything like Faulkner's relentless consistency. The reasons are to be found partly in changed attitudes towards concepts of 'character' and 'personality'; but more importantly the relationship between the poet and his audience has undergone fundamental changes.

Many recent interpretations seem to take insufficient note of the fact, hardly disputed these days, that Chaucer's poetry was written, first of all, to be read aloud to a live audience. As far as we know Chaucer himself originally read his poems to a courtly or aristocratic audience, such as the one shown on the well-known frontispiece to a fifteenth-century manuscript of *Troilus*.[3] We are not as sure today as some earlier critics were that this picture depicts an actual occasion or, indeed, that it can be trusted as a faithful representation of Chaucer's audience at all; but, even if his audience was quite different from this formal courtly gathering, it seems safe to assume that Chaucer read his poems to a group of listeners many of whom would have known him personally. This situation would obviously exclude a number of elaborate devices possible in later fiction to be enjoyed by the solitary reader in his study. It does not imply, of course, that the poet's first-person narrator can only reveal facts about himself that are demonstrably true. What it does imply, however, is that the audience will always relate the first-person narrator to the author, who may well be physically present.

In this situation a complete separation of narrator and author is neither probable nor indeed practicable. It is therefore perfectly legitimate to make some inferences about the author from what the narrator says; but in practice this is almost impossible because we hardly know anything definite about the degree of truth or deliberate falsehood of the portrait in any particular case.[4]

One obvious example is Chaucer's self-portrait in *The Canterbury Tales*. Judging by the impression he makes on his fellow-pilgrims, the poet–pilgrim is not exactly an imposing figure. The host draws a rather condescending picture of him:

> 'What man artow?' quod he;
> 'Thou lookest as thou woldest fynde an hare,
> For evere upon the ground I se thee stare.
>
> 'Approche neer, and looke up murily.
> Now war yow, sires, and lat this man have place!
> He in the waast is shape as wel as I;
> This were a popet in an arm t'enbrace
> For any womman, smal and fair of face.
> He semeth elvyssh by his contenaunce,
> For unto no wight dooth he daliaunce.'   (*CT*, VII. 695–704)

If we keep in mind the nature of oral delivery, it seems highly unlikely that this humorous description did not in some way or other point at certain obvious similarities or striking contrasts between the pilgrim and the poet known to his audience and perhaps even present at the very moment. But the range of possible nuances of allusion is unlimited, and any attempt at a precise conclusion would amount to no more than pure speculation.

It is perhaps more interesting and of a more general importance to take a look at the literary accomplishments of Chaucer's first-person narrator. The contemporary audience's eager expectation must have been aroused by the fact that Chaucer himself takes part in the competition for the prize promised for the best story.[5] Now Chaucer, the creator of the whole cosmos of *The Canterbury Tales*, does not portray himself as the superior master of the art of storytelling, or, as is sometimes assumed, as an unskilled innocent. In contrast to all the other pilgrims he gets the chance to tell two stories. The first one (the 'Tale of Sir Thopas'), cut short by the indignant host, is Chaucer's most brilliant parody, an outrageous string of popular clichés, made to sound grotesquely stupid by their sheer number and inanity and yet revealing in every line a highly conscious artist who knows how to place his effects. At the same time this is the funeral march of the orally transmitted ballad-like romance of chivalry. The clumsy use of traditional formulas, for instance, only highlights by contrast Chaucer's own skilful use of similar conventions in other contexts. Here is the salesman-like pose of the popular entertainer:

> Now holde youre mouth, *par charitee*,
> Bothe knyght and lady free,
>   And herkneth to my spelle;
> Of bataille and of chivalry,
> And of ladyes love-drury
>   Anon I wol yow telle.   (*CT*, VII. 891–6)

In a very similar manner Chaucer had announced the second book of *The House of Fame*:

> Now herkeneth, every maner man
> That Englissh understonde kan,
> And listeneth of my drem to lere.
> For now at erste shul ye here
> So sely an avisyon,
> That Isaye, ne Scipion,
> Ne kyng Nabugodonosor,
> Pharoo, Turnus, ne Elcanor,
> Ne mette such a drem as this!   (*HF*, 509–17)

From the standpoint of modern theories of the novel, it would perhaps in this case be tempting to suggest a naive narrator, himself unaware of his brilliant parody, which he takes to be serious art. This seems to me, however, an abstraction which does not illuminate this humorous self-portrait at all; nor does it account for the complex impression we, as readers, receive. The genuine charm of the 'Tale of Sir Thopas' lies in the very absence of a clear-cut and unequivocal relationship between

13

Chaucer and his fictional self. When, after the romance is cut short, the poet presents an extraordinarily long, slow-moving and blatantly didactic prose tract, hardly a tale at all, we might be tempted to take it for just another joke or as a demonstration of his incompetence; but it is surely more appropriate to see the 'Tale of Melibee' as an attempt to counter the sample of primitive popular poetry with the opposite extreme: a specimen of learned, bookish exposition.[6] It is the only tale announced as a work of literary art. Not even the most enthusiastic interpretation will ever manage to endear this sententious dialogue to the modern reader; but for today's audience, much depends on realizing that this is the result of a fundamental change in taste. For Chaucer, we may be sure, the 'Tale of Melibee' was undoubtedly an important part of *The Canterbury Tales*, one of the few places where moral 'sentence' is offered in undiluted form. It is difficult to deny, on the other hand, that this 'tale' somehow looks like a conspicuous oddity within the collection and does mark Chaucer as distinctly different from all the other storytellers. Whatever might have been the final verdict on the quality of the individual performances, there can be no doubt about Chaucer's intention to emphasize the special status of this particular pilgrim, without either putting himself in the centre by consummate artistry or playing the incompetent fool showing off exaggerated modesty. The whole episode shows Chaucer's acute literary consciousness at work, as revealed in the ambiguous irony he employs to introduce himself to his audience as a writer and a poet.

This kind of playful treatment of the autobiographical possibilities of first-person narrative can be found nearly everywhere in Chaucer's works, and time and again it invites questions as to his attitude towards his art and his subject-matter. Does the mask of the modest, but acutely observant, humorous and detached, companion give us any idea of his real personality? There are examples in the history of literature which permit a more detailed comparison of the author's character and its fictional counterpart, and still by and large suggest that not much is gained by a more reliable knowledge of the poet's character and by confusing the two aspects; but the existence and vitality of Chaucer the narrator is not at all affected by such reservations. On the contrary, it is only after having freed ourselves from these more or less ephemeral autobiographical problems that we can appreciate the real advantages of this personal way of telling a story.

What we gain is, above all, the recognition that all narrative literature is essentially sociable. For Chaucer, the art of storytelling is first of all a form of communication. This seems to be stating the obvious because it may be true, to some extent, of any literary document, but only a few poets have given shape so consciously and successfully to the idea. To study the artistic means by which Chaucer achieves the reconciliation of this principle with all the other expectations and claims he finds himself faced with as a poet seems to me one of the most rewarding approaches to his poetry. The two traditional objectives of poetry, pleasure and profit – 'best sentence and most solas' – become much more meaningful when the conversational aspect of poetry, as Chaucer sees it, is taken into consideration. The discovery, often emphasized by modern literary theory, that a fictional text only comes to life through the cooperation of the reader is particularly important and helpful for an understanding of Chaucer's poetry.

All of Chaucer's longer poems can be described as first-person narratives. Even in *Troilus and Criseyde*, which deals with the events of a distant past and which does not present the narrator as an eye-witness, the act of storytelling and the relationship between the author and his subject-matter are so clearly the major concern that we see all the characters and their fates largely through the eyes of the narrator. This may be a form of authentication – not, of course, in the sense of a claim to literal truth, but as a way of ascribing to the poet's words the authority and reality of personal experience. The endeavour to give authority to the narrator's message was most likely one of the reasons for the popularity of the dream–vision, and Chaucer's variations of this form show him struggling again and again with the problem of literary authority and the validity of personal experience. By contrasting the magnitude and weight of his subject-matter with the limitations of his own experience, and by emphasizing his own difficulties in understanding his sources, he invites the reader or listener to an intelligent cooperation. The truth and the importance of his subject are not merely stated as facts; they come to life for us as we watch the poet's own exhausting struggles and doubts.[7] He does not address the reader with the aloofness of a teacher in the possession of superior wisdom, but makes him participate in his own efforts to come to terms with the material. We shall keep coming back to this aspect of Chaucer's narrator in the following chapters, where the poems will be discussed in more detail.

The pervading impression of a personal narrator deprives authorial statements of the air of neutral pronouncements. Each story is retold by someone who pretends to have heard it from someone else and who is eager to pass on his own enjoyment or admiration. Whatever the information or philosophical insight may be, it is voiced by someone who is deeply impressed by its relevance and profundity, and each rhetorical flourish seems to be informed with the author's striving for a mode of expression adequate to his subject-matter. This decidedly personal tone is by no means confined to Chaucer's poetry alone. Others among his contemporaries, too, assume the role of a very individualized speaker in addressing us – in particular Langland in *Piers Plowman* and the Gawain-Poet in *Pearl* or *Sir Gawain and the Green Knight*. But on the whole they do not talk to the reader in their capacity as authors, but rather as fellow-men seeking after some deeper insight into the nature of man and God's government. Chaucer is the first English poet to discuss his own literary activity and its particular problems in his poetry, the first to refer to his own works, and he could obviously assume his audience's familiarity with large parts of his *oeuvre*.

This is perhaps the most important aspect of Chaucer's narrator-figure. Almost everything he says about himself has some direct bearing on his literary production and is subordinated to the particular subject of the poem in hand. Never is he concerned merely with Geoffrey Chaucer the private individual, but always with his capacity as a poet and reader. Chaucer the poet is behind all his references to his inexperience, his attitude towards women and his dedicated, if unsuccessful, efforts in love's service; all of this refers first of all to his poetical ambition, and it is in this sense that all his poems may be taken as poetological statements.[8] What is it that constitutes the authority of the poet? This is the all-important question for Chaucer, and it is very closely related to the problem of the authority of what is on the page; many of his seemingly autobiographical references are of a more fundamental relevance in this wider context.

The Prologue to *The Legend of Good Women* is particularly instructive in this respect. Chaucer's willingness to offer his literary production for public discussion, unprecedented in his age, is nowhere more apparent than in this poem. For the last time he uses the traditional dream–vision, and more than ever before does he exploit its autobiographical possibilities. Here the dream is not used, as it traditionally was, to introduce some didactic revelation, but to serve as a justification for the tales to follow and as a pretext for a discussion with his audience.[9] It seems hard to believe that it was altogether Chaucer's own idea to present in a series of uniform tales the sad lives of betrayed or forsaken women. The stories themselves, at least, have made some critics suspect that they were not composed with particular enthusiasm; they seem rather to be competent routine performances. Whether Chaucer really wrote them to answer critical and moral reservations against his earlier love-poems, whether he wrote them in obedience to some royal or aristocratic command, or whether he just used the Prologue to publish some early productions we shall perhaps never know. Be that as it may, when it comes to Chaucer's original idea of linking these stories to his earlier poems, apparently well known to his audience, these questions seem to be of minor interest. The God of Love's charging Chaucer with slander against Love himself by his portraits of women, along with the poet's deferential attempt to justify what he did and Alceste's well-meaning intercession on his behalf, provide the author with the splendid opportunity of presenting three different critical reactions to his work side by side. The angry God of Love obviously gives a one-sided interpretation of some of Chaucer's poems. In fact, neither the translation of the *Roman de la Rose* nor *Troilus and Criseyde* strikes the unbiased reader as particularly anti-feminist, and there must be some point in the fact that many of the books recommended to the poet for special study contain very outspoken anti-feminist satire. Queen Alceste, on the other hand, credits the poet with offending in ignorance of the real meaning of his own poems, a particularly witty form of authorial modesty on the part of Chaucer. More relevant is her argument that most of the poet's other works cannot really be understood as heresy or slander against the doctrine of courtly love service. When the poet himself, with abject modesty, begins to answer the charges brought against him, his defence has very little effect and is firmly put down as insolent forwardness; for the reader, however, it is a clear and serious profession of the moral purpose of poetry, which we are meant to take at its face value:

> For that I of Criseyde wrot or tolde,
> Or of the Rose; what so myn auctour mente,
> Algate, God wot, it was myn entente
> To forthere trouthe in love and it cheryce,
> And to be war fro falsnesse and fro vice
> By swich ensaumple; this was my menynge. (G, 459–64)

Most readers, I think, will be inclined to assume that this prologue had some well-considered meaning for Chaucer's audience, a meaning we cannot recover. In spite of that, what makes this autobiographical episode particularly interesting for us today is to see how Chaucer succeeds in creating the impression of a close relationship between himself and his audience. Not only does he make us give our undivided attention to the poem he is introducing; he also invites us to reconsider our own judgement of his earlier poems. In spite of the humble tone, what emerges from this public debate of his own artistic work is the definite claim to be taken seriously as an artist and as a reliable judge of what he is doing. There is no reason to assume that Chaucer wanted to parody the genre of the dream–vision as a literary convention. On the other hand, the general spirit of the Prologue hardly suggests an uncritical acceptance of the traditional form. It would be hazardous to draw far-reaching conclusions from the fact that, as far as we know, Chaucer wrote no more allegorical dream–visions after *The Legend of Good Women*, but turned to the more flexible and direct mode of *The Canterbury Tales*. The Prologue shows, however, Chaucer no longer employing the dream–vision seriously as a didactic form of poetry, but transforming it in a highly personal manner, at the same time emphasizing and making evident its artificial character. Chaucer's earlier dream–visions, original as they are, remain much more within the traditional pattern. It is the poet's relation to his subject-matter that is their chief concern, not the effect of his poetry on his audience.

Chaucer's self-portraits in *The Canterbury Tales*, especially in the 'Retraction', are again expressions of his deep interest in the relationship between author and audience as a factor that cannot be separated from the creative act. Thus, in the 'Introduction' to the 'Man of Law's Tale', the Man of Law discusses at some length Chaucer's qualifications as a love-poet, along with a humorous reference to his alleged clumsiness in matters of metre and rhyme:

> But nathelees, certeyn,
> I kan right now no thrifty tale seyn
> That Chaucer, thogh he kan but lewedly
> On metres and on rymyng craftily,
> Hath seyd hem in swich Englissh as he kan
> Of olde tyme, as knoweth many a man;
> And if he have noght seyd hem, leve brother,
> In o book, he hath seyd hem in another.
> For he hath toold of loveris up and doun
> Mo than Ovide made of mencioun
> In his Episteles, that been ful olde.
> What sholde I tellen hem, syn they been tolde?   (CT, II, 45–56)

It is interesting to note, by the way, that 'Chaucer the poet', who is being discussed here, is nowhere expressly identified with 'Chaucer the Pilgrim', who, in *The Canterbury Tales*, is present all the time. Chaucer evidently wanted to add a somewhat different literary self-portrait to the autobiographical account given in the 'General Prologue' without tying himself down by suggesting that the reporting pilgrim and the author are identical; this might have brought on him a set of new problems.

Here, as in the Prologue to *The Legend of Good Women* and in the 'Retraction', we get a kind of Chaucer bibliography, again a very substantial expression of the artist's self-confidence, of his assured view of his poems as a very personal achievement and of the themes they have in common.

While the Prologue to *The Legend of Good Women* and *The Canterbury Tales* are chiefly concerned with a just representation of the relationship between men and women, the 'Retraction' indicates that for

Chaucer any literary activity has become a matter of acute moral relevance. It is because he is so convinced of the importance of books as a means of education and of passing on wisdom and knowledge that the question of the poet's responsibility assumes such urgency. Interpretations of the 'Retraction' have often concentrated unduly on the question of its sincerity. Chaucer's personal convictions, however, seem to me less relevant here than his attitude towards his literary activity as implied in the text. He knows the amount of good or evil that books may bring about and he therefore tries to define his own moral standards in relation to his poems and his audience. He does not reject his earlier poems in a fit of puritanical revulsion against all fiction, but only insofar as any such immoral tendency can be read into them as might convert their influence into the opposite of what is for him the only end that justifies serious poetry. I have the strong impression that this, again, is a very personal document demonstrating a new way of achieving insight into the most central concerns of poetry. But more tangible and more important for the modern reader is the poet's awareness of his responsibility towards his audience and the possible effects of his poetry. And I find this to be quite without parallel in the age of Chaucer.[10]

The reasons for Chaucer's strikingly original attitude towards his own literary activity are to be looked for in his special connection with the royal court and in his extensive reading and familiarity with international literary trends, but also in the rise of a literary vernacular as a new medium, not inferior to French and acceptable even in courtly circles. Chaucer's language is perhaps the first deliberate attempt to create a literary idiom capable of incorporating the rhetorical conventions developed in Latin, Italian and French, and thus holding its own within the classical tradition. This is confirmed by Chaucer's influential work as a translator, which was for him, no doubt, an important part of his literary activity. The fact that he translated two such fundamental texts as the *Consolatio Philosophiae* of Boethius and the *Roman de la Rose* and adapted the *Treatise on the Astrolabe* for the use of a child shows how much he saw himself as a transmitter of knowledge and traditional wisdom, as one whose mission it was to make books available to a large audience. This helps to explain his importance for the development of the English language.[11]

His impact on the language of English literature is not diminished by the fact that he was not the creator of a new standard, for this had been gradually evolving over the preceding centuries. Even without him the dialect of London would have become the seed and foundation of the new received standard. His poetry, however, demonstrated for the first time the flexibility and subtle nuances of expression that could be derived from this dialect. His style certainly profited from the absence of a rarefied literary jargon. The language still had the colloquial fluidity and openness of a primarily oral and not strictly regulated idiom, and this left the poet with a remarkable freedom for creativeness and experimental originality. This partly accounts for the strong impression Chaucer made on his immediate contemporaries and successors, and it is a significant fact that many of them referred explicitly to his stylistic virtuosity and his impact on the development of the English language. Thus Lydgate, a little later, apostrophizes him as 'the first that euer elumined our language with the flowers of rethorick eloquence'. Lydgate returns to the appraisal of this particular merit of Chaucer's in several of his works. Eighty years later, Caxton uses quite a similar expression: 'the worshipful fader & first foundeur & embelisher of ornate eloquence in our english'.[12] Such seems to have been the general notion for a whole century, while some of those qualities we find most characteristic of Chaucer's poetry were obviously recognized only much later. This is true in particular of his original adaptation of traditional subjects and literary source-material and of his humour, which apparently did not strike many of his early admirers as anything worthy of particular comment. Five hundred years of Chaucer criticism offer highly illuminating and often surprising instances of remarkable changes in literary taste and can serve as a warning against any kind of dogmatism in the field of literary criticism.

Chaucer is not only the first English poet to whom a considerable number of later poets refer by name and whom they try to imitate. He also seems to be the first to be seriously concerned about the survival of his literary heritage and about its faithful transmission. His little poem to Adam his scrivener, whom he admonishes to be at pains to make correct copies, and the conclusion of *Troilus*, where he prays to God that nobody might 'myswrite ... / Ne ... mysmetre for defaute of tonge' (v. 1795–6), reveal an astonishing degree of literary consciousness. This also proves, of course, that Chaucer did not have only his immediate courtly audience in mind or write solely for oral recitation, but that he wanted to earn a place within the literary tradition handed down from generation to generation. He seems to invite an audience innumerable and anonymous, and readers who, like the narrator at the beginning of *The Book of the Duchess*, enjoy their solitary book. For the majority of his contemporaries, however, contact with literature meant listening rather than reading, and this is not only important for our attitude towards Chaucer's narrator; it also greatly influences his narrative style. Some knowledge of the conventions of oral narrative helps us to understand certain stylistic peculiarities in Chaucerian storytelling: not only his explicit references to the construction of his tales, the deliberate transitions from one set of characters to the next, the digressions and learned showpieces, but also sudden changes of key – the abrupt switches from pathos to irony, from intellectual debate to light-hearted fun. To follow all this is sometimes more difficult for the reader than for the listener. In this respect Chaucer is quite close to his predecessors and the tradition of popular romancing.[13] But his poetry, even though primarily intended to be read aloud before an audience, is yet basically literary in origin and meant for a public not only interested in exciting yarns but ready and fit to appreciate his brilliant handling of traditional rhetorical devices and having an ear for nuances of irony, parody and unexpected changes of perspective.

English narrative poetry before or contemporaneous with Chaucer (with very few exceptions such as *Sir Gawain and the Green Knight*) is much less subtle in its appeal to the reader or listener. The audience knows all the time what the poet is up to and does not very often feel called upon to discern variations in the narrator's tone or degree of seriousness. Chaucer, however, keeps confronting his reader with these questions. The very personal idiom of his narrator continually frustrates any attempt to pin him down to simple meanings and only too often makes most analytical explications sound grossly oversimplified. This is so even in his earliest poems. In *Troilus and Criseyde* and in *The Canterbury Tales* Chaucer achieves a degree of complexity which has surprises and new pleasures in store even after many careful readings. Not many poets have succeeded in giving such full measure of sheer delight to generations of readers, and a great part of this delight comes from encountering an individual who is so much more experienced, stimulating, intelligent and tolerant than most of the people we come across in literature or in our own lives. This experience is common to all readers of Chaucer and is the most convincing proof of the living reality of Chaucer's narrator, who hardly needs any substantiation by external biographical fact.

3

Convention and individual style: *The Book of the Duchess*

THE BOOK OF THE DUCHESS IS THE FIRST OF CHAUCER'S MAJOR works we know about. It is in many ways a very characteristic document of Chaucer's individual style at the outset of his literary career, even though the modern reader may find its world much more alien at first than, for instance, that of *The Canterbury Tales*. Moreover, in comparison with the foreign models by which Chaucer was obviously inspired, it may seem much less original than his later poems. The approach to this text requires some critical effort, some readiness to reconsider one's literary standards and to question conventional preconceptions. Without such an effort, however, large areas of Chaucer's later poetry too will always be inaccessible to us.

According to an old tradition, hardly ever questioned these days, Chaucer wrote *The Book of the Duchess* on the occasion of the untimely death of the duchess Blanche, John of Gaunt's wife, who died of the Plague in 1369. Chaucer refers to this poem as 'the Deeth of Blaunche the Duchesse' in the Prologue to *The Legend of Good Women*, and in *The Book of the Duchess* itself the deceased is significantly called 'White' (948–9) – a fairly obvious allusion to the duchess it seems. This, however, is all we know. We cannot be certain whether John of Gaunt commissioned the poem or whether it was a kind of unsolicited tribute from the poet to his patron, nor are we able to date it with any confidence. There is no evidence whatever to support the speculation that it might have been part of an official commemoration ceremony,[1] and it does not really help our appreciation of the poem to emphasize its private and personal nature unduly. Grief and consolation are discussed (or indeed celebrated) here as public matters – not by way of a tearful expression of sympathy among friends, but rather in an attempt to make this personal loss the occasion for a lasting poetical monument. The actual event is thus sublimated within an admittedly conventional framework. Chaucer, no doubt, follows the method of his French models fairly closely, but at the same time he sets out to discover new ways of shaping his material that strike even the modern reader as distinctly individual. I do not want to go again over the old question of how far Chaucer was dominated by the influence of French poetry and what departures from his sources in each particular instance can be quoted as evidence of his originality and individual style.[2] The concept of originality is a most unreliable criterion for judging works of medieval literature, and Chaucer would certainly not, any more than his contemporaries, have had any ambition of departing as far as possible from his models, from traditional standards or from the literary trends of his time in general. Almost every ingredient of his poem – the dream–vision, the hunting-party, the description of the lady, the lover's complaint – has some traditional ancestor. It is their distinctly original combination, as well as many variations in detail, that creates the impression of individuality and unconventional spontaneity.

The plot of this relatively short poem, which may easily be read in one sitting, is simple enough: the poet, suffering from insomnia, seeks relief in a book where he happens on a tale from Ovid's *Metamorphoses* in which the God of Sleep plays a prominent part. This helps him to a deep slumber and a vivid dream. He finds himself among a cheerful hunting-party from which he is led away by a little whelp to meet a knight in black lamenting the death of his beloved. The poet induces him to give full expression to his grief and to go over the story of his courtship. This seems little enough in terms of dramatic action, and it is mainly the elaborately embroidered rhetoric of the mourning knight's narrative, as well as the introductory tale from Ovid, that accounts for the length of the poem. Its proportions seem a little incongruous at first sight, but the attentive reader will soon discover a carefully planned structure, even though the rhetorical embellishment takes up more room than he may be accustomed to.

Even a cursory summary of the poem, such as this, shows that Chaucer has here adopted a number of well-established literary conventions – most prominently the dream–vision, which had been used, with many modifications, by European poets almost continually ever since Boethius' *Consolatio Philosophiae*. It opens up new areas of experience to the poet, with the authority of a heaven-sent dream, that suggests the nature of a divine revelation. The purpose of the dream–vision was in most instances didactic: the poet may either become the witness of a dispute between opposing principles, moral, philosophical or political, or he himself may be the object of explicit instruction, like Boethius or like Chaucer himself in *The House of Fame*. Very often the dream–vision included allegorical elements or the use of personification, as in the *Roman de la Rose*, probably the most influential of all dream–visions after Boethius, and translated into English by Chaucer himself. It constitutes almost a manual of courtly love, although one should be very careful not to overrate the authoritative claims of the love-doctrine laid down in it.[3]

In *The Book of the Duchess*, however, Chaucer combines the dream–vision with the tradition of the lover's complaint, and he does without explicit allegory. Though the characters who appear in the dream are markedly stylized and in no way comparable to the more precisely outlined actors in *The Canterbury Tales*, they should not be understood as personifications. Nevertheless, there have been critical attempts to interpret them as such and to read the poem as a veiled allegory.

Chaucer is not the first to introduce a dream–vision with an account of the poet's insomnia, but he does it in a way that not only provides a dramatic motivation for the narrator's falling asleep but also prepares us for the theme of the whole poem. It is, at the same time, a characteristic feature of Chaucer's narrative method that he keeps his own person in the background, though not without some teasing hints. He professes to be unable to give any specific reason for his insomnia and confines himself to allusions that conceal more than they tell us. His reference to eight years' sickness for which there is but one physician (36–40) has been understood by most commentators as the typical pose of the unhappy lover – a pose elaborated much more explicitly in some French poems of the same type, and one that makes the poet particularly susceptible to the revelations in store for him. Other critics have understood the passage as the expression of the poet's grief for some loss, putting him in the same position as his patron, John of Gaunt.[4] The explanation of such contradictory interpretations lies in the simple fact that Chaucer deliberately avoids an unambiguous statement. The question is brushed aside because the narrator does not wish to place himself in the limelight. The nature of his own sorrow is obviously irrelevant to the purpose of the poem in hand. Unlike the dreamers in the majority of such poems, he is not himself made the recipient of any specific instruction or consolation, and what is more he does not even ask for any. It is, of course, quite possible that the real meaning of this passage depended on a knowledge of the precise circumstances of its publication. If it was really intended as a contribution to some official mourning ceremony it would be quite appropriate for Chaucer to join the community of mourners by some introductory remarks. The tone of the poem, however, rather suggests a lover's complaint, and the narrator's brief sigh characterizes him clearly as an unhappy lover or bereaved mourner bewailing the loss of his lady and, in deference to somebody else's sorrow, not wishing to make too much of his own misery because he does not want to compete with the black knight's anguish. Never again in the course of the poem does he return to his own state of mind, and nowhere does he claim to have any personal experience in matters of love.

This is quite in keeping with the impression the narrator gives of himself in Chaucer's later poems. It is possible, of course, that his contemporaries recognized some actual relationship between this self-portrait and Chaucer's personal connections with the court and the aristocratic world, but it would be naive and not really to the purpose to draw any conclusions about the poet's personal experience in love and marriage. The conventional pose of the unhappy narrator, though very much played down here, serves, within the framework of the poem, to make the poet particularly responsive to complaint and sorrow. He has reached a point where he is no longer able to help himself but needs some help from outside, and the poem's introduction makes the reader expect that the poet will be granted such help and some consoling wisdom.

But the preparation for the dream is even more elaborate. The idea that the narrator hopes to find relief from his insomnia by resorting to a book is original enough in this context. It characterizes him as a man more interested in his solitary book than in the society of others. This must have had a special point within a community for whom reading was essentially a sociable occupation and for whom the lonely enjoyment of a book in private seclusion must have been the exception rather than the rule. The pose of the sleepless sufferer is thus combined with that of the retired, unsociable bookworm.

This also prepares the ground for a subject brought even more forcefully to the attention of the reader by the story from Ovid and recurring in nearly all of Chaucer's later poems: the elusive relationship between the theoretical knowledge contained in books and the reality of our daily experience. The sleepless poet reads an old story in which sleep and personal loss by the death of a beloved person figure prominently. The story is retold with vividness and humour; it is much more than a literal translation of Ovid's text. The parallels between this introduction and the main subject of *The Book of the Duchess* are (deliberately, I am sure) kept vague, and there is no good reason to compare the details of the story step by step with the situation of the dreamer or of the mourning knight. It is clear, however, that the experience of death is introduced and the subject of grief discussed more explicitly here than at any point later in the poem. The departed husband admonishes his disconsolate widow in her sleep:

> My swete wyf,
> Awake! let be your sorwful lyf!

For in your sorwe there lyth no red.
For, certes, swete, I nam but ded;
Ye shul me never on lyve yse.   (201–5)

Even before he falls asleep, the poet has had some important instruction from the ancient author that may justly claim the authority of
classical wisdom. Consolation must come from the knowledge, imparted
by the time-honoured text, that the mourner is part of a larger community embracing every generation. For many centuries before him, men
and women have lost what was most dear to them and have tried to come
to terms with their sorrow. But this traditional solace in the face of
personal misery is not enlarged on, and the story is broken off just at the
point where the consolation should begin to prove effective. Such
deliberate about-faces in the course of the narrative are often particularly
intriguing marks of Chaucer's way of telling a story, eluding those
readers who attempt to make the poem conform to a neat pattern by
ingenious interpretation. Chaucer's extensive digressions are hardly ever
related to the 'real' work in the direct and unmistakable way of an
exemplum; they often act as variations on the poem's themes, enriching it
by rhetorical embellishment and providing additional authority.

In the case of this tale from the *Metamorphoses*, Chaucer leaves out
what in Ovid is precisely the point of the story, i.e. the reunion of the
couple through death by their transformation into two birds. His main
concern was evidently the encounter between the bereaved wife and her
dead husband and the ideal love-union. The text of Chaucer's poem does
not make clear whether the narrator realizes the 'message' of the story.
For him at this point the idea of sleep is more important than the problem
of death and bereavement. There is no doubt, however, that Chaucer
himself deliberately reshapes Ovid's story (used already by Machaut and
Froissart) by placing Halcyone and her grief in its centre and emphasizing
the simple pathos of her situation rather than heroic dignity and formal
decorum. At the same time he 'lowers' the tone of the whole story by
humorous scepticism and realistic directness. Classical mythology is
treated not with awe and wonder, but rather with an amused curiosity
and with an eye to its relevance in the poet's own life. This is why the
concept of a God of Sleep immediately reminds him of his own insomnia.
After a playful vow to Morpheus – or to whoever might be able to send
him sleep – he is indeed overtaken by slumber, even before he has had
time to lay aside his book.[5]

Critics have often praised the amount of vivid, realistic detail Chaucer
has added to the conventional material in the dream–vision that follows.
The morning in May, the song of the birds and the delightful scenery
were, of course, among the stock ingredients of the genre, almost a

hallmark, and it would be misguided either to overemphasize Chaucer's departures from the traditional scheme or to turn every sign of overt conventionality into a fault. Chaucer's contemporaries, most probably, would have admired above all his effortless mastery of literary conventions and his easy adaptation of French formulas in English. On the other hand, it is certainly not without reason that the modern reader keeps discovering an individual tone and the impression of sensitively observed reality even in the clearly traditional passages of this poem. This probably has something to do with the fact that Chaucer's language, in spite of all stylized rhetoric, has preserved some of its colloquial directness and immediacy; in addition, the poet keeps enriching conventional descriptions with little concrete details which, often, inform a cliché with unexpected vitality.

The cheerful, swiftly moving hunting-party that opens the dream serves as another vivid preparation for what is to follow. The deer-hunt, as aristocratic, almost ritually formalized pastime and at the same time traditional metaphor of love, provides a courtly background essential for the poem's theme. The poet enters a world of which he is not really an organic part, and he is met with an atmosphere of cheerful activity which is in complete contrast to the static grief of the ensuing dialogue and may be taken as another form of indirect consolation. The courtly audience addressed by the poem is apparently invited to forget the sorrow referred to in the first lines for the time being and enter into the carefree spirit of the hunt. The same is true of the dreamer himself: he is the same person as before, but he seems to be all of a sudden freed from his oppressive malady. The dream world has brought about a complete change of mood, which again prepares us for the consolation offered and effected by this poem. Whatever the dreamer's own suffering might have been, the dream has diverted his thoughts from his personal state of mind so thoroughly that he can be a sympathetic listener and enter into another man's grief as if it were his own.

The form in which this is presented also seems to reflect something of the peculiar mode of perception associated with dreams – in particular, the abrupt transitions and the somewhat shadowy and unreal character of the chase. The dreamer can only register isolated, fleeting impressions, momentary glimpses, until, obviously guided by some invisible power, he encounters the black knight. Here, too, however, one should not see such allegedly modern features of the poem in isolation or in an imaginary contrast to its more conventional aspects. What Chaucer's poem does indeed prove is the extent to which the impression of experienced reality can be created even within the framework of a literary form which to the modern reader seems extremely artificial. Even the highly stylized and rhetorically 'alienated' reality of the dream–vision permits the poet to express himself very clearly and pertinently about everyday experience; thus, in the midst of all the conventional form and artifice, there is this simple encounter between two men and the impression of a real human fellowship in suffering such as is the true basis for any lasting consolation.

The meeting with the disconsolate knight is the centre of the whole poem to which all the careful preparation has led up. The reader will notice very soon, however, that this dialogue, too, does not take a very straightforward course, but again illustrates Chaucer's individual narrative strategy – his love of wide-ranging exposition and of seemingly aimless digression, and a deliberate delaying of the climax. The whole poem, just like the tale from Ovid, ends rather abruptly. As in many other Chaucerian narratives, there seems to be an unusually long-winded approach leading up to a conclusion whose brevity takes the reader by surprise and may even disappoint him a little by its concise suddenness. It is only in retrospect that we realize that the journey was more important than the goal. The unfolding of the poem and the development of the dialogue between the mourning knight and the dreamer constitute the real consolation, not the few compassionate words of the narrator at the end of the poem. Critics have repeatedly pointed out that there is something like a consciously applied therapy in the way the black knight is made to relate the history of his courtship and to talk freely about his sorrow, living through it all again and thus relieving himself of some of the pain he had shut up within himself.[6] In confiding the story of his love, of anxiety, hope and fulfilment to the dreamer, the knight once again experiences each stage of his progress from first falling in love to the moment of perfect union. This re-creation of past felicity takes up far more room than the brief explanation of the cause of his grief, and thus the poem unobtrusively turns from a lament for the dead into a description of former bliss and a celebration of the ideal beloved. All this creates a decidedly positive and, for an elegy, almost joyful mood.

Critics have sometimes pointed out that Chaucer could hardly have taken the liberty of offering explicit consolation to his patron, who was socially so far above him, without appearing rather presumptuous. This may be true, but it would in any case be rather simplistic to equate the black knight with John of Gaunt throughout the text and to read the whole poem as a kind of *roman à clef*.[7] If there were parallels and personal allusions, they surely would not relate to individual personalities as much as to the general situation, the experience of loss and despair, above all the problem of death which underlies the whole poem and is by no means confined to the dialogue between the knight and the dreamer.

Nor is the important question what consolation the narrator can offer to the mourner, but rather in what way the poem as a whole comes to terms with the precarious state of human happiness and the inescapable fact of death and bereavement. The personal relationship between Chaucer and John of Gaunt presumably made it necessary for him to offer sympathy and consolation unobtrusively and without any air of knowing superiority. Chaucer uses this restriction, if he felt it as such, to advantage by creating a highly original form of elegy in which lament and sympathetic listening are subtly correlated, and in which consolation does not consist in traditional commonplaces but in the free expression of grief and the relief provided by a compassionate audience.[8] The comforting effect of sympathy is reinforced – not for the black knight, but for the reader – by the fact that even before this encounter the poem has prepared us for it, by the attitude of the poet who humorously accepts his own 'sickness' and by the story of the deceased husband returning in a dream. All this is probably more important for the general effect of *The Book of the Duchess* than are the therapeutic aspects of the dialogue alone. The psychological disposition of the knight is not really a subject for discussion in the poem.

The problem of the relationship between the two speakers, much discussed by critics of the poem, should therefore not be made too much of. Within the stylized world of the dream–vision, it is not the individual characters that matter most; at least, the text does not encourage any kind of psychological analysis. There is, of course, the vivid impression of a very personal human relationship, but this is only relevant insofar as it helps to express the actual theme of the poem.

The figure of the dreamer has often been interpreted as a deliberate persona, the poet portraying himself as distinctly naive and obtuse in order to break through the reserve of the mourning knight. Can he really be so dense as not to realize what the reader has gathered from the very first words of the black knight, namely that he laments the death of his lady? Or does he only pretend to be ignorant for therapeutic reasons?[9] Such questions are in the context of the poem rather misleading, because they seem to imply that the author wanted to present a psychologically consistent character drama, which was obviously not his intention. The information that the beloved is dead is meant for the reader who needs to know a little more than the dreamer to be able to appreciate the following dialogue. The fact that the dreamer, too, has heard this information and yet seems to be ignorant of it later on would not have seriously troubled Chaucer's contemporaries; it only worries modern readers whose sense of character realism has been sharpened by two centuries of psychological novels. But even by the standards of natural human reactions the scene presents no real difficulty. Simple courtesy alone would have prevented the dreamer from directly touching upon the knight's most personal circumstances, and he therefore begins the conversation with innocent discretion until the mourner himself gives the cue. It is not simple-mindedness or lack of comprehension that direct the dreamer's behaviour, but rather tactful distance and considerate modesty, if indeed there is any need to look for this kind of motivation. Apart from that, the dreamer's alleged ignorance is not confined to the lady's death; he does not know anything about the black knight's history, about his experience of love and the real nature of his loss; his few comments make abundantly clear that the finer details and conventions of courtly love are quite new to him. For all their fellowship in suffering, the experiences of the two men are evidently very different, and the dreamer never offers expert advice or even the sympathy of one who knows all about the subject.

This pose – only roughly outlined in the text – of a man quite ignorant in courtly matters, links this poem with Chaucer's later work and accounts for an important difference between *The Book of the Duchess* and many other dream–visions in which the poet receives explicit instruction. Chaucer's dreamer is not systematically initiated into the secrets and laws of courtly love, like the dreamer in the *Roman de la Rose*, but rather indirectly, by listening to the personal experiences of a courtly lover who has had his full share of hope, fulfilment, and loss. It is more than likely that behind this personal dialogue we can catch a glimpse of the actual situation: Chaucer, the bourgeois, or non-aristocratic poet, does not presume to pontificate about the aristocratic conventions of *amour courtois*.[10] He remains an outsider, and he puts his own knowledge of these matters into the mouths of others, casting himself in the role of the uninitiated receiving instruction. This enables him as a poet to look at the conventions of courtly love-poetry from the point of view of a detached observer and even to expose their limitations without appearing impudently presumptuous. It is perhaps for the same reason that his unaffected expression of sympathy, sounding almost a little rude next to the elaborate rhetoric of the knight, makes such a strong impression on the reader as a mark of genuine compassion.[11]

The ending of the poem shows Chaucer's brilliant sense of dramatic narration and, at the same time, of the pointed effect of simple, unadorned discourse, here heightened by the contrast to the stylized elaboration of the knight's idiom:

> 'Sir,' quod I, 'where is she now?'
> 'Now?' quod he, and stynte anoon.
> Therwith he wax as ded as stoon,

And seyde, 'Allas, that I was bore!
That was the los that here-before
I tolde the that I hadde lorn.
Bethenke how I seyde here-beforn,
'Thow wost ful lytel what thow menest;
I have lost more than thow wenest' –
God wot, allas! ryght that was she!'
  'Allas, sir, how? what may that be?'
  'She ys ded!' 'Nay!' 'Yis, be my trouthe!'
'Is that youre los? Be God, hyt ys routhe!'
And with that word ryght anoon
They gan to strake forth; al was doon,
For that tyme, the hert-huntyng.   (1298–1313)

The contrast between the two speakers, the swift exchange and the abrupt intrusion of the hunters' signals make this a particularly effective demonstration of Chaucer's narrative skill right at the beginning of his career. The incredulous queries of the dreamer are not an expression of slow comprehension, but rather an indication that he is genuinely moved and only now begins to grasp the full extent of the knight's grief. Though he may have heard about the lady's death as an isolated piece of information when he first encountered the mourner, it is only now that he can really feel what this loss must mean for him, after faithful service, hope, fulfilment and perfect happiness. Following so immediately on the intense re-living of all this exhilarating experience, the sudden breaking-in of death comes indeed as a surprise for which the dreamer – and perhaps even the reader – is unprepared. The moment of helpless pain and compassion marks at the same time the end of the cheerful hunt and of the dream.

The lamenting knight then, rather than the narrator, is the poem's real protagonist. He has by far the greater share in the dialogue, to which the dreamer only contributes a few cues and some telling comments. The description of an extended courtship and of a selfless devotion is the longest coherent narrative portion of the poem and its true centre.

The black knight has sometimes been interpreted as a kind of *alter ego* of the poet, embodying an aspect of his own suffering, which he has objectified so as to relieve himself of some depressing personal experience.[12] In this case there would indeed be an element of dream psychology, in the modern sense, underlying the poem, but in view of the stylistic conventions and of the historical background it would perhaps be a little anachronistic to make that kind of identification. At least it can be said that Chaucer nowhere encourages such an interpretation – which is far more likely to occur to the modern reader accustomed to explaining dreams as acts of unconscious self-liberation or wish-fulfilment. The very possibility of this sort of reading shows, however, to what extent Chaucer has succeeded in attuning the artificial fiction of a courtly dream-poem to the actual working of human consciousness and mental associations. With all its conventional trappings and stylization, the poem presents a situation that is at once simple and basic to our common experience, and this gives it its immediate appeal.

It is important to stress this point, because the poem's form evidently belongs to a literary tradition the contemporary reader is not familiar with and may find rather far removed from his own way of thinking about the themes treated; and this applies not only to the framework of the dream–vision, but to the whole method of presenting the knight's experience of love and courtship. As far as this particular convention is concerned, it would be especially misguided to look for literal equivalents in real history, be it in the marriage of John of Gaunt – which, from all we know about it, must have taken a very different course – or even in the daily life of the fourteenth century in general. The traditional form of the courtly love-poem demanded idealizing abstraction: the knight is turned into the prototype of the ideal aristocratic lover and his lady becomes the very image of each beloved. The whole story of their love proceeds along almost ritual lines, with each stage carefully described as a necessary part of the full experience: the long silent devotion from a distance, then an equally prolonged period of abject courtship, culminating in fulfilment, that is in the lady's acceptance of the lover's service. The question of marriage hardly arises or is at least not explicitly discussed. The practical consequences of the lady's generosity and pity are, in the context of this kind of love-poetry, of little concern. This idealized image of love must not, as I said before, be brought into a superficially literal relationship with reality. The basic experience of love, and of death for that matter, is transposed into the conventionalized formula of ennobling service in the cause of love, of unconditional dedication to something one has elected as the highest goal and to which one wishes to devote all of one's life. Having decided on this formula, Chaucer employs many of the conventions developed and passed on by poets in many European countries before him and recurring time and again in medieval love-poetry.

For a long time it was a kind of scholarly axiom or creed that the poets of the European Middle Ages had created a widely accepted doctrine of courtly love, an elaborate set of rules, rooted firmly in the feudal structure of society, which regulated in detail and with the authority of a religious system every aspect of behaviour in the service of love, that is in devotion to one's chosen lady. Didactic works, like the *Roman de la Rose* or Andreas Capellanus' treatise *De Amore* (whose claim to be a serious authority or manual of courtly love has often been grossly overstated), seem, if read in isolation and with some critical prejudice, to support this theory. It has, however, during the last two or three decades come increasingly under attack and is today accepted, if at all, only in a very modified and tentative form. The first thing that can be adduced against it is the simple fact that some of the most characteristic elements of courtly love are by no means confined to the literature of the Western Middle Ages or to feudal societies; perhaps even more important is the observation that, even within the poetry of the Middle Ages, there is an astonishing variety of formal, social and moral conventions in matters of aristocratic love.[13] What the poet of a Middle High German lyric means by *minne* is not the same as the service expected of the ideal knight in one of Chrétien's verse novels, and Dante's or Petrarch's idea of love is again of quite another order. Neither the principle of extra-marital love or of devotion to a married lady, nor the alleged law that love can never find acceptance or fulfilment, has any general validity or applies to the whole range of courtly love-poetry. In particular, the relationship between *amour courtois* and marriage is a question that has led to considerable confusion. The view held by earlier critics, ostensibly endorsed by Andreas Capellanus among others, that true love was incompatible with matrimony, is at least not applicable to English medieval literature. It is quite true, of course, that social conditions did not exactly favour what later generations understood by a 'love-match'. Marriage, as a social fact and as a religious sacrament, was viewed as belonging in a different category from the emotion of love, but this need not lead to a general moral conflict or even to a universally felt contradiction. In England, especially, we find many authors celebrating courtly love within the context of marriage and thus trying to establish some (often utopian) harmony between a literary ideal and the hard fact of social reality, as Chaucer does in the 'Knight's Tale' and in the 'Franklin's Tale'.[14] The pattern of courtly love implied in these works, and also to a large extent in *The Book of the Duchess*, is first of all a literary and stylistic phenomenon, a poetic fiction that never claimed to be a literal reflection of reality and may be better described as the appropriate form of speaking about love in courtly poetry.[15] This does not by any means exclude some mutual impact: conventions can influence reality when they are, as it were, taken at their word. Examples can be found in many of the chivalric ceremonies of the late Middle Ages, which often seem to be inspired by the literature of the romances.

The Book of the Duchess is a good instance of the fundamental division between poetic convention and political reality. Its description of aristocratic love must not be confused with an account of a particular historical situation; rather it is to be appreciated as an attempt to put into

words some of the highest human qualities, manifested and activated in
any genuine love-relationship, a disinterested pursuit of what one has
recognized as an ideal and a willingness to let any other considerations
and desires take second place to this wholehearted devotion. In a
stimulating essay on Chaucer's attitude towards the conventions of
amour courtois, Dorothy Bethurum gives a definition of courtly love that
perfectly fits the black knight and many other lovers in medieval
literature: 'Courtly love was probably the purest form of sexual love the
western world has known, being unmixed with social ambition, pride,
desire of wealth, or even the laudable interests of the family.'[16] This
explains why the exclusion of marriage as the decisive motivation only
demonstrates the moral strength of this convention, in which it is the
service of love that is celebrated, irrespective of any material interests. I
think it is only when we recognize this moral centre of courtly love, as a
metaphor for man's highest aspirations and their fulfilment, that we can
understand what made Chaucer return time and again to this subject. It is
at the centre of his great epic *Troilus and Criseyde* and of many of the
Canterbury Tales. Convention and 'message', form and substance,
cannot be separated here and this is why it must have occurred naturally
to Chaucer to describe the sorrows of a courtly lover, accepted after long
and unrewarded service by his lady, only to lose her again at the moment
of supreme happiness, and at the same time to celebrate the marriage of
John of Gaunt.

It is also very important in this connection that the black knight's lady
is praised not only for her conventional beauty, but also, and more
importantly, in moral terms. Love is defined as an ennobling emotion
that makes the lover a better man. The lady is explicitly dissociated from
more vulgar concepts of courtly love. She is far above sending her knight
abroad to go through glamorous adventures for her sake. Service for her
does not mean what some of the popular romances tend to suggest:
colourful and dangerous hardships endured on her behalf and for her
greater glory. This cheaper version of courtly love is emphatically
repudiated:

> Ne, be thou siker, she wolde not fonde
> To holde no wyght in balaunce
> By half word ne by countenaunce,
> But if men wolde upon hir lye;
> Ne sende men into Walakye,
> To Pruyse, and into Tartarye,
> To Alysaundre, ne into Turkye,
> And byd hym faste anoon that he
> Goo hoodles to the Drye Se
> And come hom by the Carrenar,

And seye 'Sir, be now ryght war
That I may of yow here seyn
Worshyp, or that ye come ageyn!'
She ne used no suche knakkes smale. (1020-33)

This seems a very clear verdict on many of the popular romances and their concept of love. The black knight's lady was of very different moral stature.

In view of this background and the whole character of the narrative, it seems rather forced to explain the knight as a symbol of misguided devotion to a false ideal and of inactive despair, as Robertson does, thus flying in the face of practically all previous interpretations.[17] It is easy to produce evidence of medieval moralists pointing out the dangers of idolatry in the idea of courtly love, and it clearly appears from some of Chaucer's later work, in particular *Troilus and Criseyde*, that he himself was not unaware of this less than ideal aspect of courtly love, especially its potentially disastrous consequences for the lover when his devotion turns into blind obsession and the idol is revealed as humanly fallible and elusive. *The Book of the Duchess* does not, however, imply any kind of direct criticism of the black knight's courtship or his grief, even though the narrative situation and the conventional rhetoric create a perceptible distance between him and the reader. His sorrow is taken entirely seriously, without overt irony or satire, but also without complete identification. Spontaneous sympathy is the only convincing reaction left to the poet in the face of such loss. It is worth noting that he does not offer any of the traditional arguments against excessive grief provided by classical authors. The poem's close sounds like the frank admission that in a situation like this any verbal consolation must fail, but this conclusion would be meaningless if Chaucer had intended to denounce the knight's suffering as futile or misdirected. Any moral verdict on the mourner would have seemed improper and in any case irrelevant with regard to the central theme of the poem.

This is one of the fundamental differences between *The Book of the Duchess* and some of the homiletic poems of consolation written about the same time, such as *Pearl*,[18] where the bereaved narrator is explicitly berated and his sorrow is exposed as a sign of stupid blindness and of sad ignorance about the temporary nature of death and the eternal rewards promised to the faithful. There is no doubt whatsoever that Chaucer and his contemporaries were familiar with these ideas, but this does not mean that a poem as different from *Pearl* as *The Book of the Duchess* must be interpreted in the same way. The conventional form Chaucer decided to use for this commemorative work rather suggests the opposite: a courtly dream-vision is hardly the place for theological discussion or homiletic didacticism. Chaucer, at any rate, refrains from any explicit hint in that direction, and this is why it seems wrong to overemphasize the significance of the poem as an act of consolation. This significance is largely confined to the sociable courtly community it addresses, and it does not attempt – or only very hesitantly – to reach out to those areas from which alone lasting consolation can be hoped for by the true Christian. It is paying this poem, for all its freshness and human warmth, too much honour to associate it with the liturgy of the Mass for the Dead or with Henry Yvele's alabaster tomb for John of Gaunt and Blanche, which, to be sure, it has survived.[19]

The real importance of *The Book of the Duchess* does not lie in any theological message or even in some clearly definable moral argument, but rather in the distinctly personal and suggestive appeal the poet has succeeded in creating out of an unpromisingly conventional literary form. He neither describes a psychologically consistent process of consolation nor, indeed (apart from some tentative gestures) produces more than commonplace clichés of condolence and comfort. In spite of all this, the poem does not leave the reader with the impression that he has only listened to a depressing lamentation; rather he has the sense of a helplessness humorously accepted and a genuine fellowship based on compassion. This truly individual combination could only have been created by a poet who was able to discover new modes of expression within the literary conventions at his disposal which could be explored by original variation and personal poetic idiom. This proves the vitality of poetical traditions as long as their adaptability is recognized and made use of.

4

Traditional genre and personal message:
The Parliament of Fowls

THE RECEPTION OF CHAUCER'S POETRY THROUGHOUT THE centuries shows that *The Parliament of Fowls* has, from the beginning, enjoyed particular favour with readers. It is preserved in fourteen manuscripts; it was highly esteemed during the Renaissance, and it is probably much easier to approach and to appreciate for the modern reader at first sight than *The Book of the Duchess* or *The House of Fame*. Most books on Chaucer praise the neatness of its structure, its vitality and its unconventional humour. There is, however, much more unanimity on the high valuation of the poem than on the actual interpretation of its specific qualities, and the surprising diversity of readings suggests that the unpretentious and seemingly transparent form can easily deceive and make us overlook the wealth of themes and questions concealed by it. The poem is evidently part of a lively discussion on problems very close to the heart of courtly society, not necessarily in the sense of rational debate and argumentation, but as an ingenious and undogmatic juxtaposition of established attitudes, inviting further reflection. The astonishing variety of conventions used within such little space prevents us from assigning it to some clearly defined genre or even from pinning it down to a precise theme with any confidence; it certainly is not a treatise in verse, and for this reason alone it is safe to distrust any interpretation that would tell us what the poem is all about. The most convincing accounts are those that clearly recognize the exploratory and experimental character of the poem, its relaxed inconclusiveness.[1]

The poem may well make us wonder about the usefulness of such concepts as genre, theme or meaning as tools for a genuine appreciation and understanding of what it attempts to do. It is certainly not a cut and dried message, capable of being summarized in a few lucid sentences, that makes the poem still worth reading today. At the same time, the text raises the problem of a narrowly historical approach. It is not particularly helpful for the modern reader to be told exactly how Chaucer's contemporaries would have understood the poem, because such 'historical' readings, more often than not, are only a projection of the critics' own convictions or preconceptions back into a period which, from all accounts, was by no means monolithic but had some distinctly pluralistic aspects.[2] On the other hand, modern critics sometimes lose sight of the simple fact that Chaucer's poetry is based on conventions which are no longer part of our living literary culture and on attitudes most of us would no longer seriously entertain.

The first difficulty we encounter is the question of genre. If we look for precedents in literary history we find a good many forms Chaucer seems to have made use of, but none of the traditional labels will quite fit this work. This is not entirely a Chaucerian problem, because it is quite characteristic of Middle English literature in general that poets tend not to conform to well-defined genres as closely as is the case in other periods. In lyric poetry as well as in verse narrative we find an often bewildering diversity of forms, an unorthodox disregard of poetic rules, and only few genres that seem to have remained fairly stable for any length of time. This is particularly noticeable in the poetry of Chaucer. None of his major works is a repetition or even a closely related variation of any other, as far as its form is concerned. Even with those of the *Canterbury Tales* that belong to the same type, be it legend, romance, exemplum or fabliau, their differences are far more interesting than what they have in common.

The framework of *The Parliament of Fowls* belongs again to the tradition of the dream–vision, but a glance at *The Book of the Duchess* reveals that Chaucer has only made use of a few basic conventions; apart from that, he seems to have been chiefly interested in exploring new areas of his subject-matter and new ways of expression within the formal conventions of courtly love-allegory. After the dream-introduction, Chaucer proceeds with an original version of the time-honoured mode of didactic allegory and of humorous debate in the form of a spirited dispute among animals; the combination of all these well-tried devices is a highly individual achievement and a very personal comment on clichés that might easily become meaningless by mere repetition.

Like the narrator of *The Book of the Duchess*, who made it quite clear that he viewed courtly conventions with some detachment, the poet in *The Parliament of Fowls* assumes a very definite persona and is even less prepared to identify himself with his subject: the whole concept of courtly love is something he only knows from books; he sees it only as a great storehouse of metaphors and theoretical ideas, and this means that all he can do is to make some reverential gestures from a distance, because he is totally unable to offer any opinion that is based on personal experience. This is how, modestly and tentatively, he approaches his subject:

The lyf so short, the craft so long to lerne,
Th'assay so hard, so sharp the conquerynge,
The dredful joye, alwey that slit so yerne:
Al this mene I by Love, that my felynge
Astonyeth with his wonderful werkynge
So sore, iwis, that whan I on hym thynke,
Nat wot I wel wher that I flete or synke.

For al be that I knowe nat Love in dede,
Ne wot how that he quiteth folk here hyre,
Yit happeth me ful ofte in bokes reede
Of his myrakles and his crewel yre.
There rede I wel he wol be lord and syre;
I dar nat seyn, his strokes been so sore,
But 'God save swich a lord! – I can na moore.   (1–14)

This introduction is a particularly good example of the way the poet not only describes a specific situation, but makes it appear as the result of an imaginative process: the conventional symptoms of love are at first listed like abstract items or like so many quotations, but these commonly accepted properties of love begin to confuse the narrator to such an extent that he hardly knows whether he is waking or dreaming. Although he has, so far, only heard about the effects of love on others and in literature, without being himself emotionally involved, he is fascinated by the subject and, for all his inexperience, cannot but recognize its universal appeal. It is not just that Chaucer, being polite and unassuming, does not claim any intimate knowledge in matters of courtly love; rather he transforms the conventional pose of the lovesick poet into that of the inexperienced reader in need of instruction. This raises the question of the nature of courtly love in a far more provocative manner; and it is characteristic of the direction the poem takes that the narrator should turn to a book 'a certeyn thing to lerne' (20), because it is from literary tradition that he expects an answer to his questions, not from experience or direct observation.

It has often been assumed that what the poet is looking for is some particular point in connection with his general theme; 'a certeyn thing', however, could also mean something constant and authoritative, some really reliable piece of information.[3] It is interesting to note, especially in view of other thematic connections, that the phrase 'a certeyn thing', also occurs in Chaucer's translation of Boethius' *Consolatio Philosophiae* (as the English word for *certum*), as the term used for something that is not subject to mutable Fortune and can thus be depended on as a fixed point in the midst of a constantly changing reality.

The following lines about the creative and fertilizing power of the written word constitute one of the most revealing statements on the

39

relationship between the poet and literary tradition in the whole of Chaucer's work.[4] As in science and all intellectual pursuits progress is only possible on the basis of a vital contact with the achievements of the past, so in literature there is no genuinely new contribution without the inspiration of 'olde bokes'; but it is precisely this inspiration and the creative reference to the great authors of all ages that brings forth original and truly instructive literature:

> For out of olde feldes, as men seyth,
> Cometh al this newe corn from yer to yere,
> And out of olde bokes, in good feyth,
> Cometh al this newe science that men lere.   (22–5)

Scipio's dream, the first book the narrator happens to light on – and he is immediately fascinated by it – does indeed claim to reveal to the reader 'a certeyn thing'. It is a literary work that had been an inspiration for many, far beyond its original intention. It had been the subject of commentaries by medieval authors which invested this pagan text with a wealth of Christian significance, proceeding from the conviction that the greatest pre-Christian authors had been granted glimpses of divine wisdom even though they were not conscious of it.[5] In Chaucer's poem, the dream of Scipio is not exactly Christianized, but its interpretation is clearly influenced by a Christian world-view. It impresses on the reader the idea, familiar to all Christians, of the insignificance of this earth and our individual existence in relation to the cosmic order and the seemingly changeless universe. It is only after death, in the world beyond, that the true success or failure of our lives will become apparent.

Even before the poet's own dream had begun, the authority of the ancient author has created a spiritual background to the poem which serves as a standard by which we will have to judge what is to follow. The narrator's own experience seems more interesting and significant by virtue of this implied relationship to Scipio's dream (although there is obviously an ironic contrast), and the experience of earthly love is not entirely unaffected by what the dream has taught us even though the poem does not establish any specific thematic connection. Chaucer employs a similar technique here as he does, rather more elaborately and with a far more serious purpose, in *Troilus and Criseyde*. There, at the end of the tragedy, the human dilemma is viewed from a cosmic vantage-point, and its hopeless finality is thus seen in perspective. In *The Parliament of Fowls*, it is the other way round: from the superior wisdom of *contemptus mundi* we proceed to human comedy in the guise of an animal fable. By this order of events the undogmatic and inconclusive debate is prevented from being smothered by an orthodox solution and the thematic relevance of Scipio's dream is deliberately left vague. Any interpretation that attempts to pin it down any more definitely than the text does is in danger of substituting a moral commonplace for the teasing exhibition of contradictory attitudes. On the other hand, it would be a simplification to ignore the message of the dream: Scipio's advice to keep the mind firmly fixed on the 'commune profyt' (47) in view of this deceptive and cruel world,[6] stays with the reader as an implied moral imperative, even if it is rather general and does not seem particularly applicable in the world of this poem.

It is clear from the poet's dissatisfaction and confusion after he has put down his book that the rather extreme attitude of Scipio does not provide him with the answer he has looked for:

> For bothe I hadde thyng which that I nolde,
> And ek I nadde that thyng that I wolde.   (90–1)

The vivid reality of love described in the first lines of the poem cannot be talked away or ignored by turning one's back on the world of daily experience. In view of this, it is rather ironic that the same Africanus whose revelations seemed so little to the purpose now makes his appearance again in the poet's dream and begins to offer far more mundane instruction. It is another half-serious indication that there is indeed some connection between the introduction and the dream proper. The venerable mentor lends a slightly humorous, but nevertheless remarkable, authority to everything the poet sees in his sleep and adds weight to the subject. This guide is prepared to descend to the narrator's less fundamental and cosmic problems, and he promises some instruction more adapted to his limited intellect. His benevolent and slightly condescending tone makes the inexperienced bookishness of the poet appear in a rather comical light. The dream is presented as a reward for assiduous reading and at the same time as a kind of substitute for the experience in love the poet has missed so far.

The complete change from the unadorned paraphrase of the classical text in the concise introduction to the dream is marked by the solemn invocation to the Goddess of Love, Cytherea.[7] It not only aims to impress on the reader the importance and dignity of the dream; it also announces the subject. The narrator, for all his ignorance and inexperience, presents himself as a poet inspired by the Goddess of Love, and the dream claims to be an authoritative contribution on the theme of love. Personal experience – as is again and again suggested in Chaucer's poetry – is not the only or most convincing source of information. There are other, perhaps more lasting, credentials for the poet: i.e. detached observation and, in particular, familiarity with the great authors of the past. An instance is the unobtrusive, but, at least for the better-read contemporaries, unmistakable allusion to Dante's *Divina Commedia*: it concerns most of all the figure of the classical guide, Vergil in Dante's poem, Africanus in the *Parliament*. There are a number of deliberate echoes and parallels that make the reminiscence quite obvious. Of course, Chaucer's narrator is not introduced to hell or to heaven, but this only shows that he has chosen a very different subject and that he does not wish to rival his great model either in scope or in seriousness. This is confirmed by the double inscription over the gate of the Garden of Love which is closely modelled on that over Dante's hell-gate. This may be meant as a humble acknowledgement, an admission of Chaucer's far more modest purpose, but at the same time Chaucer does not mind profiting by the authority of the great Italian poet; his unpretentious poem, too, claims to be in the nature of a divine revelation, although Chaucer must have been very conscious of the rather ironical contrast between Dante's encyclopaedic vastness and the modest brevity of his own poem.[8]

The wide-ranging, but in the last resort somewhat abstract, cosmic survey of Scipio's dream had not really answered any of the poet's urgent uncertainties. When the actual dream begins, the poem changes into a completely different, much less explicit form of instruction, chiefly employing allegorical modes of discourse.

Allegory has been defined in many different and often contradictory ways, and it seems to me particularly important to recognize the surprisingly varied possibilities of allegorical techniques and forms of expression. Allegory can neither be identified with a distinct literary genre – although it appears rather more frequently in some genres than in others – nor defined as a very clearly marked stylistic convention. An allegorical narrative as crystal-clear and consistent as the *Roman de la Rose* is the exception, not the rule. Far more typical and numerous are those mixed forms that combine abstract personification with 'real' characters, allegorical localities and plots with more realistic descriptions, and thus continually puzzle the modern reader by refusing to conform to any preconceived model.[9] Naturally, allegorical elements are employed more often than not in works of a didactic nature, and this is why allegory has often been misunderstood as something abstract, lifeless and therefore completely superseded by more realistic types of literature. The special attraction of allegory and its distinct claims, however, lie precisely in its power to establish a new and suggestive kind of reality and to use bits of familiar reality for the purpose of instructing the reader and of giving him such insights into philosophical and moral phenomena as are not easily provided by any other literary form. Allegory must not be read as a kind of riddle or crossword puzzle, and it does not attempt to say, in a clever disguise, what could be expressed more simply and lucidly by plain discourse: on the contrary, it enables the reader, by concrete and vivid images, to visualize ideas that could otherwise only be conveyed in abstract and theoretical terms.

Accordingly, the gate that leads into the Garden of Love, with its double inscription, is a visual image of the antithetical character of love as it was described in the very first lines of the poem. There, it was more of a rhetorical epigram to introduce the theme; here we have a suggestive allegorical setting. The description of the garden that follows is a particularly skilful attempt to give us a graphic and easily recognizable picture of the complex nature of all love experience through conventional literary devices.

The modern reader usually finds this mode of discourse rather alien and unnecessarily oblique at first, but it does not really help to a deeper understanding of this kind of medieval allegory to try and paraphrase it in prose. Rather one should make the effort, by repeated reading, to grasp something of the specific possibilities of allegorical writing. Thus, the topos of the walled garden, *hortus conclusus*, was a very popular and frequently modified device to suggest some specific area of experience. Shut off from the more complex and distracting world of daily life, this fictional plot of land enables the poet to inspect certain forms of existence in isolation and thus make them more easily intelligible. Entering this garden is a concrete image of the process of coming into personal contact with love. Whoever passes that gate, in spite of the warning and at the same time inviting inscription, accepts a challenge and commits himself to an adventure the consequences of which he is unable to foresee. The decision, at any rate, puts a wall between him and his former existence as well as his fellow-men who prefer to stay outside. To become a lover is to enter a different world and to stake everything on this single experience.[10]

Again the narrator makes clear that he is not one of those dedicated lovers, and he hesitates to pass through the gate, a sign that he has no personal experience. Africanus, his guide, explains to him, however, that an exception will be made for him: he will be allowed to look round the garden as a detached visitor without any binding obligation. It is another of the narrator's humorous self-portraits, a teasing combination of self-effacing modesty and uncommitted aloofness:

> But natheles, although that thow be dul,
> Yit that thow canst not do, yit mayst thow se.
> For many a man that may nat stonde a pul,
> It liketh hym at the wrastlyng for to be,
> And demeth yit wher he do bet or he.

And if thow haddest connyng for t'endite,
I shal the shewe mater of to wryte.   (162–8)

Thus the poet is once more reduced to the role of the curious onlooker, in
search of subject-matter for his poetry but without any active involvement. This also passes on to the reader the responsibility for a correct
interpretation of the allegory. The description of the garden is clearly
personal, and we are time and again reminded of the narrator's presence,
but he does not claim to offer a final explanation of what he sees, and the
guide disappears without giving any further assistance either to the
narrator or to the reader.[11]

The garden itself seems to fill the poet with deep joy, and this informs
all the following account of what he sees. There is first of all the
impression of inexhaustible fertility; frost and the change of seasons are
unknown and no darkness ever interferes with eternal day. This garden is
exempt from the natural laws of mutability and decay that were so
strongly impressed on the dreaming Scipio by his ancestor. It is the
traditional utopia of an ideal landscape, the *locus amoenus* of classical
and medieval literature, a kind of secularized Eden and a clear reminiscence of the *Roman de la Rose*, probably the most influential of all the
'sources' of *The Parliament of Fowls*. A great many literary and mythological traditions are brought together in the description of this park;
many of its items must have seemed like old acquaintances to some of
Chaucer's first readers, although their combination and, above all, their
specific function within the whole structure are highly original and often
give new meaning to well-used clichés.

In contrast to the *Roman de la Rose*, allegory and personification are
here used at first in a purely static way. The various aspects of love are not
shown as active agents; they remain completely isolated from each other
and do not enter into a dynamic interrelationship. The chief impression is
that of a surprising variety, rich in contrast and vitality. The disgusting
and the ennobling, the sensual and the ideal stand next to each other and
make this park a kind of visual commentary on the first lines of the poem.
This is not just an exhibition of courtly love; rather, courtly love is seen
within a much richer context of all possible shades of love experience. It
would not be very profitable to give an abstract explication of each single
item – this could hardly do justice to their suggestive appeal; but certain
themes and opposites become visible for the reader. The figure of Cupid
is obviously a personification of the more playful and irresponsible
aspects of love, with all the qualities that promise an enjoyment largely
confined to the senses ('Plesaunce', 'Aray', 'Lust', but also 'Curteysie').
All the sensual dimension of human love is then embodied in the image
of the temple, which is secluded from the open and life-giving nature and

clearly suggests a sultry and infertile atmosphere. Masculine con-
cupiscence and female shamelessness are contrasted in the figures of
grotesque Priapus and seductive Venus. Without any moral undertone,
these dangerously tempting aspects of love are 'placed' merely by the
contrast to the charms of the ideal landscape and the harmlessness of
Cupid, without even a rigorous line of demarcation between them. These
images are, in fact, not neatly separated and mutually exclusive forms of
love, but stimulating forces that may be operative, in varying degree,
within every human love-relationship. The list of ladies in the service of
Venus illustrates the deadly dangers of this form of love. Again, there are
no explicit accusations and the poet does not say that all these women
have put their trust in a mistaken idea of love, but they are warning
examples of the ambiguous nature of all love experience. The paintings of
classical heroines add the authority of mythological tradition to the
significance of the garden, and they suggest a close connection between
the personifications in the manner of the *Roman de la Rose*, the classical
deities of love and traditional romance stories. Allegory and literary
tradition thus illuminate each other for the poet, who leaves the temple in
a rather depressed mood to cheer himself up again in the garden. It is
important to note that the poet clearly identifies the positive aspects of
love with the invigorating vitality of open nature. Love and natural
growth belong together, and this is another indication that the subject is
not just *amour courtois* in the limiting sense. There is no suggestion either
of a particular social class or of any fixed set of rules for love's servants.

The colourful panorama of love has failed to provide the poet in search
of 'a certeyn thing' with a reassuring sense of direction. None of these
figures represents anything like the full complexity of the experience of
love. At this point the poet's eye is arrested by another personification,
the Goddess Natura, and if anything it is she who embodies something
like a synthesis of all the contradictory aspects of love described in the
poem. Looking at the poem's structure, we realize that Nature links the
two parts of the dream, the Garden of Love and the parliament of birds
over which she presides. The reader will understand this as an invitation
to look for thematic connections and to read the following part as a
pointed comment on the garden allegory and the problems raised by it.
This does not necessarily mean that the garden has to be seen as the real
centre of the whole poem; it does mean, however, that one part of the
poem should be read in the light of the other.[12] The didactic dream of
Scipio and the graphic allegory of the garden are not just introductions to
the debate of the birds: they open up themes and provoke questions that
will be further unfolded in the second half of the poem in more specific
terms and in a different literary idiom.

The Goddess Natura has a long ancestry in medieval literature; from the point of view of the history of thought, she may be described as the remarkable result of an attempt to reconcile the principle of rigorous restraint enjoined by religious moralists and the idea of natural procreation within a comprehensive concept of love and fertility.[13] There are many variations, especially in the degree of philosophical sophistication, but Natura almost always represents the creative, inexhaustible forces of life that are an aspect of God's life-giving omnipotence, his delight in his own creation; at the same time, she represents the root of all human love. Chaucer's Goddess is not, of course, adequately explained if we simply replace her by some abstract philosophical concept, and she is more than just a personification of a clear-cut idea. This is another illustration of the fact that the allegorical method enables the poet to express by suggestive images what could not be translated into the language of rational argumentation without serious loss. It is, at any rate, clear that through the figure of Nature and the part played by her during the following debate we dimly recognize the existence of some power above the various aspects of love displayed in the garden and even above Venus – a power that embraces the natural urge of fertility and transcends the conflict between the *contemptus mundi* preached by Africanus and the sensual glamour of love. This concept allows for the enjoyment of love, for fertility, chastity and abstention from love, without any of the suffering Venus brings on her servants. The poem is, of course, no philosophical treatise, and it would not be appropriate to overburden it with the fundamental themes of centuries of philosophical speculation, but it is certainly an important contribution to the debate: not the God of Love or Venus, but Natura is the final authority in the ensuing dispute.

The occasion of this dispute also makes clear that its subject is not an exclusively courtly form of love, but the natural desire of all living creatures to be mated. This is one of the chief differences between this debate and the genre of the *demande d'amour* by which Chaucer was influenced. There we usually find a more or less specialized discussion on subtleties of courtly love-casuistry, whereas in Chaucer's poem we have a far more elementary problem, the choice of a mate. At the end of the poem the great majority of the birds depart cheerfully with their new partners, without giving any further thought to the theoretical problems of love. The question raised by the poet at the outset of the poem, concerning the causes of love's misery and happiness, is placed in a much wider context: what the poet had meant by love now turns out to be only a very limited aspect of a universal law that preserves and keeps in motion the whole creation. This widening of the poem's scope from the narrator's initial query is the chief contribution of the parliament to the thematic structure. It is, however, not only a question of theme, but of literary technique as well: the static description of the Garden of Love is followed by a polyphonic debate, with the dramatic clash of controversial attitudes. The stylistic variety of the second half, too, emphasizes that we are not presented here with a concept of love that is confined to one particular group of society. This is quite a new development in Chaucer's early poetry, and it appears almost like a first foretaste of *The Canterbury Tales*, with its incomparably richer spectrum of styles and levels of sophistication.

It is only too easy to complicate the approach to this part of the poem unnecessarily by the wrong kind of question (as some interpretations show); one such question concerns the occasion. The poem gives the impression of having been written for some specific event or date, but we have no definite indication of any such occasion and no reliable evidence as to the date or the circumstances of its composition. What remains is only the vague speculation that *The Parliament of Fowls* could have been written to mark some particular St Valentine's Day. This anniversary was apparently celebrated in courtly circles with sociable games which may have led up to a more or less seriously meant choice of partners for the coming summer season – just as, according to a later popular tradition, the birds chose their mates on that day. It is probable, at least, that an originally aristocratic custom gradually became a generally accepted element of folklore. A late illustration is Ophelia's outspoken St Valentine's song in *Hamlet*. The choice of partners is also, presumably, alluded to in a charming little carol, written some two hundred years before Chaucer, from the famous collection of the *Carmina Burana*:

> Swaz hie gât umbe,
> daz sint alle megede,
> die wellent ân man
> allen disen sumer gân!

(Those going round here are all girls who intend to spend all this summer without a man.)

This was evidently accompanied by a dance and may have been a teasing invitation to pick one's partner for the summer.[14]

More difficult, but at the same time less relevant, seems to me the question of whether Chaucer meant to celebrate some particular choice of partner with his brief poem. Some scholars have, detective-like, gone through Chaucer's contemporaries in search of aristocratic ladies wooed by different suitors and, not surprisingly, have come up with a few constellations that could, with a bit of imagination, be made to fit the situation in the *Parliament*. The possibility of such topical allusions can

47

never be ruled out once and for all, because the poem was probably written for a fairly close community who would have a great number of friends and acquaintances in common; thus the conditions for a rather personal form of allegory may have been very favourable. But this would only have applied to the poem's very first audience, and the number of manuscripts suggests that it soon became known to a much wider circle who would presumably not be particularly interested in the original occasion. Even if we could discover the precise historical background to the *Parliament*, it would not add much to our enjoyment of the poem or to its interest as a particularly original treatment of the subject of love. It might perhaps explain the identity of the three eagles, but not the structure of the whole poem. If ever there was a definite occasion for the poem it must already have been lost sight of when Chaucer's contemporaries and immediate successors copied and imitated the poem. It can never have been more than a very minor aspect of the poem's appeal.

The *Parliament*'s main attraction for the modern reader lies in the particularly successful fusion of well-known literary conventions, which defies any simple paraphrase: animal fable and the *demande d'amour*, political satire and spring-song, have all contributed to the work and readers may well differ as to which is the most prominent element. The light-hearted tone and the absence of any explicit didacticism suggest to me that Chaucer leaves the reader a fairly wide margin of possible interpretations. This applies to a number of problems that have puzzled critics, especially the role of the eagles, the social hierarchy of the parliament and Chaucer's whole attitude to the conventions of courtly love in general.

The introduction of this parliament, in particular the rhetorical catalogue of birds, makes it fairly clear that the world of these birds, divided according to different degrees and functions, is meant as a mirror of human society, a mirror that makes it easier for the reader to recognize failings and ridiculous postures than many a straightforward account could do. It is also quite obvious that the eagles represent the highest 'class' in this society, not in any precise sociological sense, but – in accordance with the theory of true gentility – as an embodiment of aristocratic ideals that need not, so at least it was often claimed, be confined to hereditary titles and to one particular section of society.[15]

The speech of the first eagle, announcing his claim to the lady, is a comprehensive summary of the traditional concept of courtly love. The lover vows eternal 'trouthe'; he hopes for the reward of 'mercy' and 'grace' from the lady and he disclaims all impure motives and uncourtly behaviour, such as is 'untrewe', 'disobeysaunt', 'necligent', 'avauntour'. I do not think that we are meant to look for hidden irony or a satiric denunciation of courtly love in this speech.[16] It is only a natural consequence of this competitive situation that the eagle should think mainly of his success and not just profess his faithful service; it does not mean that he himself is offending against the laws of *amour courtois*. There is nothing in the text to suggest that Chaucer wanted to present him as anything less than a perfect representative of the conventional concept of courtly love, which the poet, to be sure, only knows from books, as he confessed at the beginning. Similarly, the formel is an image of the perfection all lovers see in their lady, the most successful of all the works of creation; even Nature herself cannot look at her without 'blysse' (377–8) and keeps bending to kiss her.

Here again, different audiences will respond differently, but it is likely that we are more inclined these days to discover comedy or subversive irony where the medieval poet would not have found any occasion for it. Our own attitude towards the ritualized forms of courtly love is naturally much more detached, and it is easy to assume that the poet must have shared our reservations. The whole balance of the debate, however, depends on the courtly position being presented with full conviction and without any suggestion of parody. The irony comes in later and is implied not in the pose of the aristocratic birds, but in the context of the whole debate.

What the three eagles declaim is by and large the same profession of an eternal devotion, based on nothing but truth and virtue, without any selfish consideration. The two speakers that come after the first eagle are 'of lower kynde', and their wooing has not quite the same rhetorical flourish. Thus, from the start, there does not seem to be any genuine uncertainty as to whom the formel should choose. If there is any suspense it concerns not so much the actual outcome as the presentation of different points of view. For the eagles, as for the ideal lover and the courtly love-poet, love is a subject for rhetorical display and endless reflection. It has to be constantly articulated, and this makes it a particularly suitable theme for reflective and argumentative poetry. The narrator is full of admiration and relishes these courtly speeches, the 'gentil ple' lasting all day. He does not give us any more extended specimens of this precious rhetoric, however, as he did in *The Book of the Duchess*. This is evidently not the subject of the poem, whose real originality lies in the way the rhetoric of courtly love is placed in a context that clearly demonstrates the possibility of very different kinds of love, and of lovers who have no taste for this sophisticated courtly code. Though to the poet, as he assures us, the time does not seem long, and he does not grow tired of listening to the rivals' pleas, the vociferous impatience of the 'lower' birds adds quite a different kind of comment. We may be all too quickly prepared to agree with the commonsense of the birds who are weary of listening to all that fine rhetoric and want to be off home; more than anything they want the practical business finished that has brought them here. For them, 'gentil ple' is nothing but 'cursede pletynge' (495), and this demonstrates again Chaucer's delight in provocative contrast. He is evidently interested by the fact that courtly love and all stylistic conventions that go with it do not exist in a vacuum, but have to face the challenge of very different attitudes, just as all literary tradition has to be confronted with the realities of practical experience.

It would, however, be rather anachronistic to conclude from this spirited clash that Chaucer meant to devalue once and for all the formal discipline and the impractical idealism of *amour courtois* or that for him all other forms of love were equally valid and admirable. He does seem to see the danger of an esoteric cult that loses sight of its real object and indulges in a devotion for its own sake. Every reader is free to descend to the level of the goose or the cuckoo, but this involves the sacrifice of everything that raises human love above the simple mating instinct of animals. It is in this spiritual and moral aspect of courtly love that Chaucer and most courtly love-poets are primarily interested. Chaucer's own attitude towards the traditional values of courtly love was neither uncritical nor simple; the very fact that he again and again returns to the subject is evidence of his fascinated interest. At the same time, he constantly chooses as one of his main subjects, be it in comedy or in tragedy, the conflict between the idealistic devotion to a lady and the primitive sexual instinct, and this again suggests that he felt very acutely the contradiction between an ideal standard and sober reality. This is, of course, a problem that the love-poetry of all ages has recognized, and it is treated much more fully in Chaucer's two major works, but it is also crucial to a fuller understanding of *The Parliament of Fowls*.

The quarrel between the birds once more directs the attention of the reader to their diversity. There are unmistakable allusions to the class differences in the English Parliament of the time and to social divisions within contemporary society in general, but a more specific equation is rather difficult and not very profitable. Actual contemporary social stratification was not so clear and inflexible that any reader would immediately have recognized the significance of each group of birds; nor does the poem as a whole give the impression of a very direct and sharply pointed estates satire.[17] The differences between the birds are not presented in narrowly social terms; rather, they suggest a diversity of temperaments and degrees of wisdom. This distinction would, however, be less relevant to medieval readers because social and intellectual divisions were often seen in close conjunction, and it is obvious that Chaucer's poem, too, associates particular mental habits with social status. The whole field of *amour courtois* is presented as the domain of the aristocratic birds – not in a strictly exclusive sense, but as a matter of historical experience and stylistic decorum. It is more difficult to place the other birds with any precision, but we do recognize clearly defined and familiar attitudes in the self-assured simplicity of the goose, the un-worldly and impractical idealism of the dove or the philistine stupidity of the duck – attitudes we shall meet again with even greater diversity among the Canterbury pilgrims. The text suggests plainly enough, I believe, that the poet has a certain sympathy for the outspoken impa-tience of the lower birds, but at the same time there is no doubt that their proposals reveal a complete lack of understanding and sensitivity towards the real issue – except, perhaps, in the case of the dove, whose uncritical and literal acceptance of the courtly idea of 'trouthe' only exposes the impossibility of a simple solution.

Many interpretations show that it is very difficult for some readers to enter into an attitude of mind that neither identifies unquestioningly with the courtly ideal as presented here nor sees it as only one among other equally valid and exemplary poses. It is simply not adequate, I think, to describe the poem only as 'a comedy of attitudes'.[18] When it comes to the point, Chaucer is surely more on the side of the eagles than on that of the other birds, and the world of courtly ideals and conventions is closer to his own standards than the purely practical pragmatism of their critics; but this does not at all imply a self-sufficient blindness to the challenge of such direct opposition. *The Parliament of Fowls*, for all its tolerant diversity, remains a courtly poem, but one that transcends the exclusive elitism of courtly convention and allows for other points of view. Readers may differ in their precise reaction to this provocative diversity, but any interpretation that attempts to simplify the poet's 'message' comes short of the poem's wise intelligence and its inconclusive polyphony.

Its tentative, rather than dogmatic or didactic, character is finally brought home to the reader by the postponing of the final verdict at the end of the debate. In spite of what Natura had laid down as a condition right at the beginning, the proper choice and the mutual consent of the partners does not seem to present any problem to the lower birds.[19] The world of their experience is so neatly ordered that each of them can pick his mate without further reflection and ado and enjoy the coming of spring with her, whereas the formel needs another year to make up her mind although the question of who is the most deserving of the three suitors had been settled from the very start. The reason for her procrasti-nation is not that the choice is so difficult, but that the code of *fin amour* demanded such a refusal to come to a quick decision and to give up her freedom and her virginity without a very lengthy process of hesitation, aloofness and distant goodwill. The fact that the three eagles have to face another year of devotion and service to their love while all the other birds, happily mated, celebrate the season, is surely not meant as a criticism of the infertility of courtly love,[20] but, rather, as an expression of its complex and ritualized nature. Final fulfilment is not as easy for those who see love as a rich and totally committing experience as it is for the simpler, unreflective creatures. The highest form of love is at the same time the most difficult and demanding for its servants. Thus the poem's outcome confirms the initial statement of love's contradictory qualities. To have to wait for another year is not a punishment and must not be understood in negative terms only, because it is an opportunity – for all three contenders at that – to prove themselves worthy of the lady by their actions, not just by fine professions:

> Beth of good herte, and serveth alle thre.
> A yer is nat so longe to endure,
> And ech of yow peyne him in his degre
> For to do wel ...
>
> (660–3)

As at the end of Shakespeare's *Love's Labour's Lost*, where again the theory and the practice of an aristocratic code of love are weighed against each other, a time is set in which the rhetoric of courtly wooing must be substantiated by the lovers' actual deeds and thus proved to be an expression of true moral endeavour. With such ethical claims, verbal declamation is not enough. In this Chaucer remains firmly within the best tradition of *fin amour*. Devotion to a lady makes the lover a better and worthier man, as Chaucer shows beautifully in *Troilus and Criseyde*, and this ennobling quality of love is its chief justification, outweighing all the lover's suffering in love's service. Thus the three eagles are not really disappointed or turned away empty-handed. Our expectation that two of them might eventually find themselves without a partner does not make Nature's verdict tragic or depressing. None of them has as yet been finally refused; each has a chance of demonstrating the sincerity of his devotion and the superiority of his claim. The spring-song at the end, chanted by the smaller birds, applies to all the assembly and must not be understood as being in any way directed against the courtly wooers. Here again there is a clear affinity to Shakespeare's romantic comedies (different as they are in many other respects), where dance and song unite the couples and society as a whole, and music becomes an expression of true harmony and reconciliation, even though this does not mean that all the questions and contradictions which have emerged in the course of the work have miraculously become non-existent.

This skilful little lyric adds another mode of poetical expression to this brief work. Coming after all the intellectual debate, rhetorical decla-mation and formal dispute of the dream–vision and the parliament, this completely untroubled song of joy is an important aspect of the poem's 'message' – or perhaps it rather emphasizes the lack of what could be pinned down as a message. Instead of a clearly defined genre we have something like a swift review of various poetical attempts to describe the nature of love, a kaleidoscope of conventions and perspectives, held together by the humour and the stylistic virtuosity of the poet.

It is in this exhilarating variety in the poem, with the experience of love not so much described in any neatly formulated aphorism as reproduced in all its cheerful energy, that we have to look for the insight gained by the poet. When, waking up from his dream, he returns again to his books, it is no longer just in a bewildered search for some 'certeyn thing': he has found real inspiration in his reading, and he has proved by his own little poem how much true wisdom and real experience can be transmitted by the written word.[21]

The Parliament of Fowls, as a whole and in its individual episodes, is an amazing demonstration of Chaucer's continual effort and achieve-ment to bring literary clichés to new life, to reactivate the meaning they were originally intended to express and to stimulate the reader's imagina-tion. As the poet's creation is compared to new corn shooting year by year out of old fields, this poem itself aspires to be a seed from which, through contact with a receptive audience, new insight and experience can grow.

5

Tradition and experience:
The House of Fame

THE HOUSE OF FAME CONTINUES THE DEBATE ON THE INTER-
relation between convention and experience which had been opened in
The Parliament of Fowls, and again Chaucer employs structural devices
similar to those he used in his two earlier poems. There are, however,
significant differences. Not only is *The House of Fame* much longer than
the earlier poems, it is also more ambitious in its wide range of themes,
and it seems to be less of an organic whole. Many recent critics have been
anxious to affirm that there is much more unity here than the reader
discovers at a first reading; but almost all interpretations that try to
demonstrate something like strict unity start from thematical preconceptions that do not really apply to every part of the poem. The fact that
most readers at first find the poem lacking a consistent plan, as to its
structure as well as its subject-matter, need not necessarily be due to their
inability to recognize subtle connections and thematic consistency, but
has to be seen as the result of the poem's particular design. On the other
hand, as in the case of *The Parliament of Fowls*, it can be shown that the
individual parts of *The House of Fame* are more than just isolated
fragments, because Chaucer is evidently concerned with similar questions and similar poetological conventions, although he goes on to new
areas of thought, treating his source-material with even more independence and originality than in the *Parliament*.[1]

The poem is, again, a dream–vision, but the starting-point is already
somewhat different: it is the very nature of dreams that the poet has
discovered as fascinating subject-matter. So, after having presented a
learned epitome of possible theories, Chaucer proceeds to suggest a direct
bearing of dreams on the personal experience of every individual human
being. The very first sentence, repeated later in the poem (58), makes it
clear that he does not intend to indulge in an academic argument: 'God
turne us every drem to goode!' The poet is not interested in a detached
debate, for the subject may have a very personal relevance for every
reader. In contrast to the *Roman de la Rose*, where the authority and

truth of dreams are emphasized in general terms to give due weight to the narrator's own dream, the poet here brushes aside all the learned theories as being beyond his judgement, but not without having elaborated them with an impressive show of expert knowledge and minute detail. It would be wrong to conclude that it was Chaucer's intention to ridicule the discussion about the origin and authority of dreams, which was very lively in this period and recurs again and again in his own poetry. Rather, he makes a point of emphasizing that this discussion ultimately proceeds from genuine experience, which in its turn makes it relevant for every individual concerned. Consequently, his own dream is announced as a real occurrence, and this again draws our attention to the provocative tension between actual experience and traditional wisdom. The singularity of his dream is further underlined by the particular date assigned to it. It is more than probable that the poet's contemporaries may have found this date less arbitrary than we do today. But what the reader of the *Roman de la Rose* or other love-allegories would at least have noticed is the time of the year (10 December), which is not exactly the most favourable season for a love-vision. The extensive, half-serious invocation of the God of Sleep, combining conventional material and inventive individuality, intensifies our expectations and creates the impression that the poem in hand is an ambitious and serious work of art. It is at the same time an amusing variation on the theme of sleeplessness already touched on in *The Book of the Duchess*.

By contrast to the two earlier poems, the narrator does not immediately put forward his own personal questions and problems, nor is his ignorance given particular emphasis at this stage; but the lavish display of literary clichés characterizes him as a poet eagerly showing off the fruits of his reading, without, however, committing himself to a firm opinion of his own on all the controversial matters he finds in his sources. From the very beginning, the impression conveyed to the reader is that literary competence and wide reading do not necessarily include practical experience and true wisdom, whereas this is usually taken for granted in most serious medieval poetry.

Nearly the whole of the first book – the book-division being another proof of the poem's demonstratively literary character – is taken up by a paraphrase of Vergil's *Aeneid*, or significant parts of it. Although it is a very free and personal version of the plot, it still remains a traditional story, which is bound to disappoint those readers who had expected a more original revelation. Again, the parallel to *The Parliament of Fowls* is very instructive. There, too, the poet in his search for knowledge is at first confronted with a specimen of classical literature, the dream of Scipio, and his disappointment is answered with the actual dream. In this case, however, the classical reminiscence is part of the dream itself, and this intensifies the contrast to the reader's expectations and makes the question of what kind of helpful experience a canonized piece of poetry could actually contain even more urgent. With either of these poems, it would be rather shortsighted to ignore the thematic links between the extensive introduction and the centre of the poem. On the other hand, a neat, literal analogy is hardly to be expected either: this would imply a much too narrow concept of unity based on literal meaning.

The history of Dido, one of the most famous love-stories the Middle Ages knew, is quite obviously introduced here as an example of the suggestive and at the same time ambiguous vitality of literary source-material. Chaucer's account is deliberately simplified and moralized, to such an extent that the reader is left with a variety of possible interpretations: has the narrator completely misunderstood the time-honoured story, or has he just trivialized it when he reduces Aeneas' pious obedience to his vocation to a vulgar breach of faith, or is his account meant to suggest that literary tradition can turn a trivial romance into a heroic pose?[2] What exactly is the 'reality' or the 'truth' behind the traditional story: is it the actual occasion or what tradition has made of it? The problem of tradition is explored here in a more fundamental and radical manner than in *The Parliament of Fowls* and with a slight shift of emphasis. Aeneas' fame is, in fact, the product of a great poet's art, it is created by words; but this is not a poetological question alone, it also concerns the very nature of love. The glassy temple of Venus in which the poet finds the history of Dido is an impressive though ambiguous image of the artificial reality generations of poets have built up around the concept of love. Dido is the most prominent example of this, but all the other figures of classical literature gathered here testify to the same experience. The reality of this world, even though it does only exist in tradition, is suggested by the fact that the poet is deeply moved and emotionally involved in it: retelling the classical tragedy he is moved to genuine compassion. Thus, without any further explanation, by the simple re-narration of the well-known story, the power of tradition to inspire real sympathy and create genuine experience is demonstrated. This is further intensified by the fact that the reaction of the reader differs markedly from that of the narrator, who confesses at the outset that the phenomenon of love is beyond his grasp and that he is unable to offer an opinion based on experience. On the other hand, he is deeply moved and cannot resist the impulse to offer the reader detailed comment, thus producing an ironic discrepancy between the heroic matter and his naive, over-simple interpretation, when, for instance, he asks the reader to take warning from Dido's fall that women should not love foreigners.[3] At the same time the narrator tries to convey his own compassion for Dido to the reader. Her complaint is the centre of the Vergil-paraphrase, which at this point expands on the source and completely changes its tone. Dido, who in Vergil's account has to suffer because of Aeneas' divine vocation, here appears as a true lover treacherously abandoned, and Aeneas' divinely inspired mission to go on to Italy is denounced as the subtle attempt of dishonest writers to justify what really is unjustifiable. Dido herself puts the crucial question of what later generations will make of her deplorable fate, and she fears, with good reason as the event shows, that she will be treated unjustly by posterity. The reader, comparing her fundamentally human dilemma with what tradition and the poets have made of it, can only join her in lamenting over the arbitrariness of 'wikke Fame'. This basic problem, presumably, was Chaucer's real motive for trivializing the heroic story. Like any other glaringly one-sided interpretation, his version of the Dido narrative must challenge the reader and make him reconsider his own attitude towards this story. It is obvious that Chaucer's narrator can see only half the truth, and his pretended inability to treat his material impartially must raise serious doubts as to the reliability of literary tradition in general. Even the faithful study of tradition is not enough for those who want to get at the truth, least of all in matters of love. And this, indeed, is a theme which recurs in all three books of the poem, however different they may be in other respects; it concerns Chaucer's highly ambiguous concept of fame.

Here again, as in *The Parliament of Fowls*, the encounter with a specimen of the great literary tradition leaves the poet in a state of perplexity. What knowledge has he gained? He certainly has not learnt anything apt to satisfy his general uncertainty about tradition or to help his lack of personal experience. The realization of the relativity and unreliability of things handed on by former generations, along with the triviality of much of his own experience, at first leads to a rather depressing dilemma, symbolized impressively by the image of the endless desert. It is not just the dilemma of a narrator who has failed to comprehend what was revealed to him, nor is it the helplessness of a poet who finds himself wanting material, but it is the expression of the general feeling of having lost his bearings amidst the rich material supplied by tradition and an ambiguous reality which very often turns out so much less imposing than the idealizing literary tradition seems to suggest.[4]

The second book provides something like the beginning of an answer for the bewildered dreamer. As to its literary form, it is, again, a dream–vision, in the course of which the ignorant poet is instructed; not only the basic setting but also a great number of substantial details gives clear evidence of its indebtedness to Boethius' *Consolatio Philosophiae* and Dante's *Divina Commedia*.[5] At a first glance, to be sure, its unconventional features are much more striking than the traditional formulas of didactic poetry. The human traits of the golden eagle, the almost colloquial tone of his conversation with the poet, and the amusing aspects of their journey through the air have often been praised by critics.[6] They inform this part of the poem with a liveliness and originality that fascinate even today's reader. But it is exactly this personal tone that emphasizes the intellectual claim and wisdom behind the instruction provided for the poet. The modest curiosity of the dreamer is confronted with the pontificating loquaciousness of the eagle, the all-inclusive cosmic subject-matter with everyday reality – a reality the poet keeps before our eyes by occasional realistic details. Just like the narrator in *The Parliament of Fowls*, he is promised an authentic experience as a reward for his faithful study and for his theoretical love-service; and here again the poet is described as someone who has had neither luck nor concrete experience in love-matters, and yet has not, from disappointment, adopted an attitude of scornful rejection. The pose of the eager though inexperienced theorist is portrayed with particular liveliness here, and thus we get a self-portrait which undoubtedly stands in some direct and suggestive relation to Chaucer's personal situation and his reputation with his audience, be it only by a pointed or ironical contrast between his real self and his literary *alter ego*:

> thou hast no tydynges
> Of Loves folk yf they be glade,
> Ne of noght elles that God made;
> And noght oonly fro fer contree
> That ther no tydynge cometh to thee,
> But of thy verray neyghebores,
> That duellen almost at thy dores,
> Thou herist neyther that ne this;
> For when thy labour doon al ys,
> And hast mad alle thy rekenynges,
> In stede of reste and newe thynges,
> Thou goost hom to thy hous anoon;
> And, also domb as any stoon,
> Thou sittest at another book
> Tyl fully daswed ys thy look,
> And lyvest thus as an heremyte,
> Although thyn abstynence ys lyte.   (644–60)

Much more important than these details, exciting as they are, is the decided profession of an attachment to the world of literature, which makes the poet forgetful even of the nearest opportunity for genuine experience. And it is this sharp contrast between two completely different sources of experience and information that constitutes the central theme of the poem. In this respect, the conversation with the eagle is something like an attempt to bridge the gap between the two areas: the eagle's appearance, as well as the revelation on which he comments, belongs with traditional wisdom, whereas for the poet himself the journey is a decidedly real adventure. This is confirmed by the tone of his account, suggesting that there is nothing supernatural or fantastic about the instruction: for him it is, on the contrary, a direct confrontation with reality. The dreamer is, for instance, positively allowed to examine with his own eyes the truth of traditional astronomical lore, and this authentic sensory perception also lends immediate authority to all the other information provided by the eagle.

It is, however, interesting to note that the dreamer is not particularly curious about these natural phenomena and declines to take the trouble to inspect the world of stars and planets personally. He declares that he is quite content to believe 'Hem that write of this matere' (1013); in other words, he trusts tradition and authority and does not feel the need of 'preve by experience' (878). It is different with the 'tydynges' 'of Loves folk' (675): here the dreamer seeks and is promised the kind of instruction, or indeed demonstration, that goes beyond what he can find in books. Unlike Dante, who is explicitly referred to as the poet of heaven and hell, he has no ambition to touch cosmic matters in his poetry.[7] He is happy to confine himself to secular aspects of fame and rumour.

The literary form of the poem, too, suggests that art and life are shown to be correlated in a disquieting manner. The division into books and the numerous intrusions of the author are unmistakable evidence of the literary and admittedly fictitious character of the poem. Thus, the dream is interrupted and the second book is announced by a *proemium* which combines the style of the popular entertainer with rhetorical ostentation:

> Now herkeneth, every maner man
> That Englissh understonde kan,
> And listeneth of my drem to lere.
> For now at erste shul ye here
> So sely an avisyon,
> That Isaye, ne Scipion,
> Ne kyng Nabugodonosor,
> Pharoo, Turnus, ne Elcanor,
> Ne mette such a drem as this! (509–17)

The reader's critical detachment in the face of all the verbal bravura displayed here again brings home to him the ambiguous relationship between literary craftsmanship, convention and real-life experience. The same is true for the eagle's comical assertion that he is using a plain and concise style in order to instruct the simple listener more effectively:

> 'Telle me this now feythfully,
> Have y not preved thus symply,
> Withoute any subtilite
> Of speche, or gret prolixite
> Of termes of philosophie,
> Of figures of poetrie,
> Or colours of rethorike?
> Pardee, hit oughte the to lyke!
> For hard langage and hard matere
> Ys encombrous for to here
> Attones; wost thou not wel this?'
> And y answered and seyde, 'Yis.'
>   'A ha!' quod he, 'lo, so I can
> Lewedly to a lewed man
> Speke ...'   (853–67)

The glaring discrepancy between assertion and practice is not just another comic effect, it again goes to show how inseparably form and theme work together in this poem. The actual information given to the poet could have been expressed much more concisely. The eagle's speech sometimes turns into a scientific treatise. The elaborate rhetoric does not only involve the clearly fictitious elements of the narrative, it also gives a stylized description of natural phenomena, making them part of the literary tradition as well, thus blurring the borderline between reality and fiction. The constant juxtaposition of different levels of style and formal structure reflects Chaucer's way of viewing the complex interplay of our various modes of perception.[8] The eagle's instruction therefore includes both experience and knowledge and in doing so he links the concept of knowledge to the scintillating image of Fame. The eagle's wordy and circumstantial scientific explanations again bring home the fact, already demonstrated in the first book, that the relationship between reality and tradition is utterly uncalculable. At this point, the concept of tradition is extended to include what the eagle calls 'tydynges', so that it now not only covers literature or the past in general but also embraces any method of transmitting experience, whether orally or in writing, whether as a realistic account of actual events or as stylized poetry. The House of Fame as it is described by the eagle is primarily a kind of collecting-point for all sorts of orally delivered accounts, as is suggested by the complicated acoustical theory propounded by the verbose instructor. Fame is made out of words; it is an aspect of language and speech.

The third book is indeed the climax of Chaucer's vision: the final revelation of the puzzling activities of Fame, which the reader has been prepared for indirectly through various hints, now takes shape in an allegorical scene which hardly needs any detailed commentary. The unpredictable elusiveness of traditional knowledge is now personified in the Goddess Fame, closely related in this poem to the Goddess Fortuna, whose capriciousness at least she shares. Fame is a gift, awarded more frequently at random or even in the heat of short-lived moods than as the reward for real merit. While the names of Fame's favourites become universally known and are handed on from generation to generation as household words, the names of many others fall into oblivion. Many worthy and deserving figures are thus irretrievably wiped out. The image of the rock of ice, with the names engraved on it melting away, represents this very vividly. Beyond that, the whole of this section of the poem demonstrates strikingly what a surprising amount of suggestive, by no means merely artificially constructed, argument can be presented within the framework of an allegory. Besides, this is not just a static icono-graphical allegory – as is, for instance the Garden of Love in *The Parliament of Fowls* – but almost a new kind of myth, a dramatic representation of a universal experience. Here, too, personifications, mythical characters and 'historical' figures, are not strictly distinguished but appear within the same context. The variety of people the poet encounters in the House of Fame illustrates particular qualities associ-ated with the concept of fame. Next to great historians and poets like Josephus, Statius, Homer and Geoffrey of Monmouth, who are the sources of our knowledge, a great number of troubadours, musicians and minstrels enter the stage, and each produces his own version of fame. It is clear, then, that Chaucer is concerned not just with the desirable fame of distinguished personalities, as it was cultivated during the Renaissance, but with any means of disseminating news. Fame and ill reputation spring from the same capricious source. Fame is a very human goddess, and her totally irrational verdicts, executed by Aeolus and his two trumpets, add a rather comical aspect to the whole scene.[9]

The fact that this comprehensive concept of fame includes the living as well as the dead becomes suddenly clear when the dreamer finds himself confronted with the question whether he himself has come to apply for fame. His cautious and at the same time very sensible answer shows that he is not just a naive observer, but that he has already benefited from this lively demonstration of Fame's unpredictable nature and is not over-whelmed by the traditional lure of glory:

> 'Nay, for sothe, frend,' quod y;
> 'I cam noght hyder, graunt mercy,
> For no such cause, by my hed!

Geoffrey Chaucer

Sufficeth me, as I were ded,
That no wight have my name in honde.
I wot myself best how y stonde;
For what I drye, or what I thynke,
I wil myselven al hyt drynke,
Certeyn, for the more part,
As fer forth as I kan myn art.'   (1873–82)

This is not the only point at which the immediate relevance of the vision to the dreamer himself is made clear; the whole of the third book is presented in terms of a very personal experience. We are continually reminded of the fact that it is the narrator in person who is actually living through all this and that his impressions are decidedly real, indeed sensual – not just an intellectual experience, as his study of books is. The realistic tone is achieved not only by many verbs suggesting sensual perception, but most of all by the critical and at the same time amused tone that informs his whole account.

Here, again, it would be misguided to overrate Chaucer's parodic intention. The irreverent presentation of personified fame is not merely directed against earlier allegories or the allegorical method as such; it reactivates the potentially rich expressiveness of the allegorical mode by establishing a very close relationship between allegorical and realistic accounts. It is only if we attempt to translate the poetical vision into plain discursive prose that we shall find the narrative abstract or lacking in precise plan. In the case of Chaucer's allegories, however, this would indeed be particularly pointless and would virtually bar our way to a better understanding of this kind of poetry.

This is true in particular of the final part of the poem, which returns to what the poet was actually looking for and to the revelation promised by the eagle. The House of Fame has largely disappointed his expectations, because the unreliability of posthumous fame is in no way new to him and therefore is of no help to him in his lack of experience. The ultimate instruction now seems to be at hand in the House of Rumour, where he is led by the eagle, who has suddenly reappeared. This continually revolving house is the focus where all events of the world, as they are communicated by word of mouth, converge. Here, at last, authentic experience and solid information should be available to the poet; but the prevailing impression he gets is that of absurd chaos and aimless movement rendering any kind of reliable orientation impossible. The restless, unstructured and transparent house is an allegorical image of the utter impossibility of grasping reality by any simple formula. The 'tydynges' the poet has been in search of turn out to be nothing but an inextricable tangle of truth and lies, of no more use to him than all the preceding revelations. Past events and facts do only exist in the form in which they are transmitted by word of mouth, so that any hope of reaching a place where unveiled truth is to be found ultimately turns out to be an illusion. And just as illusory, it seems to me, is the conviction of some critics that the 'man of gret auctorite' who appears in the closing lines of the poem would have settled the matter satisfactorily by producing some few words of wisdom. It is more likely that this information, too, would have failed to satisfy the poet once and for all; at best it would only have brought home to him once again the immense variety of possible manifestations of love and fame. Otherwise, *The House of Fame* would be the only one of Chaucer's poems to end with a kind of epitome of its theme.[10]

The poem's transmission does not permit any confident statement as to whether Chaucer actually finished it, whether he lost interest in it, or whether there were any other reasons why the text was left unfinished.[11] It is only natural that this state of affairs has set many readers guessing, but a glance at *The Book of the Duchess* and *The Parliament of Fowls* suggests that the interpretation of the whole would hardly have been affected by some few additional lines. In view of Chaucer's usual narrative practice, speculation as to the possible end of the poem seems to be hardly profitable, but it is most likely that here, too, the only thing left for the poet awaking from his dream would have been to return to his books again and to go on looking for experience and for 'tydynges' there. Be it as it may, it is difficult to believe that anything was meant to be revealed in those missing last lines that had not already been implied by the whole course of the poem.

Chaucer in the end seems to have come no nearer the ultimate aim of his endeavours, to discover truth. He just has to go on trying to make the best of the material provided by capricious tradition. Reality, in the last resort, has proved in no way more reliably available than book-knowledge. The poet's scepticism towards literature, at any rate, has done nothing whatever to improve his knowledge; on the contrary, reality urges him on towards a fresh, though more wary and sophisticated, study of books.

Chaucer's poem does not propose an intellectually consistent line of argument; but as a whole it is a particularly lively exposition of a problem central to Chaucer's art, and, in its highly successful combination of learning, brilliant rhetoric, humour and observation, it embodies a kind of synthesis which contradicts the poet's scepticism. As the great number of controversial interpretations show, the poem itself has become a most inspiring and ambiguous instance of literary tradition. And, although it does not present any clear-cut solutions for the problems it touches upon,

it nevertheless invites our active participation in the process of questioning and exploring those issues by suggesting a direct correlation between
experience and literature; in this context it seems irrelevant to ask
whether love or poetry is the actual subject of the poem. The love-poet
depends on a reasonable experience of reality, but an intelligent analysis
of tradition, founded on experience, is much more important for any true
insight than an uncritical registering of sensual impressions. Exploring
this complex matter by means of time-honoured conventions and modes
of expression, the poet has not only found a particularly fascinating
subject, far more interesting at least than most of the 'tydynges' aimlessly
whirling around, but has at the same time created a new piece of reality
complete in itself, which can be of great help to the reader in his own
search for reliable experience.

6

The storyteller and his material:
Troilus and Criseyde

TROILUS AND CRISEYDE IS THE ONLY LONGER POEM CHAUCER
ever finished. And looking at *The Canterbury Tales*, with its obvious
gaps, at *The Legend of Good Women*, breaking off apparently half
finished, and at *The House of Fame*, ending in mid-air, it might well seem
as if the unfinished narrative was Chaucer's favourite literary genre. True
enough, in most cases the actual reason may well be a rather simple one;
but it still remains a remarkable fact that Chaucer usually preferred
shorter narrative units, as *The Canterbury Tales* illustrates clearly
enough, and that, as a rule, he was more interested in the basic situation
of the storyteller and individual modes of presentation than in the
carefully balanced structure of a whole poem. Thus, whenever he adapts
a particular model, he invariably gives us an abridgement or selected
passages from his source. Only in the case of *Troilus and Criseyde* has he
expanded and rearranged his source-material on a large scale, to create a
finished work of art with an elaborately balanced structure which has no
equal in Middle English literature. There is no English poem before
Chaucer of equal size which is comparable to *Troilus and Criseyde* in its
careful construction, its variety and wealth of stylistic devices and its
intellectual stature. The poem has been associated with the classical epic,
it has been described as a medieval romance, and interpreted as a
predecessor of the modern novel. This variety of interpretation alone
suggests that it is not strictly modelled on any particular conventional
genre but attempts something new: an ambitious and rhetorically
heightened but in no way exclusive presentation of a classical story which
allows discussion of almost all the fundamental problems of courtly
love-poetry that occupy such a prominent position in Chaucer's early
poetry. The intellectual richness and variety of this work make every
fresh reading a challenging and often surprising experience, and this
explains, too, why the critical debate about the poem is not likely ever to
be concluded, although, browsing through the vast number of critical
studies, one is tempted to feel that most of the basic problems of

interpretation have been formulated and that it is now up to the individual reader to decide for himself.

More than any other poem by Chaucer, *Troilus* has provoked critical disagreement about its central message.[1] Does it glorify or condemn courtly love? Is it based on an orthodox view of the world, or written in an unorthodox and questioning spirit? Any reader who tries to define his own attitude towards the poem is confronted with the problem whether the variety of possible interpretations is due to his own inability to read a medieval text, whether the text itself is wanting in explicitness, or whether many interpretations simply make the wrong kind of claim. The fact that the poem has inspired such a colourful debate gives clear evidence of its inexhaustible intellectual appeal; on the other hand it seems worth pursuing the question why this debate has produced so few reliable results and often reflects little more than the plurality of critics. It seems to me, at any rate, more sensible to keep this in mind and to resist the impulse to propose just another interpretation, which could at best be little more than an anthology of previous interpretations with minor modifications in detail.

The narrative material of Chaucer's poem has a long tradition. The fall of Troy had inspired the imagination of many poets, especially in England, because according to a time-honoured belief, frequently expressed and elaborately presented even in Spenser's *Faerie Queene*, the British traced their descent from the Trojans. Thus in romances and chronicles the destruction of Troy is often treated as a part of English history, usually with a strong bias towards the Trojan side and a rather derogatory view of the Greeks.[2]

The story of Troilus and Criseyde is obviously a medieval addition to the original account. It first appears as an episode in the comprehensive kaleidoscope of the legend of Troy by Benoît de St Maure, two hundred years before Chaucer. But it is only in Boccaccio's *Il Filostrato*, Chaucer's primary source, that it becomes the centre of an independent work, with the fall of Troy only providing a general, sinister background for the story. Boccaccio is also the first poet who, as far as we know, gives a detailed account of the earlier history of this love affair up to the moment when the exchange of Criseyde is arranged; only with him did the main course of the action take the shape familiar to the modern reader from Chaucer but also from Shakespeare's *Troilus and Cressida*.

The relationship between Chaucer's poem and Boccaccio's *Il Filostrato* has often been discussed in detail, and I shall confine myself to an illustration of some of its most characteristic features.[3] Chaucer's poem is almost one and a half times as long as Boccaccio's, but only half of his text is directly taken from Boccaccio; the greater part is either Chaucer's own contribution or derived from other sources. This brief summary can give only a rather rough idea, yet it confirms that Chaucer's poem is a very free adaptation. Chaucer himself repeatedly alludes to his source; he never refers to Boccaccio by name, but he deliberately gives the impression that he is no more than a humble translator, the faithful reteller of a given story.[4] This, in my view, is one of the essential facts necessary for a true understanding of the poem. At almost every crucial point in his narrative Chaucer insists on the fundamental difference between the traditional material and his treatment of it. This makes *Troilus and Criseyde* an almost classic example of the technique of 'interpretation' in the medieval sense of the word. The poet embellishes his material; he invests it with fresh meaning – or, rather, he tries to rediscover its real meaning. The notion that he has to relate everything in obedience to his 'auctor' is time and again restated and is obviously meant to be an essential part of the intended effect on the reader. The comparison with Boccaccio also reveals to what an extent Chaucer felt free to give a very personal interpretation, and it shows how utterly different two works can be, even though they draw on the same material.

THE LOVER'S SORROW

The way the two poets introduce themselves and their stories is already completely and significantly different. Boccaccio assumes the stance of an unhappy lover who, bewailing the absence of his lady, resorts to old books for comfort. For him, Troilo's suffering is a reflection of his own grief, and he deliberately suggests autobiographical associations in his story. Like Troilo he recalls his former happiness, and by describing the grief of his protagonist as movingly as possible he hopes to move his lady, to whom the poem is addressed, to compassion. Consequently, he writes largely from the point of view of Troilo, with whom he does not identify throughout, but has in common grief over lost happiness and the belief that love is an ennobling experience demanding all intellectual and moral resources. This attitude determines the tone of the whole poem, and above all our view of its protagonist, who is presented as a warning for all lovers. For them the poet, at the end of the story, has this advice: that they should not waste their love on inconstant women, but should choose noble ladies who alone can be relied on.

Chaucer's attitude as a narrator is completely different. As in his dream–visions, he presents himself as an outsider who faithfully sticks to his source and relates matters he knows nothing about in terms of actual experience. From the outset, he views his subject-matter from a detached standpoint, which sets the tone of his work and enables him to give an unbiased and undogmatic evaluation of the events. Moreover, on the basis of this alleged impartiality he is free to vary his emotional distance according to the intended effect on the reader, playing now the role of the scrupulous chronicler, now that of a reader who is himself overwhelmed by the power of his story. Yet, although at times he seems unable to escape the impact of his own subject, he never identifies with Troilus. His own experience of love always remains theoretical and has no direct bearing on his personal life.

This also modifies his attitude towards his audience. As a mediator who is not personally involved he can appeal to his audience to receive his narrative in the proper spirit, to show compassion with unhappy lovers, to act wisely in matters of love and to pray for those who suffer as Troilus does. This explicit appeal to the audience, to their freedom and responsibility, has not always been taken seriously enough by critics. It is, I am sure, more important for any adequate understanding of the whole standpoint of the poem than the question of what might have been Chaucer's personal judgement of the events; because, although this judgement, if we look at the poem's conclusion, is much more radical than Boccaccio's, its claim is at the same time more modest and less dogmatic. The poet does not step forward as one who has any special authority, but from the very beginning invites the reader to look at the story for himself and to form his own judgement. The undeniable fact that he actually handles his material with much more freedom and individuality than he gives us to understand, and thus manipulates the reader's response even more effectively, is quite another question, to which we shall return; but this is no reason to interpret the narrator's modesty, which clearly is one of the most distinctive features of the text, as an ironic mask to disguise his authoritarian control of his audience. Many critical accounts oversimplify the problem by assuming that Chaucer's own attitude, contrary to his explicit statement, is far more self-assured and dogmatic than is borne out by the introduction and indeed the whole poem.

The introduction also makes it clear that Chaucer places his version of the story in a much wider context than Boccaccio does his. Boccaccio appeals primarily to his lady, who is also the addressee of the traditional invocation of the Muses, because she actually is his Muse. Chaucer, by contrast, associates his solemn invocation of the Muses explicitly with the great European epic tradition, with Dante and with Statius' *Thebaid*, apparently highly esteemed by Chaucer. At the same time he underlines the universal character of the tragedy he sets out to relate: the 'double sorwe of Troilus' goes directly *in medias res*. The hero's double sorrow, from the outset explicitly linked to the specific problem of love, is the theme of the poem, but the course of his fortune is of no less importance than the actual subject-matter: 'Fro wo to wele, and after out of joie'. This describes a full turn of Fortune's wheel, and it implies the idea of a 'fall', characteristic of the medieval conception of tragedy as Chaucer had encountered it in Boethius.[5] At this stage there is no question of guilt or punishment: the problem is simply not touched on here. It is, however, closely related to the issue of human free will in the face of divine providence or the capriciousness of Fortune, and this is indeed for Chaucer, as the fourth book shows in particular, one of the central themes of his story.

As later in Shakespeare's play, though to a lesser extent, the love of Troilus is depicted against the background of the inevitable fall of Troy. The law of Fortune's inconstancy governs the fate of human communities as well as the life of the individual. Chaucer's audience knew well enough how the siege of Troy ended and how Criseyde betrayed her love. The close interrelation between the tide of war and the love-story is brought out in the very first episode. Criseyde is the daughter of the seer Calchas who, foreknowing the fall of Troy, seeks to leave the sinking ship in time. Within the walls of this doomed city no lasting happiness can be expected, and Calchas anticipates his daughter's betrayal by becoming a traitor in order to avoid being dragged into the inevitable catastrophe, a fact made more poignantly clear in Chaucer than in Boccaccio. This scene, which bodes nothing good, opens the poem; but the beginning of the love affair between Troilus and Criseyde, too, is presented in such ambiguous terms that a straightforward judgement is made impossible.

A first comparative reading of Chaucer's and Boccaccio's versions suggests that, for long stretches, Chaucer really did no more than translate the Italian text into English, because long passages are nearly identical. True enough, it would be rather unwise to interpret every minor difference as a deliberate departure from the source or a meaningful comment. Undoubtedly, the demands of metre, inadequate means of expression in the English language, a somewhat superficial reading of the original, or here and there just a simple misunderstanding, are very likely to account for certain discrepancies. On the other hand, Chaucer has placed some of his stresses so consistently differently that even the minor differences, taken together, produce a rather original picture.[6]

He has, for instance, deliberately heightened the suddenness and the elementary power of Troilus' love, to emphasize his role as an exemplary courtly lover even more clearly. The conventions of courtly love-poetry, the concept of the absolute power of love and the exclusive demands of love-service are intensified, and their implications taken more literally. This is already implied in Troilus' first meeting with Criseyde.

Boccaccio's protagonist, like Troilus, has been scorning all lovers, but not because he does not know anything about love; in fact, he has been in love before, and he is quite certain that what comes of it is grief rather than happiness. Chaucer's Troilus has never loved before. He is an outsider, imagining himself immune against this disease and therefore hit all the more suddenly. Both poems add a warning against arrogance, and both formulate a moral which is something like the traditional 'pride goes before a fall'. Chaucer, in his version of the story, however, attaches much more importance to this aspect, and even though it is the power of love in particular that is demonstrated here, Troilus is, at the same time, something like a representative of all human beings who consider themselves independent of blind Fortune and divine providence. This is the first 'fall' Troilus has to suffer, the first stage of his double sorrow, as the first line of the poem calls it.

The long and passionate lament of Troilus, who is deeply struck by the image of Criseyde, expands on the source and is even more rhetorically stylized, in particular by the insertion of a Petrarchan sonnet. On the one hand Troilus is more thoroughly disturbed than Boccaccio's hero, on the other his actual goal is at first much less definite: he does not so much want to win the lady's favour as to serve in the cause of love pure and simple. Boccaccio's account suggests that this is not much more than just another love affair for Troilo. For Troilus, it is a totally new experience, and this further underlines the striking contrast with his preceding attitude of uncomprehending arrogance: 'Blissed be Love, that kan thus folk converte!' (1.308). What this line suggests, and by no means unintentionally, is a parallel with religious experience; it also expresses the narrator's sympathy. For the narrator, who frankly admits his lack of experience in such matters, the history of Troilus is a particularly striking example of the real power of love, and he makes it very clear that as far as Troilus is concerned this is a positive experience, because personal commitment and understanding take the place of blind arrogance. The exemplary character of the process is underlined by the elevated and, in the best sense of the word, conventional style. Troilus finds himself in the position of the typical courtly lover in the opening stages of his service: he is deeply moved and suffers without any hope of being accepted and, indeed, without even any personal contact with the object of his passion. The style of this whole section makes it quite plain that it would be wrong to see it as a particularly individualized and detailed portrait of Troilus' character, although Troilus is sufficiently differentiated from Boccaccio's Troilo to suggest that Chaucer had his own concept of the exemplary courtly lover.[7]

The question of distinct personal traits of character does, however, arise in the ensuing scenes, where Troilus is contrasted with Pandarus. And it is here that the difference between Chaucer's version and his source becomes more obvious. Pandarus is one of the most original 'additions' of Chaucer and in fact one of his most fascinating creations. Boccaccio's Pandaro, Criseida's cousin, is a friend of Troilo and of the same age. He is himself an unhappy lover, who therefore understands his friend only too well. Between the two, there is, from the beginning, no doubt as to Troilo's ultimate intentions. When Pandaro first learns who the lady is that has set Troilo's heart on fire he enthusiastically affirms that she is worthy of his friend's love, with only one thing standing in his way: her piety and virtue; but he is convinced that this obstacle can soon be overcome.

In Chaucer, this dialogue takes a completely different course, although its actual result is very similar. Pandarus is Criseyde's uncle, and even though his age is not explicitly specified he is certainly not a friend of the same age but a senior adviser who knows the world. The fact that he, too, is introduced as an unhappy lover only serves to testify to his experience in these matters, and at the same time casts him as a kind of outsider, which connects him, in a teasing way, with the narrator. Chaucer again, as in his earlier dream–visions, tries to come to terms with the phenomenon of love by looking at it from varying points of view. In the first book, there is on the one hand Troilus, the passive victim incapable of clear-sighted reflection or action, and on the other Pandarus, who lacks such genuine experience, but being (like the narrator) not directly involved, is able to recognize the symptoms and to foresee the practical consequences. It seems to be a characteristic feature of Chaucer's portrayal of courtly love in his poetry that for him only one or the other of these attitudes is possible. The narrator, and Pandarus as well, can only observe the effects of love on others with compassionate sympathy because he does not share this experience. Pandarus is ready to do anything pity and commonsense can do, but it is clear that he has only a very abstract and inadequate idea of Troilus' real state of mind. This mixture of compassion and a general readiness to help, along with emotional inexperience, is, within the context of this poem, the only response possible for an outsider unable to enter into the emotional dilemma of the lover.

The contrast between these two figures is one of the most brilliant achievements of Chaucer's poem, and it marks one of the most fundamental departures from his model. We bar our way to an understanding of this profoundly original creation if we immediately look for its moral function and for Chaucer's own attitude to the two characters.[8] The artistic success of this lively confrontation does not lie in a clear-cut

moral judgement, but primarily in the intellectual and emotional challenge and the much more comprehensive view of experience it offers.
This, too, is to a large extent reflected in the style of the work. The
stylized pathos of the lover's lyrical complaints is contrasted with
Pandarus' commonsense, the passive lamentation of Troilus with Pandarus' delight in resourceful plotting and his inventive manipulation of
people, and the rhetorical calm of the lovers' soliloquies with the vigour
and restlessness of the dialogue. The scene, for instance, in which
Pandarus virtually squeezes out of Troilus all he wants to know, is a
masterpiece of dramatic rhetoric, unequalled in Middle English literature. Carefully calculated argument and verbose rhetoric combine with
precise gestures and direct personal address. The following passage, in
which Pandarus, wanting to get at the lady's name, throws out the
question whether he knows her at all, shows how very consciously he
manipulates the conversation. Troilus' reaction immediately tells him
that at last he has hit a weak spot and that he has almost succeeded:

> Tho gan the veyne of Troilus to blede,
> For he was hit, and wax al reed for shame.
> 'A ha!' quod Pandare, 'here bygynneth game.'
>
> And with that word he gan hym for to shake,
> And seyde, 'Thef, thow shalt hyre name telle.'
> But tho gan sely Troilus for to quake
> As though men sholde han led hym into helle,
> And seyde, 'Allas! of al my wo the welle,
> Thanne is my swete fo called Criseyde!'
> And wel neigh with the word for feere he deide.   (1.866–75)

In Boccaccio, the scene is much shorter and lacks this dramatic vividness
on the brink of comedy. Its main function here, however, is not just to
present an interlude of comic realism, but also to accentuate the sharp
contrast between two levels of style. Pandarus' gestures and diction are
related to the comic fabliau rather than the courtly epic. The effect of this
juxtaposition of two completely different modes of expression is difficult
to describe and will no doubt differ with every reader, but it would be too
superficial and simplistic to take it as a plain comment on Troilus' love.
The character of Pandarus does, of course, influence the reader's attitude
towards Troilus and his love. The realism of the scene makes the idealized
artificiality of his love-sickness all the more conspicuous. Pandarus'
frequent reminders of the practical consequences cast a sobering light on
the basic unreality of the stylized courtly pose. The poem thus suggests
that the idealizing convention is not the only way to describe the
experience of love – that, at least, it does not cover its full range and

richness. Troilus' attitude is by no means devalued, but he is certainly viewed with much more detachment than in Boccaccio. The intensity, as well as the limitations, of his experience is conveyed to the reader with far more precision by Chaucer's refusal to confine himself to one particular level of style. In Boccaccio, Troilo's suffering is but the generally accepted, normal condition of a lover, whereas in Chaucer it is an exaggerated, passive and unresistingly endured obsession which needs the help of the practical plotter to achieve its end.

Yet neither the narrator nor Pandarus voices any explicit criticism of Troilus; it is genuine compassion that determines their attitude. Pandarus' occasional levity is not directed against Troilus' passion but against his inability to face its practical implications. Beyond that, it is often just a tactical means to cheer him up or to manipulate him for his own good. Many critics have found it necessary to defend Troilus against the reader's contempt and to present him as the perfect courtly lover.[9] To a certain extent this is reasonable, because today's readers are only too easily inclined to take Chaucer's overemphatic description as a caricature of courtly conduct and, in consequence, consider Troilus a weakling and a passive sentimentalist, which is certainly not the intention of the poem. Troilus' larger-than-life lover's stance is a very conscious attempt at poetic stylization. Its remoteness from ordinary experience is overemphasized by Pandarus' knowing pragmatism; but the delicate comedy of incongruity always remains on the surface of outward behaviour and does not cast any fundamental doubt on the sincerity of Troilus' attitude. The poem is very clear about the positive change in Troilus brought about by the intensity of his love-experience:

> And in the town his manere tho forth ay
> Soo goodly was, and gat hym so in grace,
> That ecch hym loved that loked on his face.

> For he bicom the frendlieste wight,
> The gentilest, and ek the mooste fre,
> The thriftiest and oon the beste knyght,
> That in his tyme was or myghte be.
> Dede were his japes and his cruelte,
> His heighe port and his manere estraunge,
> And ecch of tho gan for a vertu chaunge. (I.1076–85)

This moral aspect of courtly love as an energy that can bring out the very best in a man is very strongly emphasized by Chaucer, as against Boccaccio, and so, at the same time, is its slightly absurd remoteness from reality – the artificiality of some of its conventions, which does not, however, call in question its positive effect on the lover. Above all, the remarkable development of Troilus' character is a matter of public interest, involving everybody around him, whereas all that could be described as overemotional weakness is confined to himself and his relation with Pandarus. To the society of Troy only the positive change in him is visible.

Thus the comic or, at times, satirical elements are decidedly subdued and do not question the foundations of the courtly love-experience. The tone and the spirit of the poem do not encourage quick and confident judgements; they are informed by an undogmatic openness and vitality and by the conscious attempt to define the experience of courtly love within the widest possible human context, instead of presenting it as an isolated, exclusive emotion removed from all other areas of life.

Face to face with such wholehearted love, Pandarus too, like Troilus, is inspired to disinterested service. The whole of the second book and part of the third describe his inventive and energetic endeavours to help Troilus reach his goal. A comparison with *Il Filostrato* shows that Chaucer has expanded this part of the poem much more than the rest, so that the description of Troilus' suit occupies just as much space as Criseyde's betrayal. One effect of this change is that the happy aspects of love, the hope of fulfilment and the bliss so strenuously worked for, are given much more weight, though this, at the same time, makes the final disappointment all the more shattering. In addition, the comic realism of certain scenes helps to bridge the gulf between conventional idealization and genuine experience. It is not left to the reader to discover that, when all is said and done, what is behind all the fine conventions of courtly veneration is simply the desire for sexual satisfaction: the poem itself, namely Pandarus, hints at such a possibility.

A number of direct interventions by the narrator give clear evidence of the fact that Chaucer is very anxious about the appropriate reaction of the reader. Two possible objections, both of which concern the nature of his presentation, are anticipated and then explicitly rejected. At the very beginning of the second book, the narrator points to those fundamental changes of language and habit which have their origin in the natural succession of generations and which might well stand in the way of a spontaneous emotional participation of the audience:

> Ye knowe ek that in forme of speche is chaunge
> Withinne a thousand yeer, and wordes tho
> That hadden pris, now wonder nyce and straunge
> Us thinketh hem, and yet thei spake hem so,
> And spedde as wel in love as men now do;
> Ek for to wynnen love in sondry ages,
> In sondry londes, sondry ben usages.

And forthi if it happe in any wyse,
That here be any lovere in this place
That herkneth, as the storie wol devise,
How Troilus com to his lady grace,
And thenketh, 'so nold I nat love purchace,'
Or wondreth on his speche or his doynge,
I noot; but it is me no wonderynge.   (II.22–35)

As Chaucer explains, these differences of manner, due to the distance in time, are not basically different from those which may also occur between people of the same generation. This is, above all, an appeal to the reader not to miss the substance of the events by concentrating too much on their outward conventional appearance. Behind those antiquated patterns of conduct there are basic experiences which all generations have in common. Wonder or amusement about unfamiliar modes of expression must not prevent genuine sympathy with the historical characters, because their sorrows and their happiness are, from their own point of view, no less genuine and deeply felt than our own and therefore must be taken seriously.

Thus the problem of the historical dimension of poetry is held up for discussion with a clarity unequalled in Middle English literature, and it is passed on to the reader. He himself is called upon to bridge the historical distance by a conscious act of sympathetic understanding and to perceive the unchanging human emotions behind all external differences. Thus sympathy and compassion, not an amused or censuring detachment, are what Chaucer expects and demands of his audience. This reminder of the historical distance to be overcome by the reader does not only apply to the re-living of events from the distant past, but is relevant, in the last resort, to any kind of fictional reality. Chaucer makes it clear that all narrative poetry demands of the reader the ability to discriminate between timeless substance and varying forms of presentation: that he must not confuse literary conventions with the real argument behind them.

A little later, the narrator defends Criseyde against the possible criticism that she may have granted her love too suddenly, a criticism rather more appropriate in the case of Boccaccio's account in which the action moves forward much more swiftly. Chaucer, again, refers the reader to the problems of presentation. Everything, he says, has its beginning and its end, and so the poet, too, has to concentrate on selected points of particular importance, whereas in everyday life everything develops far more smoothly and with often imperceptible transitions. Again the reader is called upon to distinguish between the shortcomings of the presentation and the real substance the poet wants to convey.

75

Critical awareness of the poet's problems thus should combine with a sympathetic solidarity with the fictional characters.

This is the appropriate perspective for a sensitive appreciation of the comedy of Pandarus' wooing on behalf of Troilus. And comedy it is, in parts at least, as Chaucer's exuberant narrative clearly suggests. Pandarus' purposeful cunning and resourcefulness inform the scenes between him and Criseyde with dramatic intensity and speed. Again, gestures, brief interjections and extensive rhetorical declamation are employed side by side, and the conventions of the courtly novel are contrasted with those of the comic fabliau. Pandarus is a disinterested friend who makes every effort on behalf of Troilus, but at the same time, he has already something of the prurient pander of later tradition. His sense of the rather prosaic reality behind all the conventional forms of courtly conduct is one of his main characteristics. This becomes quite obvious when, towards the end of his first conference with Criseyde, after all his solemn declarations to the effect that all he has been talking about is an honourable love from a distance, he suddenly, in an uncontrolled outburst of triumphant delight at his first success, lets the cat out of the bag:

> 'Ther were nevere two so wel ymet,
> Whan ye ben his al hool, as he is youre:
> Ther myghty God yet graunte us see that houre!'

> 'Nay, therof spak I nought, ha, ha!' quod she;
> 'As helpe me God, ye shenden every deel!'
> 'O, mercy, dere nece,' anon quod he,
> 'What so I spak, I mente naught but wel,
> By Mars, the god that helmed is of steel!
> Now beth naught wroth, my blood, my nece dere.'
> 'Now wel,' quod she, 'foryeven be it here!'   (II.586–95)

Here, again, it would be too simple to interpret this only as a straight-forward parody of courtly patterns of behaviour. On the contrary, the love-convention, often presented in too abstract terms, is treated as something very real, by the very admission of its slightly absurd aspects. The fact that Pandarus clearly recognizes the rather profane desire at the bottom of Troilus' love-sickness does not at all make him a sneering cynic, but prevents the impression on the part of the reader that this is but a world of disembodied ideals. The ritual patterns of formalized behaviour are in no way devalued by the poet's refusal to accept them as the only kind of reality. Troilus, as well as Criseyde, would in fact deserve much less of our sympathy if from the start either of them adopted Pandarus' attitude, which is appropriate only for the outsider.

The portrait of Criseyde, in particular, which combines stylized convention and individual features, is so complex that it does not permit any quick judgement. There is nothing in the text to suggest that the narrator's warning of a hasty condemnation of Criseyde is to be understood as irony. On the other hand, it directs the reader's attention to the moral implications of her conduct and thus encourages him to observe her critically. The poet seeks to convince us that Criseyde does not give in easily and thoughtlessly, but is brought round by a variety of outward influences and inward considerations. Pandarus' strategy is supported by the visual impact of Troilus' personality, by the astrological constellation and by Criseyde's own reflections. In Boccaccio everything happens far more swiftly and Pandaro has much less trouble. Even after his first preliminary conversation with her, Criseida agrees to grant Troilo the favour of allowing him to cast a glance at her, and the two friends pass by her window for that purpose. At this moment she falls in love with him and regrets the time she has wasted in ignorance of his love. In Chaucer, Troilus passes by her window on horseback quite accidentally while Criseyde is contemplating his proposal, and his appearance does much to sway her in his favour. It is just one of those coincidences that form an alliance against Criseyde. But her concessions are much harder to win and take much longer to materialize than in Boccaccio. Nevertheless, it is precisely Chaucer's more extensive and colourful description that makes the reader take a more thoughtful view of her actions. Is it only her respect for outward form and concern for her reputation that motivates her strong resistance, or does she really act in keeping with the demands and expectations of the courtly convention? Is she, behind all her demonstrative reserve, in secret league with Pandarus? Such questions come up again and again for the reader, and they prove that Chaucer's narrative method, in spite of its numerous conventional elements, engages our interest in Criseyde as an individual character.[10]

A very instructive example in this respect is her extensive soliloquy in the second book (703–808), which, again, shows Chaucer employing the stylized method of the courtly novel. It is not so much a complex portrait of her state of mind or a psychologically motivated account of her secret thoughts, as a compilation of all sorts of reflections appropriate in her situation. There is certainly an affinity to the modern novel and its attempt to represent intellectual processes, but the stylized character of this soliloquy must not be ignored. It would be unreasonable, for instance, to try and discover something like a calculating nature in Criseyde behind this orderly weighing of arguments. Her reflections are in keeping with her situation and are not meant to reveal a particularly complex or unconventional state of mind. If anything, the monologue suggests that Criseyde still considers herself completely free, and what is more the loss of freedom through love or marriage, a fabliau-theme which enjoyed great popularity, appears to be her greatest problem, while on the other hand it seems to her an enticing prospect to have Troilus, the most highly esteemed prince next to Hector, as her secret worshipper and, indeed, dependant. The soliloquy is one of the poet's attempts to protect Criseyde against the accusation of wantonness and at the same time to stress her human free will. She obviously tries hard to consider all the consequences of her situation, and this is a distinctive feature of her character, just like the weakness and timidity pointed out with such insistence by the narrator.

Here, again, the realization of her complex behaviour is much more important than any moral evaluation or a groping for secret motives. It would be an undue moralization of the text to accuse Criseyde of seeing through Pandarus. Her whole way of acting combines conventional stereotype, commonsense and calculating caution. She is another example of Chaucer widening and modifying the concept of courtly love, which embraces, in this poem, a variety of contradictory emotions and considerations which render the protagonists' actions and reactions largely unpredictable and discourage confident moral verdicts.

The same applies in particular to the roundabout, indeed fussy, way Pandarus goes to work. His task is all but easy, although at heart the lovers, without realizing it, both really want exactly the same as he does.

> But theron was to heven and to doone.
> Considered al thing it may nat be;
> And whi, for shame; and it were ek to soone
> To graunten hym so gret a libertee.
> For pleynly hire entente, as seyde she,
> Was for to love hym unwist, if she myghte,
> And guerdon hym with nothing but with sighte.
>
> But Pandarus thought, 'It shal nought be so,
> Yif that I may; this nyce opynyoun
> Shal nought be holden fully yeres two.' (II.1289–98)

The imaginative, as well as complicated, manipulation of the first meeting of the lovers must have had a slightly comic effect on Chaucer's audience, well acquainted with courtly romances, because it unexpectedly illuminates a new dimension of a conventional situation. The contrast between the sophisticated tactics and the comparatively simple result corresponds to the opposition of reality and convention, and yet it does not deprive the convention of its authority. The sympathy of the reader is deepened by this linking of the narrative to a familiar reality.

There is no section in Boccaccio's poem comparable to the ending of Chaucer's second book, where the tension is so purposefully heightened, with Troilus lying in ambush waiting for Criseyde, who has been so cunningly manoeuvred into this meeting.[11] By a direct address to the audience, pointing out that Troilus' situation is quite an extraordinary one, but most of all by the brilliant handling of narrative time, we become directly involved in the action, and the distance between audience and protagonist is effectively reduced:

> But now to yow, ye loveres that ben here,
> Was Troilus nought in a kankedort,
> That lay, and myghte whisprynge of hem here,
> And thoughte, 'O Lord, right now renneth my sort
> Fully to deye, or han anon comfort!'
> And was the firste tyme he shulde hire preye
> Of love; O myghty God, what shal he seye? (II.1751–7)

The time-scheme is stretched beyond the inconclusive ending of the book; the course of action is suddenly brought to a halt, and the question in which the narrator seems to join Troilus (1757) puts the audience on a level with the lover, almost bursting with expectant excitement. At the same time, however, the ending of this book re-establishes the distance between the reader and the world of the poem, which is further increased by the hymnic invocation at the beginning of the next book. When at last the thread of the action is picked up again, the mechanism of the narrative is made deliberately obvious: 'Lay al this mene while Troilus' (III.50). The narrator here manipulates his material almost as Pandarus manipulates the lovers.

Pandarus' prosaic intrigues have brought about the first meeting of Troilus and Criseyde. Although this does not go very far, remaining on the level of respectfully detached declarations, Criseyde's basic consent to accept Troilus' offered love-service does actually mean that all that is left for Pandarus to do is to remove a few minor obstacles in the way of the final union of the lovers. And this, perhaps, is why this conversation is already part of the third book, which is devoted to the blissful climax of their love.

REALITY AND ILLUSION OF LOVE'S BLISS

Chaucer's third book, in contrast to Boccaccio's less symmetrically structured novel, is clearly the centre of the poem. There has always been much disagreement about its interpretation, especially about the problem of the relationship of this part of the poem to the tragic ending. The first and most striking aspect is indeed the seemingly unconditional praise of

love as an enchanting experience which can be described adequately only
by means of religious metaphor. The glorification of love is the recurrent
theme throughout the whole of this book – from the emphatic invocation, singing the praises of love as an energy enlivening all created
nature, to the delighted hymn of Troilus at the zenith of bliss that takes
up the same idea, enlarging on it in the words of Boethius:

> Love, that of erthe and se hath governaunce,
> Love, that his hestes hath in hevenes hye,
> Love, that with an holsom alliaunce
> Halt peples joyned, as hym lest hem gye,
> Love, that knetteth lawe of compaignie,
> And couples doth in vertu for to dwelle,
> Bynd this acord, that I have told and telle.　　　(III.1744–50)

A comparison of these verses with their source, however, also reveals
possible difficulties. Whereas Boethius in this context definitely speaks of
a Christian marriage, Troilus is thinking only of his relationship with
Criseyde.[12] The question whether Chaucer here implies a criticism of
extra-marital love seems to me of little relevance. The real concern of the
poet is his emphatic picture of love as an overwhelming experience.
Many critics have joined C. S. Lewis in claiming that Chaucer unreser-
vedly celebrates human love as a reflection of divine love as Boethius
describes it.[13] It leads the lovers to the very summit of happiness and
changes them into human beings who are everything to each other. Again
and again the poet returns to the way Troilus' whole personality is
transformed and enriched by this experience: he becomes the embodiment of kindness, modesty, helpfulness, and courage to all those around
him. In all essential points, Troilus' concept of love corresponds to that of
Boethius: love is the divine energy emanating from the Creator; it holds
together the whole universe, determines the course of the stars, controls
the elements and keeps the powers of chaos in check. Thus Troilus comes
as close to a Christian concept of God's love as, according to a medieval
view of a pre-Christian world, a heathen possibly can. His loving union
with Criseyde has given him insights reaching far beyond his individual
destiny, to the ultimate source of all love, not just its manifestation in one
particular human partnership.

　　This glorification of love is continued so consistently throughout the
whole of this section of the poem that for the reader there seems little
reason to distrust the narrator or to regard Troilus' bliss as a delusion. A
great many recent interpretations, however, have pointed to the discrepancy between this uncritical idealization of human love and the catastrophe of the last book with its radical repudiation of earthly joy. From
the point of view of this orthodox homiletic conclusion, Troilus' love is

indeed deeply flawed and must necessarily lead to complete disappointment. But the perspective of that last book is not the same as that of the whole work, and at the climax of the poem the reader is by no means expected or encouraged to judge Troilus' behaviour only in the light of the tragic conclusion. The portrayal of his blissful state would lose all its emotional impact if we were reminded from the outset that all this happiness is but hollow and illusory.[14] Neither the reality of this experience nor the sincerity and truth of Troilus' new insight is called into question. Whatever moral condemnation of Troilus has been read into this book comes from the reader's own mind and not from the spirit of the poem itself, which at no point sanctions an attitude of moral superiority or a readiness to pass final judgements.

True enough, the reader knows from the very first lines of the poem that Troilus' trust in Criseyde is doomed to be disappointed, and this undoubtedly determines our response to the ecstatic bliss of the third book. We are conscious of an element of tragic irony of which the protagonists are completely unaware, and this may well provoke the question whether Troilus' love has not been misguided from the beginning. The point, however, is not so much the subjective misjudgement of the protagonist; what really matters is the basic discrepancy between the ideal conception of divine love and its very human manifestation. Troilus clearly perceives the divine origin of love, its far more than individual energizing force, but he is bound to be disillusioned when he equates this universal power with its very limited manifestation through his love of Criseyde. His experience has shown him how the transitory world of appearances, of which Criseyde is but one part, may serve as an image of divine truth. The crucial precondition which he ignores is, however, that this basic principle must not be confused with any specific manifestation within this world. Not the smallest part of the enthusiastic definition of love is invalidated or refuted by Criseyde's eventual breach of faith. What actually is refuted is Troilus' belief that in the person of Criseyde he has a permanent and reliable share of divine love. Chaucer presents this 'tragic error' not as a flaw in Troilus' character and definitely not as a new fall of Adam,[15] but as an example of the precarious and threatened state of all human love, owing to the discrepancy between ideal and reality.

Within the range of this general theme Chaucer's presentation allows for a variety of responses. As a comparison with other Middle English narrative poetry will confirm, his attitude is marked by his refusal to provide a clearly formulated and unmistakably authoritative interpretation that saves his audience the effort of an individual decision; and, what is more, he deliberately accentuates discrepant elements in his story to make a smooth and inoffensive interpretation even more difficult. No attentive reader, for instance, can fail to notice that Chaucer not only presents Troilus' unclouded happiness and the harmony of his union with Criseyde in more glowing terms than Boccaccio, but that, in striking contrast to Boccaccio, he also brings out the all too human, often anything but courtly, and even trivial or vulgar aspects of this love affair. The effect of the intrusion of such rather surprising elements into the conventional description of successful wooing at first seems to be that of disillusioning comedy and good-humoured criticism of courtly exclusiveness. It would be wrong, though, to overrate the importance of such contrasts as a means of authorial comment. The point is, again, as I have suggested with regard to the second book, Chaucer's intention to widen the range of experience presented in this poem, to confront convention and everyday life, and to avoid any kind of exclusive idealization. And again it is mostly Pandarus who represents a completely different perspective and thus underlines and makes us more conscious of the unreflecting idealism of Troilus. The description of his strategy for bringing the lovers together is so obviously exuberant that it must have produced a comic effect for the majority of medieval audiences, much as it does for the modern reader. Pandarus' bustling activity clearly recalls the burlesque fabliaux. He is indeed much more than just a devoted friend who does his best on Troilus' behalf. His inventive mind manipulates events in a way that makes Troilus' passive and unworldly innocence stand out all the more glaringly, and, at the same time, it brings home to the reader the rather commonplace goal of his desire. There is no courtly novel before Chaucer in which the lover is physically pushed into the bed of his beloved, as he is here. The poem quite evidently wants to suggest in plain terms that as far as the action is concerned there is no basic difference between this pretentious courtly love-scene and the straightforward bedroom-comedy of such episodes in a frivolous fabliau. Pandarus knows from the outset what Troilus' pining boils down to; for him, as for the Wife of Bath, love remains nothing but 'the olde daunce', despite all stylized trappings. When his work is done he goes to sleep contentedly. And yet there can be no doubt that in the last resort he is excluded from the real experience of love, and that Troilus' insight into the divine power of love will always be beyond his comprehension. Thus Troilus' love is by no means put on the same level with the sexual escapades of the 'Miller's Tale'; the outward similarities, which are certainly not glossed over, do not devalue his love at all, but bring home to the reader the real if rather prosaic nature of Troilus' ecstasy.

The whole course of the third book, with its continual variation of stylized rhetoric, lyrical interludes and dramatic comedy, suggests that Chaucer is very anxious not to give undue prominence to any one of these divergent elements. However vividly the manipulations of Pandarus are described, his disinterested motives are given equal emphasis. His admonition to Troilus, greatly expanded in comparison with Boccaccio, not to endanger his niece's reputation reveals that he is well aware of the ambiguity of his position and his activity:

> 'That is to seye, for the am I bicomen,
> Bitwixen game and ernest, swich a meene
> As maken wommen unto men to comen;
> Al sey I nought, thow wost wel what I meene.
> For the have I my nece, of vices cleene,
> So fully maad thi gentilesse triste,
> That al shal ben right as thiselven liste.
>
> 'But God, that al woot, take I to witnesse,
> That nevere I this for coveitise wroughte,
> But oonly for t'abregge that distresse
> For which wel neigh thow deidest, as me thoughte.
> But, goode brother, do now as the oughte,
> For Goddes love, and kep hire out of blame,
> Syn thow art wys, and save alwey hire name.' (III.253–66)

These lines give a very clear definition of Pandarus' role within the poem. They make evident that he himself (and the poet as well) feels the need to justify himself and that he is not blind to the possible dangers of his intrigues; but his genuine concern for Troilus' happiness and the latter's gratitude serve as a positive, though not altogether unambiguous, balance to the more trivial elements of the situation.[16] Farce, wishful thinking, and blissful idealism alternate in abrupt succession, without, however, one cancelling out the other. Many studies of the poem only express the understandable desire of readers and critics for a simple reading that resolves all the contradictory elements of this work; but such simple interpretations usually ignore the creative variety and generosity of Chaucer's presentation and largely fail to do justice to the text.

The same applies to Criseyde's part in this section of the poem. Depending on how we interpret the concept of love at this climax of happiness, the heroine appears as an innocent victim, a worthy object of adoration, or the calculating niece of Pandarus who sees through his plans from the start. As frequently in the novels of Henry Fielding, the reader is presented with a variety of attitudes and possible explanations, but in the end – as in our daily intercourse – he has to form his own ideas about the characters. A particularly instructive illustration of this technique is the controversial scene in which Pandarus invites Criseyde to his house and she asks in return whether Troilus will be there too. It is a telling example of how Chaucer involves the reader in the process of characterization:

> Soone after this, she gan to hym to rowne,
> And axed hym if Troilus were there.
> He swor hire nay, for he was out of towne,
> And seyde, 'Nece, I pose that he were;
> Yow thurste nevere han the more fere;
> For rather than men myghte hym ther aspie,
> Me were levere a thousand fold to dye.'
>
> Nought list myn auctour fully to declare
> What that she thoughte whan he seyde so,
> That Troilus was out of towne yfare,
> As if he seyde thereof soth or no;
> But that, withowten await, with hym to go,
> She graunted hym, sith he hire that bisoughte,
> And, as his nece, obeyed as hire oughte.
>
> But natheles, yet gan she hym biseche,
> Although with hym to gon it was no fere,
> For to ben war of goosish poeples speche,
> That dremen thynges whiche that nevere were,
> And wel avyse hym whom he broughte there;
> And seyde hym, 'Em, syn I most on yow triste,
> Loke al be wel, and do now as yow liste.'   (III.568–88)

In the face of this roundabout and deliberately ambiguous description, the effort of the critic to defend Criseyde against the accusation of acting in a calculated manner seems a little pathetic.[17] The passage means exactly what it says: the narrator refuses to look behind the curtain of Criseyde's solemn declarations by offering a clumsy, unambiguous explanation. It is obvious that Criseyde is not completely convinced of her uncle's simplicity; she cannot openly accept a proposal the consequences of which are perfectly clear to her, and therefore she makes absolute discretion a precondition before she will go any further. Within the world depicted in the poem, there is no reason whatsoever for moral disapproval. Having made sure of Troilus' worthiness, the protection of her reputation remains the only consideration to determine her conduct; and, as in many courtly love-poems, the crucial point to consider is not only the kind of gossip an independent character just has to ignore, but also how to act in accordance with the approved standards of society. The moral value of such conformity is rated much higher than it is in many Western communities today.[18]

These considerations, however, should not lead to an interpretation of Criseyde as a minutely portrayed character who can always be expected to act in a psychologically consistent way.[19] The narrator wants most of all to discourage a premature verdict on the part of the reader by withholding precise information and giving him to understand that large areas of our human nature cannot be satisfactorily illumined by a fictitious narrative; the impulses and motives at work here are too diverse for that. Thus Fortune promotes the careful scheme of Pandarus even beyond his own preparations: the particularly rare constellation of the planets Saturn and Jupiter makes the rain foreseen by Pandarus swell into a great flood that turns out to be particularly favourable to the final coming together of the lovers. While this seems to suggest that super-natural powers direct the course of the lovers' destiny according to a predetermined plan ('fro wo to wele') the ambiguous and modest attitude of the narrator leaves room for human free will and thus prevents the impression that everything has been decided in advance. It is true that Criseyde is pressed from all sides, but it is never suggested that she could not have acted differently.

However, the reader who thinks that Criseyde's betrayal is already foreshadowed at this stage – so that, from the beginning, she has been an unworthy object of Troilus' veneration – can actually cite a number of instances where Chaucer, without any hint from Boccaccio, throws in occasional touches really incongruous with the innocent harmony of the blissful scene. Troilus' completely unfounded jealousy, for instance, elaborates on the theme of disloyalty and of an alleged rival with an insistence hardly called for in view of the actual occasion.[20] Of course, this is to be interpreted only in terms of a general thematic anticipation and not as a direct contribution to the characterization of Criseyde, who in this case is the completely unsuspecting victim of consummate deception. Her startled rejection of the false insinuations turns into a general complaint about the treacherousness of all human prosperity: he who realizes the transitory nature of earthly happiness will never enjoy perfect bliss because all the time he foresees the loss of it. Her resigned conclusion – 'Ther is no verray weele in this world heere' (III.836) – is in pointed contrast to the happiness she is to enjoy immediately afterwards, the constancy of which she herself claims to guarantee (see III.1492ff.). The note of tragic irony in her emphatic vows of loyalty, when we look at the well-known ending of the story, will hardly be missed by any reader. Yet this irony must not be understood as if it were directed against Criseyde's honesty, but as a reminder of the great variety of problems raised by this story, in particular the fallible nature of human self-assurance and foresight.

Another means of involving the reader in the intellectual process of the narrative is the direct intrusions by the narrator, particularly frequent in this third book. They prevent the reader from identifying too easily with the protagonists or condemning them too hastily, because they keep reminding him of the distance between himself and the world of the narrative and, at the same time, of the problems of adequate representation. This applies, in particular, to the description of the consummation of the protagonists' love: the fictional character of this scene is repeatedly insisted on by the continually shifting distance from the events reported. The narrator time and again points out that his account can give but a feeble impression of the true emotions and the heavenly bliss of the lovers; he emphasizes again and again that in everything he says he is completely dependent on his source, thus underlining his inexperience and his eager efforts. On the other hand, he is so deeply affected by his own narrative that at times he forgets all distance between himself and his characters and abandons himself to an unreserved glorification of such a love:

> O blisful nyght, of hem so longe isought,
> How blithe unto hem bothe two thow weere!
> Why nad I swich oon with my soule ybought,
> Ye, or the leeste joie that was theere?
> Awey, thow foule daunger and thow feere,
> And lat hem in this hevene blisse dwelle,
> That is so heigh that al ne kan I telle! (III.1317–23)

The tone of this stanza is not easy to describe. The obvious approach seems to be to take refuge in the fiction of a naive narrator who speaks in the ironic pose of simple-minded credulity.[21] From this point of view, the narrator's innocent enthusiasm can be seen as meant to alert the reader to the virtual confusion of all standards. Like Troilus, the inexperienced narrator indulges in an uncritically exaggerated glorification of love which, as the conclusion of the poem shows, turns out to be totally unjustified. Such an interpretation, however, rests on the assumption that the third book has to be seen primarily in the light of the poem's ending, and this is surely only part of the intended effect. The love-story would be reduced to a mere commonplace if it were not to be taken very seriously at this stage. If Troilus' happiness were but a naive illusion, his fall would be little more than a simple homiletic exemplum. I am convinced, however, that the emotional involvement of the narrator at this point serves, on the contrary, as an effective means of engaging the reader's sympathetic understanding; it creates the impression – surely not un-intended – that the poet too is overwhelmed by the intensity of this ecstatic happiness and that he envies the lovers their experience, without any regard to the final conclusion. Chaucer's irony is very rarely so direct as to simply imply the contrary of what he says, and his narrator's stance is much more delicate than the theory of the naive simpleton allows for. It lets him take each individual moment entirely seriously and makes us forget, for the time, the author's omniscience. At the same time, the emotional reaction of the narrator is a living instance to demonstrate the potential impact of literary tradition on later readers. Even an ancient story, handed on from author to author, has the power to move narrator and audience to genuine emotional participation.

This does not, of course, alter the fact that the poet here assumes the role of a narrator and that everything he says must be seen within the context of the whole scene. Thus, immediately following his emotional outburst, he again protests his own inadequacy and his indebtedness to his source, thereby at once reaffirming the distance between himself and his material, and at the same time bringing forward for discussion the problem of the mediatory function of the artist.[22] This constant change of perspective and distance also prevents the impression that we as readers are just playing the part of voyeurs, watching a scene of embarrassing intimacy, because all the time we are kept actively involved in the narrator's efforts to give an adequate representation of the scene and to inform the bare events of his source with the reality of a strong emotional experience. Such unpredictable variations of narrative technique are much more likely to make the audience recognize the moral implications of the story than a plain moralizing account could achieve. The richness of the third book lies in its technical virtuosity and its imaginative treatment of the traditional motif of the union of lovers, the experience of the highest bliss within a most imperfect world.

THE TRADITION OF CRISEYDE'S BETRAYAL

The third part of the poem, relating Criseyde's breach of faith and the downfall of Troilus from the height of his bliss, takes a similar course in both Chaucer and Boccaccio. No extensive episodes have been inserted by Chaucer, and the material has been much less expanded. The speed of the action has markedly increased in comparison with the first part. By this shift in the poem's structural balance, Criseyde's betrayal still remains a central, but not the most decisive, aspect of the story, and Troilus' desperate grief is not, as in *Il Filostrato*, the real core of the whole poem, but becomes part of a cycle of human experience that embraces happiness, disillusionment and the possibility of consolation.

This part of the poem, too, gives evidence of the motivation behind Chaucer's very often deliberately ambiguous narrative method: to invest his neutral material with a multiplicity of meanings, to explore every aspect of the story and to suggest a variety of possible reactions. And with the course of action being, as it were, not at all to the taste of the narrator – or, moreover, in harmony with the general idea of his work so far – the problem of presentation and meaning now becomes even more urgent for the poet. In fact, he seems to have increased the difficulties of his task deliberately: after the eloquent glorification of love, the tragic conclusions must look like a revocation of everything he has said before. Because love, as Troilus has experienced it, brings out what is best in man and refines his whole personality, a betrayal of such faith must mean more than just the proof of women's frailty as in Boccaccio. It casts doubt on the very reliability of any experience and on the possibility of lasting happiness. At the same time, and much more insistently than in previous versions of the story, which only record the bare fact of Criseyde's disloyalty, Chaucer goes into the question of her character. His rather provocative solution to the problem gives the conclusion of his poem its very personal and, for many readers, puzzling quality, and has aroused a spirited controversy among Chaucer scholars.[23]

The treatment of the same material in Shakespeare's *Troilus and Cressida*, two hundred years after Chaucer, illustrates how easily Criseyde's unfaithfulness could be prepared for from the very beginning of the story. At no time at all is Shakespeare's Cressida a worthy object of the prince's extravagant adoration. Chaucer, however, in spite of some interpretations to the contrary, has not taken this simple line. Criseyde is by no means portrayed as the kind of woman of whom nothing better is ever to be expected anyway, and it seems to me totally inappropriate to keep looking for signs in her character that might 'explain' her unfaithfulness, because this ignores the most distinctive quality of Chaucer's presentation. Criseyde is not at all an unworthy partner for Troilus, despite the deliberately accentuated human touches in her personality. The sincerity of her love for Troilus is again and again stressed by the narrator, and there is no reason whatever to suspect his words. The perfect harmony of the lovers' union is not a deplorable illusion of the deluded Troilus, but is felt by both lovers with equal conviction. How, then, is Criseyde's sudden change to be explained? The closer one looks at the text the more one is struck by the way Chaucer consistently emphasizes the shattering turning-point in his story. He neither starts with a critical portrait of Criseyde, as Shakespeare does, nor, contrary to our first superficial impression, tones down the suddenness of her reversal, which he could have done quite easily by slight modifications of the source. Instead, as a close comparison with Boccaccio makes abundantly clear, he does just the opposite: Chaucer's Criseyde forgets Troilus even more quickly and offers even less resistance to Diomede's aggressive suit than Boccaccio's Criseida. Moreover, the contrast between Troilus' diffident efforts to obtain even the slightest mark of her favour and Diomede's straightforward demands is much more sharply underlined and more disturbing. A great number of minor alterations proves that Chaucer has increased the discrepancy in full consciousness of this effect.[24] The massive assurances of his sympathy with Criseyde, therefore, do not at all mean that he wants to reduce her guilt so as to make it easier to find some excuse afterwards. In fact, his whole way of dealing with the story suggests very strongly that he has indeed made his task 'unnecessarily difficult',[25] – not, I am sure, to press his own interpretation all the more forcefully, but to intensify the tragic impact of the story and its disquieting effect on the reader. Various possible explanations for Criseyde's way of acting are offered to the reader, but none is adequate to account for all the provocative discrepancies of the story. Philosophical, artistic and human questions combine to make the search for an appropriate presentation all the more urgent. In terms of psychological characterization, some plausible explanations seem to be available, such as Criseyde's defenceless weakness, her loneliness among the Greeks and her 'fearful' character, as well as her understandable desire to be protected and her presentiment of the hopeless situation of Troy. But the narrator reluctantly admits that the favours she grants to Diomede by far exceed what might be excusable. And, in view of his conspicuous reticence when it comes to pass judgement on her, his short exclamation, 'and that was litel nede' (v.1040), sounds almost like a final damning verdict. Criseyde's letters, too, as they are formulated by Chaucer, make her heartless and flippant brutality appear inexcusable. The only attitude possible for the narrator in this disturbing situation is not one of forgiving lenience, but of simple compassion: 'I wolde excuse hire yet for routhe' (v.1099). Her breach of faith can be neither glossed over nor whitewashed; in her moment of horrified self-knowledge, however, she deserves compassion rather than moral condemnation. Thus this section of the poem is linked to the beginning, where the narrator has already made a moving appeal to the humanity and sympathetic imagination of the audience. It is the chief aim of this narrative, in the face of such a terrible guilt, not to encourage aloofness and righteous indignation, but to accept fallibility and suffering as the common property of all mankind. There is no soft-pedalling on moral issues; but the seriousness of the offence and the irrevocable decline render humble solidarity all the more needful.

On this basis Chaucer is able to present not only the tragedy of Troilus but also the tragicomedy of Diomede's seduction of Criseyde much more poignantly than Boccaccio. Troilus' terrible pain at parting from Criseyde is depicted with the same exuberance as are his love-sickness and the joy of his union with Criseyde. Every recollection of his former bliss is now turned into agony, and yet, in his self-tormenting passion, he cannot help recalling again and again everything he has lost. His complaint in front of the empty house of Criseyde, the highly emotional description of a certain locality, reminds one of much later romantic and 'sentimental' poetry.[26]

The helplessness of Pandarus, who up to this moment had never been at a loss for a way out, underlines Troilus' perfect isolation. As he has completely lost control over the course of events, his theoretical arguments of consolation are but useless commonplaces. His pragmatic view of the new situation and his dispassionate foresight give him a rather depressing superiority, but they also confirm, in retrospect, that he has never really understood Troilus' wholehearted devotion. His almost perfunctory attempts to cheer him up cannot obscure the fact that he has already abandoned every hope of altering the course of events by his own activity. For him, too, there is nothing left but compassion.

The reader realizes very soon that Troilus' misfortune is even greater and more definite than he himself is aware, because no sooner has Criseyde turned her back on him than she is courted by Diomede. The change of scene is much more pointedly employed as a means of ironic contrast than in Boccaccio. Thus, after Criseyde is handed over, the narrator does not return to Troy with Troilus, as in *Il Filostrato*, but goes on to describe Diomede's man-of-the-world way of preparing the ground to press his suit with Criseyde. He makes it clear that it is not the God of Love who has inspired Diomede to a disinterested admiration for Criseyde, as was once the case with Troilus, but that his is a much more direct purpose. His crafty cunning is in no way inferior to that of Pandarus, and like Pandarus he looks upon the woman in terms of a sporting trophy: 'To fisshen hire, he leyde out hook and lyne' (v.777). What drives him on is not genuine affection but the prospect of being reputed a lady-killer:

> But whoso myghte wynnen swich a flour
> From hym for whom she morneth nyght and day,
> He myghte seyn he were a conquerour. (v.792–4)

At the same time, he has at his disposal, no less than Troilus, the whole repertoire of conventional terminology and gestures of courtly love; coming from his mouth, however, they sound like the well-contrived mask of a most profane purpose. Whenever he talks about the irresistible power of the God of Love and begs Criseyde to show 'mercy', or when he blushes with brilliant timing, we suddenly become aware of a completely new way of interpreting the traditional formulas. His resolute, but in its outward forms courtly, wooing appears almost as a parody of the first two books of the poem.

In consequence of this frank introduction to the final stage of the drama, the innocent complaint of the still unenlightened Troilus becomes even more disturbing for the reader. The effect is repeated when, after Criseyde's breach of faith has become an irrevocable fact, Troilus is described waiting for her in vain on the city-wall. For the reader, who knows that Criseyde will never come back, his painful attempts to justify her staying away and Pandarus' knowing smile are all the more pathetic. There are other instances too where Chaucer accentuates tragic contradictions and emotional intensity, but also the more trivial aspects of his story, very sharply. He is evidently anxious to present the simple course of events from as many points of view as possible, to provoke simultaneously a variety of conflicting reactions on the part of the reader: not just compassionate sympathy with the protagonists, but also doubts about the traditional interpretation of the story, uncertainty about the real motives of the chief actors, uneasiness about the workings of providence, and a critical reflection on the function of the poet as the transmitter of all these far-off events.

This last aspect is of particular importance for an appropriate understanding of the fifth book. There is no other part of the poem in which Chaucer reminds the reader so insistently of the fact that what he has in front of him is not a faithful mirror of reality but an attempt to bring back to life the actuality of a distant past, with the inadequate means at the poet's disposal and an insufficiency of reliable information. This is particularly true of Criseyde's betrayal. The narrator knows the bare facts of the plot from his source; but, try as hard as he may, he cannot find there a convincing explanation of her behaviour. Again and again he brings his narrative to a halt to insert personal comments or references to his source, to produce critical detachment and prevent any unreflecting emotional identification. The reader is constantly forced to discriminate between the course of the events actually related, the narrator's difficulties in presenting them and their historical substance. Since there are many instances in the poem to prove that Chaucer is by no means in principle reluctant to enlarge on his source-material by inserting invented details or to fill in apparent gaps in the motivation, the anxious obedience to his source at this point is obviously part of a deliberate strategy for the sole purpose of bringing out the aesthetic problem. What can the poet do who has to report events which are not only incompatible with his own sympathies but also with the course of his narrative as related so far? Chaucer passes this question on to the reader by putting before him the bare facts of the story with seemingly complete honesty. At the crucial point he hides behind his source: 'the storie telleth us' (v.1037, 1051). His pose of undecided and helpless perplexity becomes most prominent in the stanza, frequently quoted, that reports Criseyde's final change of allegiance:

> I fynde ek in the stories elleswhere,
> Whan thorugh the body hurt was Diomede
> Of Troilus, tho wepte she many a teere,
> Whan that she saugh his wyde wowndes blede;
> And that she took, to kepen hym, good hede;
> And for to helen hym of his sorwes smerte,
> Men seyn – I not – that she yaf hym hire herte.　　(v.1044–50)

As the narrator cannot alter the facts recorded in his source, he is anxious to assure the reader that at least he has not added anything. He does not tell us whether Criseyde really transferred all her love to Diomede or whether she only outwardly surrendered to his aggressive wooing, because, he claims, he does not know. This is fully in accord with his later statement: 'Ne me ne list this sely womman chyde' (v.1093). He also refuses to join the chorus of all those historians and poets who have made her name a synonym for disloyalty in women. Thus the question is left open how her notorious betrayal can be reconciled with the character she has shown up to this moment. Chaucer carries his pose so far as to withhold, somewhat over-elaborately, information which he could have found in his sources or, at least, could have deduced from them quite easily. For instance, he deliberately leaves the question of the exact time-sequence open:

> But trewely, how longe it was bytwene
> That she forsok hym for this Diomede,
> There is non auctour telleth it, I wene.
> Take every man now to his bokes heede;
> He shal no terme fynden, out of drede.　　(v.1086–90)

As a matter of fact, Chaucer could have found in Benoît, from whom he accepts very precise information elsewhere, that the interval must have been at least two years. The intended effect of these lines and of similar statements can only be that the reader should turn his attention more sharply to the narrator and to his attitude towards his material, to observe his method of interpretation more closely while at the same time drawing his own conclusions from the facts made available to him. This, in my view, is the only reasonable interpretation of the narrative technique of the fifth book.

There is yet another issue emerging from his material to which Chaucer does not offer a cut and dried answer, again appealing to the reader's own judgement. This is the problem of predestination raised by Troilus himself when he reflects on the reasons for his downfall. His extensive analysis of all the traditional arguments, largely based on Boethius, ends with the resigned conclusion that man is absolutely powerless to alter his fate. This, of course, has to be understood as an expression of Troilus' agonized despair, not as an opinion offered by the author himself.[27] As its translator, Chaucer knew very well that Boethius' *Consolatio* solves the dilemma by proposing a way completely in accordance with the ortho-dox concept of God's omniscience, which largely determined the position of the Church on this question.[28] Even if Chaucer's audience failed to notice that Troilus evidently did not read far enough in his Boethius, they must have realized that, despite all seeming indications to the contrary, decisions based on human free will are made in the course of the poem more than once. Even the most sympathetic account of Criseyde's unprotected loneliness in the Greek camp and her timid disposition cannot absolve her from all responsibility for her betrayal, and Troilus, too, quite deliberately refuses to take the initiative actively to try to prevent the handing-over of Criseyde. Chaucer, like Boccaccio, devotes a remarkably large section of his narrative to the discussion of possible ways of circumventing their separation, either by flight or by use of force. Every proposal is rejected by Troilus himself or by Criseyde because it would either lead to even more difficulties or be harmful to Criseyde's reputation. The detailed discussion obviously anticipates possible objec-tions by the reader, who might form the impression that the lovers have resigned themselves too easily to their fate. Chaucer makes a point of showing that any imaginable alternative has its own difficulties; at the same time, however, he suggests that Troilus and Criseyde had at least certain options, so that, in the last resort, they freely chose to accept the risk of separation. This general affirmation of the possibility of free decisions and genuine options is of much more relevance than the hypothetical question whether there really would have been an effective way out or whether the lovers are to be blamed for their passive inactivity. The narrator's assertion that both lovers, and Criseyde in particular, have acted in good faith and with the best of intentions, is placed side by side with their complete misjudgement of the whole situation, as proved by the course of the following events – when, for instance, Criseyde talks about the possibility of peace negotiations or imagines herself in a position to guarantee her return in the near future.

But what is more important is that the reader sees all those apparently free decisions frustrated by the predetermined course of events. Although, subjectively, the characters feel absolutely free, the story itself has assigned to them roles from which they cannot escape. In this sense they are indeed subject to the law of predestination, and this holds true for any narrative relating past events. Narrator and reader foresee the final conclusion from the outset, and, since for them all decisions have already been made, they can only watch the pathetic ignorance of the actors and their vain efforts to look for alternative courses with a kind of superior compassion.[29] Although Chaucer does not explicitly mention the analogy between the position of the reader and that of divine providence, the reader knows from his own experience that, as Boethius argues, divine omniscience and human free will can be perfectly compatible. Just as God stands completely outside space and time, totally unaffected by the law of chronological succession, the reader, too, moves in a dimension categorically different from that of the fictitious characters and can see their situation in its entirety, while they themselves are still in the midst of the dilemma of practical and moral decisions for which they themselves are responsible. This aspect of the story is clearly demonstrated by the emphasis on the temporal and intellectual distance of the events, by the constraining force of the source-material felt by the poet, and by the lovers being inextricably involved in the notorious fate of Troy.[30]

All these issues are taken up again in the concluding section of the fifth book. And it is only because their significance for the poem as a whole has often been overlooked that the question could arise whether this elaborate coda is really an organic part of the whole work or an appended afterthought. Whereas earlier critics, under the powerful influence of Chaucer's apotheosis of love earlier in the poem, saw his final rejection of worldly love as a perfunctory tribute to orthodox Christian morality, in contrast to the intellectual attitude of the rest of the poem, more recent interpretations have insisted that, on the contrary, this section really contains the quintessence of the whole poem and all other parts are to be subordinated to it. According to the most consistent and influential interpretation from this point of view, the fifth book shows 'the hell on earth which results from trying to make earth a heaven in its own right'.[31] This is true, up to a point; however, such a glib description argues on the basis of a moral self-assurance about the symmetry of guilt and punishment that is absolutely alien to the tone and spirit of Chaucer's whole poem. True enough, Chaucer makes us aware of the fundamental moral relevance of all the lovers' experiences and decisions throughout the poem – and this is an important difference from *Il Filostrato*; but earlier critics certainly touched upon a real problem when they took exception to the discrepancy between this smooth moral conclusion, presented with homiletic directness, and the sophisticated narrative technique of the poem in general, which clearly seems to suggest that simple judgements are inadequate in view of the complex nature of reality.

This does not mean that the conclusion of *Troilus and Criseyde* must be inconsistent with Chaucer's own religious beliefs or with the moral and intellectual basis of the whole work. What it does mean, however, is that it should not be read as a sort of final summary of the poem. The theological claims formulated here would hardly have been new to any member of Chaucer's audience, and his narrative would be little more than unimaginative commonplace if it were only an exemplum of misguided passion. The provocativeness and richness of the work rest on the unresolved and almost unbearable tension between the unpredictable mutability of reality, the beauty and misery of human passion, and the uncompromising rigour of an ethical standard that seems to demand a world quite different from that which we all encounter in our daily lives. The rigid and unmitigated moral conclusion comes as a surprise to most readers because it assumes a much simpler view of reality than anything that has gone before – but not, I am sure, because it really contradicts it in principle.[32]

To explain this difficulty there is no need to take refuge in the assumption that Chaucer himself was undecided as to his own attitude towards his material. The stylistic contrasts of the final part of the poem are an important aspect of Chaucer's narrative technique; he is deliberately experimenting with very different forms of presentation. Without unduly overemphasizing the individuality of the narrator-figure or separating it from the author altogether, we may say that Chaucer here rehearses different narrative stances one after the other, creating the impression – obviously intended – that the poet is struggling, helplessly and uneasily, to come to terms with his subject.[33] Neither a polite excuse to the ladies or some conventional literary formula nor even an orthodox moral provides an adequate exit. The combination of all these, however, once again focuses the reader's attention on the narrator and appeals to his own critical judgement. It goes without saying that Troilus was misguided in idealizing Criseyde uncritically and in putting all his confidence in human steadfastness; but at the same time his love opened up to him the experience of supreme earthly happiness and the highest moral effort in his absolute devotion to an ideal chosen by him as his ultimate goal. The poem does not raise the question that seems to have troubled many critics: whether Troilus could have spared himself his 'double sorwe' by a different choice, such as the rejection of worldly lust or, perhaps, marriage. The tragedy of his fall – and this is not so very different from later concepts of tragedy – for all the unhesitating affirmation of human free will, nevertheless leaves room for an element of inevitability. At least it would be hardly possible to pick out one particular point in the story where Troilus takes the wrong decision and thus causes his own downfall. Within the moral framework established by the poem, Troilus has proved himself a worthy lover, and whatever his fate in the other world may be (Chaucer deliberately leaves this rather vague), the text leaves hardly any doubt that his vision is meant as a reward rather than a punishment for his sinful life.[34] The poet's warning not to put undue confidence in created and therefore transitory things concerns all mankind and does not point at Troilus as a particularly wicked example. On the contrary, he experiences what the poet, at the beginning of the poem, wishes for all unhappy lovers:

> And preieth for hem that ben in the cas
> Of Troilus, as ye may after here,
> That Love hem brynge in hevene to solas   (1.29–31)

The meaning of these lines is not entirely unambiguous and at first sight might well point to the earthly heaven described in the third book. In the end, however, they gain a deeper significance: from a standpoint similar to that of divine providence and, at the same time, to that of the audience, Troilus is made at last aware of the real dimensions of human suffering and the transitory quality of all that the poem has glorified.

And it is to this final, crowning experience, and not only to the pitiful end of the love affair (as possibly was the case in an earlier version, and similarly also in Boccaccio) that the following lines, with their primitive rhetoric and their surprisingly untroubled homiletic assurance, refer:[35]

> Swich fyn hath, lo, this Troilus for love!
> Swich fyn hath al his grete worthynesse!
> Swich fyn hath his estat real above,
> Swich fyn his lust, swich fyn hath his noblesse!
> Swich fyn hath false worldes brotelnesse!   (v.1828–32)

The bald 'moral' of the story does not indulge in pharisaical gloating but embraces the whole course of the poem, the tragic conclusion as well as its qualification by the sudden change of perspective. And it is in this sense that the warning addressed to all young lovers has to be understood: as an invitation to interpret this pagan narrative in the light of the Christian doctrine of salvation and thus to learn wisdom for their own lives. The traditional prayer at the end, too, is not just a dutiful appendage, but the final result of a process of reflection. This gives it a more profound significance and at the same time makes the reader aware of its literary and conventional character.

This apparently experimental sequence of possible conclusions and narrative attitudes is in accordance with Chaucer's method of presenting his material right through the whole poem. Time and again the poet retreats behind a distinctly subjective, often very limited, and therefore inconclusive, stance;[36] he presents the story in quotation marks, as it were, and keeps qualifying it by frequent shifts of tone and perspective. But in spite of this alienating effect of the literary medium, or perhaps rather by the deliberate use of it, he succeeds in engaging the reader's critical attention and in bridging the temporal distance. Chaucer was one of the first to be fully aware of some of the problems every author of a longer narrative finds himself faced with, and his solution is not so very different from that of Fielding, Sterne and many other modern novelists: the difficulties of presentation are made part of the text itself and are openly explained to the reader.[37]

The Canterbury Tales gives proof of the central significance Chaucer attached to the problem of presenting a story in narrative poetry; and what in *Troilus* seems to be primarily a question of rhetoric, sophisticated variation of levels of style, surprising changes in the narrator's pose and a playful attitude towards possible reactions of the audience, becomes in *The Canterbury Tales* an essential principle of the whole structure. However exciting or moving or instructive the poet's material may be, its potential qualities are realized only when given a distinctly individual shape by the poet in the act of presentation and in the presence of a critically attentive audience.

7

The storyteller and his audience:
The Legend of Good Women

CHAUCER'S FIRST COLLECTION OF STORIES, *THE LEGEND OF GOOD Women*, was evidently written between *Troilus and Criseyde* and *The Canterbury Tales*, because it explicitly refers to the Trojan epic and is in turn quoted in the 'Introduction' to the 'Man of Law's Tale'. Of all the narrative poems discussed in this book it is probably the least popular although it is by no means less original than the others, but shows us Chaucer in as experimental and exploratory a mood as in any of them. Many accounts of the *Legend* start from an openly apologetic position or begin with the admission that this is indeed an inferior and uncharacteristically conventional work.[1] It is not entirely Chaucer's fault, however, that we have lost the taste for brief and fairly unadorned narrative or that we find the provocative reinterpretation of classical stories whose original versions we are no longer familiar with less exciting than Chaucer and many of his contemporaries must have done. Twelve manuscripts preserve *The Legend of Good Women* or parts of it, almost as many as in the case of *The Parliament of Fowls* and four times as many as in that of *The Book of the Duchess* or *The House of Fame*. 'Comparisons are odorous', as Shakespeare's Dogberry knew, and there is nothing to be gained by demonstrating that *The Legend of Good Women* is inferior to *The Canterbury Tales*. It will certainly never enjoy anything like the same popularity, but then it does not claim to be the same kind of story collection and its appeal is more limited by its very subject and, perhaps, by its confessedly more literary character. Form and subject-matter suggest that Chaucer was consciously attempting something beyond the scope of his earlier work, a decisive extension of the concept of courtly love (if indeed this is still the right term), with a choice of material that invites comparison with the famous poets of Rome and Italy.

THE PROLOGUE

Viewed superficially, the Prologue once more harks back to the earlier love-visions, but it is even more personal and free from the restraints

98

imposed by the traditional genre. The legends themselves are, for the most part, based on Ovid, that is, they take their subjects from pagan antiquity, and whatever 'modern' issue they are meant to illustrate, they do so in a deliberately detached and generalizing manner. The same applies, of course, to *Troilus and Criseyde*, but the *Legend* goes a step further by virtue of the variety of stories and the greater number of characters, all of whom have this in common: 'And yit they were hethene, al the pak' (G, 299), as the God of Love says, choosing a rather provocative colloquial turn of phrase. If we look at the nine tales in the light of what Chaucer had attempted and achieved before he started on this collection, we are in a better position to appreciate their originality and their experimental qualities. Not only did Chaucer succeed in introducing a wealth of new material to English literature by opening up the rich storehouse of Ovidian mythology, with its inexhaustible variety of character and incident; this material also presented him with the challenge of an unorthodox diversity of male and female characters who would not fit into the traditional roles of courtly love-literature. He had to find new ways of drawing such unexpected and unpredictable figures, in situations not to be found in his earlier poetry. In this he may not have been quite as successful as in many of the *Canterbury Tales*, but if we compare the *Legend* with any of the earlier narratives, including even *Troilus and Criseyde*, we are bound to see a definite advance in scope and variety, even though the subject does not allow for unlimited freedom of stylistic experiment.

What makes the Prologue so different from the earlier dream–visions is the way in which the new subject is introduced. Even more distinctly than in *The Parliament of Fowls* or *The House of Fame*, the narrator sees himself, and is seen by others, not as an unsuccessful lover, but as a poet with a respectable number of works to his credit. In fact, the Prologue contains the earliest bibliography of Chaucer and a particularly valuable one at that because it lists some titles we would otherwise know nothing of, like 'the Wreched Engendrynge of Mankynde' (G, 414) and 'Orygenes upon the Maudeleyne' (G, 418). It cannot be ruled out, of course, that these are only fake titles, but it is more likely that the works are lost. In any case, the list is impressive enough, and it is clear that the real subject of the Prologue is Chaucer's reputation as a poet and, in particular, the critical reception of his works.[2]

The Prologue begins with a wonderful account of the true function of literature and the truly indispensable contribution of books to our whole culture. One of the most important services of written texts is that they can tell us about things we have not seen ourselves and thus widen our knowledge beyond the scope and the possibilities of our own experience:

> A thousand sythes have I herd men telle
> That there is joye in hevene and peyne in helle,
> And I acorde wel that it be so;
> But natheles, this wot I wel also,
> That there ne is non that dwelleth in this contre,
> That eyther hath in helle or hevene ybe,
> Ne may of it non other weyes witen,
> But as he hath herd seyd or founde it writen;
> For by assay there may no man it preve.
> But Goddes forbode, but men shulde leve
> Wel more thyng than men han seyn with ye!
> Men shal nat wenen every thyng a lye,
> For that he say it nat of yore ago.
> God wot, a thyng is nevere the lesse so,
> Thow every wyght ne may it nat yse. (G, 1–15)

Chaucer goes beyond his earlier poems in his emphatic claim that there are things we will never see with our own eyes but in whose existence we should nevertheless believe because the poets testify to their reality. Truth is much wider than our own experience and literature acts as a kind of collective memory preserving the knowledge and thus the very existence of a whole world of facts and ideas that would otherwise be lost irretrievably:

> Thanne mote we to bokes that we fynde,
> Thourgh whiche that olde thynges ben in mynde,
> And to the doctryne of these olde wyse
> Yeven credence, in every skylful wyse,
> And trowen on these olde aproved storyes
> Of holynesse, of regnes, of victoryes,
> Of love, of hate, of othere sondry thynges,
> Of which I may nat make rehersynges.
> And if that olde bokes weren aweye,
> Yloren were of remembrance the keye.
> Wel oughte us thanne on olde bokes leve,
> There as there is non other assay by preve. (G, 17–28)

The examples mentioned by Chaucer (21–4) are the subjects of all kinds of narrative literature, be it saints' legends, history or romance, but perhaps the most significant item is the one mentioned in the very first lines of the poem, where 'joye in hevene and peyne in helle' are instanced as undisputable facts. Nobody has ever been there and yet everybody believes in the existence of heaven and hell. This may be a pointed tribute to Dante's *Divina Commedia*, whose narrator does indeed claim to have visited hell and heaven, if only in a divinely inspired poetic vision.[3] Whatever the realistic basis of his experience, we have no doubt about its truth and validity. At the same time, this may be one of Chaucer's modest disclaimers: his own subject is so much less lofty and yet the stories he is going to tell also have the truth and reality which is attested by books. The narrator's passion for reading is cheerfully admitted and not, as in earlier poems, presented in a slightly comical light as an inability to cope with the demands of actual experience.

The narrator goes on to confess – and this is a surprising change of direction – that there is one area of experience that makes even him forsake his books: this is the season of spring, with its renewal of nature and the budding of flowers. The worship of May is here presented as a lively activity, placed in sharp contrast to the world of books:

> Farewel my bok, and my devocioun! (F, 39)

The (presumably later) G-version is a little less sweeping and suggests that the poet's devotion to books is interrupted just for this particular season:

> Farwel my stodye, as lastynge that sesoun! (G, 39)[4]

Of course, the traditional month of May, the month of love, is in a way as literary an experience as the books are; it can certainly not be regarded as an instance of real life versus books. After all, as every reader of Chaucer knows, the springtide with all its traditional paraphernalia is a literary convention as far removed from actual reality as many other subjects we read about, and at the same time just as near to some deeper levels of experience. Any reader will perceive that the object of the poet's delight, the daisy, is not some particular flower but an image of love, of wholehearted devotion to virtue and honour, and of the poet's wish to praise it with all the rhetorical gifts at his command.[5] Even after he has left his books, the narrator immediately returns to literary considerations and to his own poetical efforts. His references to other poets and to the courtly party-game of the Flower and the Leaf must have meant more to his contemporary audience than it can possibly mean to us, but it is still evident that he is talking about his own position as a love-poet in this courtly society and wants to introduce his own stories, taken from old books, as a subject of at least as much relevance and authority as the new-fangled conventions of love-poetry.

In the later version (G), the poet goes to bed after roaming the meadows and has a dream that is the subject of the rest of the Prologue. He wakes up in the last two lines and begins to write the legends. The earlier version (F) has over a hundred lines more, mainly devoted to daisy-worship, and this makes the transition a little more awkward, as well as perhaps overdoing the conventional praise of love, although I am not at all sure that this should be taken as a straightforward parody of courtly love. It may be deliberately conventional to contrast it with the highly original and personal sequel. The narrator's idea of love is clearly a limited one, not really informed by an experience of life's unpredictable variety, and there is something curiously artificial about his going to rest – as if the conventional sleep, usually introduced at this point of a dream–vision, were deliberately staged:[6]

> Hom to myn hous ful swiftly I me spedde,
> And in a lytel herber that I have,
> Ybenched newe with turves, fresshe ygrave,
> I bad men shulde me my couche make;
> For deynte of the newe someres sake,
> I bad hem strowe floures on my bed. (G, 96–101)

This sounds almost like Orsino's self-indulgent devotion to love:

> Away before me to sweet beds of flowers!
> Love-thoughts lie rich when canopied with bowers.
> (*Twelfth Night*, I.1.41–2)

It is, at any rate, quite different from the introductions to the earlier dream–visions, where sleep comes far more naturally to the narrator. We have heard so much about the importance and the truth of books that we begin to look for vestiges of literary source-material everywhere. The narrator behaves as if he had read some of the more conventional dream–visions, like *The Book of the Duchess*, and this literary aspect is underlined by the subject of the dream itself. It begins, unremarkably enough, with the joy of the birds who happily remember St Valentine's Day, almost like an echo of *The Parliament of Fowls*; but it is not long before the God of Love is announced, and he is rather different from any of the allegories of the earlier poem. He is not at all like the Goddess Nature and even less like Venus, but, rather, like a bad-tempered monarch who is more respected for his imperious manner than for any true authority. Nor does he offer any conventional instruction, and his appearance, like that of his followers, hardly conforms to the clichés of courtly love. The 'Balade' sung by the ladies in praise of the Queen anticipates the subject of the stories the poet will be condemned to compose, and its refrain is a superlative praise of Alceste, whose 'trouthe' in love puts all other heroines to shame. The concept of love is defined not, as it usually is, by the idea of faithful service and ennobling devotion, but by woman's loyalty and innocent suffering. The narrator is treated in a far less pleasant and more condescending manner than in any of his previous dreams. Instead of being rewarded for his naive interest in the subject he is turned away as 'my mortal fo' (G, 248), and his most distinguished love-poetry is held against him as heresy and a disservice to love's cause.

Again, Chaucer has created a highly individual and teasingly ambiguous self-portrait. It is tempting, but in view of our limited knowledge unprofitable, to speculate whether there was in fact any official displeasure Chaucer wanted to answer or whether the whole situation is pure fiction. The poem creates its own reality, and we shall never know just what degree of actual experience and critical discussion are behind this passage. What makes it so interesting for us is the frankness with which Chaucer enters into a public debate on the subject of his own poetry and its reception. It soon becomes clear that Chaucer's most critical reader, the God of Love, is at the same time the most biased. This God of Love is not to be taken as a serious personification of a divine principle, but rather as a form of criticism of simple models of love-religion and outworn allegorical clichés. He is not only a rather haughty and self-important character, but also a remarkably unsystematic and narrow-minded literary critic.[7] Through prejudice or obtuseness he misunderstands the poet's intentions completely; this is emphasized by the fact that he picks out two works that are the most unconvincing witnesses for Chaucer's alleged hostility to women. The *Roman de la Rose* can hardly be described as a work against women and love, and in *Troilus and Criseyde*, Chaucer, as we have seen, goes out of his way to soften the reader's predictable verdict on Criseyde and to present her as an object of pity. It is therefore not very likely that Chaucer himself would have agreed with Cupid's criticism; it makes more sense to assume that the God of Love is meant to represent a particular, limited and deplorably superficial reaction to Chaucer's poetry. He does not seem to know that at least some of the books he mentions to support his case contain some notorious anti-feminist satire and ironically undermine his argument.

The defence Chaucer puts up for himself and the Queen's apology on his behalf are interesting contributions to the discussion of the poet's purpose, although neither is answered by the God of Love, who pardons the poet only to show his royal mercy and because of the Queen's intercession. To her he leaves the final verdict and the choice of the penalty, and it becomes clear that the whole Prologue has led up to the imposition of this task on the narrator. The stories introduced by this prologue are thus announced as a literary labour undertaken by the poet, not voluntarily, but as an atonement for his earlier work. This raises a number of questions about the tone and the purpose of this collection, and the answers we give to them will largely determine our reaction to the legends.

If early readers had expressed their disapproval of Chaucer's portrayal of women, as the God of Love's attack seems to suggest, they must have found fault with the whole concept of courtly love. Their ideal of womanly behaviour, like that implied by Cupid, must have been concerned more with truth and constant relationships than with the lover's woe and his lady's pity. The modern reader may well ask which view is the more complimentary, and there is no reason why Chaucer and his contemporaries should not have asked the same question. Cupid's account of virtuous women puts the finger on whole areas of experience which were simply not the subject of courtly love-poetry, but rather of saints' legends, except that he is explicitly referring to heathen ladies whose virtue is not grounded in holiness, but is presented as a natural female quality. Cupid is interested in women not as the objects of lovers' devotion alone, but in all aspects of their relation to men. There are for him, as for many traditional moralists, three states, each with its proper code of behaviour:

> ... clene maydenes, and ... trewe wyves,
> ... stedefaste widewes durynge alle here lyves,   (G, 282–3)

This is repeated a few lines later:

> For alle keped they here maydenhede,
> Or elles wedlok, or here widewehede.   (G, 294–5)

In other words, this Cupid is not the conventional God of Love, but the patron of steadfast women. For a modern feminist, this appears a severe limitation, because women are defined only in their relation to marriage or rather to the opposite sex in general; but before we see this as a deliberate piece of social or literary criticism on Chaucer's part we must first recognize that it is at least a considerable extension of the part women are usually assigned in aristocratic love-poetry.[8] It is, of course, true that woman's role in medieval society was far more varied and included many activities outside marriage, but this is not really the point here because love-poetry does not claim to present the full range of human experience: it largely excludes the realities of professional and of domestic life. This applies to the portrayal of the lover as well as to that of the beloved, except that fighting is included in the knight's legitimate pursuits. But, apart from vaguely described off-stage fights, Chaucer's Troilus, to mention but one instance, is hardly less 'limited' than Criseyde. It is only with his role as a lover that the poet is concerned, and it would be quite irrelevant to point out all the aspects of his personality on which the poem is silent.

It seems equally beside the mark to fasten on the restrictive aspects of the Prologue and to read an anti-feminist bias into its portrait of women. Within the context of traditional literary ideas about women, Cupid's praise of them is unexceptional. At least they are presented here in more than one capacity and more than one age-group. To praise their steadfast purity and 'trouthe' is to give them credit for moral qualities and firmness of character rather than for beauty, attractiveness and the passive virtue or the power to ennoble their lovers. This is certainly not in itself an anti-feminist point of view. On the other hand, there is something in the tone of the dialogue that suggests that the god's line of argument is not taken entirely seriously by the poet himself, even though the narrator is forced into submission and agrees to the penalty with as good a grace as he can manage. The flaw in the ideal picture presented by the God of Love is not that it fails to do justice to the full range of women's activities or that it is too patronizing, but rather that it is too simple and too good to be true. To praise women in such fulsome and wholesale manner is hardly more adequate than to denounce them *in toto*, especially when the eulogy includes a sweeping disparagement of men. Coming from a man, this might well make the reader pause and wonder whether he is expected to take Cupid's account as the full story. What the dispute does, at any rate, is to announce a complete change of subject. To celebrate faithful women and their martyrdom is to turn away from love-poetry in the traditional sense and to try out new material. At the same time there is at least a suspicion that this could lead to a monotonous string of pre-dictable biographies. The poet is told more than once that there is an inexhaustible number of women whose exemplary lives are worthy of being told, and at one point the Queen even suggests that he should devote all the remainder of his days to this task:

> Thow shalt, whil that thow livest, yer by yere,
> The moste partye of thy tyme spende
> In makynge of a gloryous legende
> Of goode women, maydenes and wyves,
> That were trewe in lovynge al here lyves;   (G, 471–5)

When Chaucer or one of his characters is as emphatic as this it is usually a signal for the reader to be on his guard, and he surely does not misread the text if he begins to wonder whether the subject dictated to the poet is as rewarding as he is told. The narrator writes his stories under compulsion; it would have created quite a different impression if he himself had offered this collection as a voluntary penance; but though 'thy penaunce is but lyte' (G, 485), the word 'penaunce' rather suggests that the idea did not come from the poet himself and that we are therefore invited to question this choice of subject. It would be a gross oversimpli-fication to say that the ideal of woman's truth and constancy is ridiculed, but it seems just as inadequate to take the poem entirely at its face value and thus to miss the irony of the title.

Above all, the choice of this particular narrative genre implies a rather limited view of the function of literature. Alceste and the God of Love evidently want to turn the narrator into a narrowly didactic poet, and their idea of the real moral impact of fictional narrative seems so much less complex and sophisticated than Chaucer's own. This is also emphasized by the God of Love's injunction to be brief: 'Sey shortly' (F, 577). Brevity may be the soul of wit, but in medieval literature very short tales are, as a rule, simple exempla, and it is doubtful whether Chaucer really felt that he could do justice to Ovid's complex stories when turning them into brief summaries.

The collection is introduced as a secular legendary, and we shall see how some of the stories had to be distorted in order to fit into this rigid scheme. Not every woman who died because of some man is necessarily a martyr, and indiscriminate denunciation of women – even if the poet had been guilty of it – cannot effectively be answered by equally sweeping glorification.[9] Thus the stories that follow are placed at a distance from the reader by the idea of penance as well as by the hesitation and humility of the narrator. We are deliberately encouraged to read them as a performance, and this should make us more critically alert than we would be without this very personal introduction. As in Chaucer's early poems and, even more, in *The Canterbury Tales*, this provocative ambiguity of the narrative point of view is more important than any specific conclusions the individual reader may draw from it. The poet, out of genuine modesty or a sophisticated detachment, withholds any authorial interpretation or presents it in such a way that it cannot possibly be taken literally.

Modern readers are at first inclined to suspect that Chaucer must have found these stories boring and that he gave up after nine legends to go on to the more exciting collection of *The Canterbury Tales*; but this is certainly wrong or at least much too simple. The importance of these legends lay first of all in the selection of classical stories, gleaned mainly from Ovid and various other authors, or perhaps from selections from classical writers, and in the adaptation of the material to a new kind of brief tale, complete in itself and yet part of a larger structure. Many or most were inspired by Ovid's *Heroides*, brief versions of classical stories, told from a personal and therefore distinctly limited angle. This makes for irony and doubt about traditional interpretations. Chaucer's treatment, similarly, suggests that there is more than one way of looking at time-honoured episodes and more than one possible judgement. The tone of the stories, and especially the narrator's personal interventions, discourage a naive and literal reading. Chaucer obviously delights in distancing stories by having them told in an ostensibly personal manner.[10] The narrator takes sides vigorously and, in accordance with the theme of his collection, acts the part of an uncritical defender of defenceless women. Excessive pity easily turns into condescension, and the heroines are often reduced to rather marrowless objects of tearful commiseration. In the case of such powerful and politically or domestically active women as Cleopatra, Dido and Medea this is particularly striking, and it is most improbable that Chaucer should not have been conscious of this consistent effect. It would be a distortion to call the narrator anti-feminist, but it is also clear that he is woman's friend only in a very narrow and biased sense; any reader who knows some of the original stories will notice the omissions.[11] Woman's role is mostly reduced to her relationship with some seductive man whom she is not able to hold as Criseyde held Troilus. Men are neither ennobled by women's company nor attracted by anything but their outward charm and quick submission. If *The Legend of Good Women* was read to an audience of women it is doubtful whether they can have been particularly flattered; it seems much more likely that Chaucer aimed at a more sophisticated effect. Any lady of half of Criseyde's quick intelligence might have resented this kind of pathetic appreciation until she saw the larger purpose of the collection and discovered some of its deeper ironies. It is obvious that the narrator is a persona created by the author and that we have to read the legends as a very personal statement. This is not meant in a strictly psychological sense, and I think it is idle to speculate whether this narrator knows what he is doing or whether he is completely serious. His personal character is not really an issue here; at least it is far more important to recognize the discrepancy between the simple voice of the narrator and the sophistication of the whole collection. The narrator is not flatly discredited, but most readers will, after a while, feel a little superior to him and believe that they can see more in the text and the story-material than he himself does. This is precisely the effect Chaucer tries to achieve; at least this seems to me the most convincing explanation of the elusive style of the Prologue and the legends.

THE LEGENDS

The first legend, that of Cleopatra, is a good example. It is, as far as we know, the first treatment of Cleopatra's story in English and if Chaucer had before him Boccaccio's account in *De Claris Mulieribus* (supplemented by the life of Antony in *De Casibus Virorum Illustrium*), which is very likely, he cannot have been unaware of the fact that he was reinterpreting the character of Cleopatra completely.[12] Boccaccio is extremely hostile, and though there were more favourable versions of her story it is still obvious that Chaucer deliberately turned her into a pathetic martyr. It has often been remarked that Chaucer opens his series of legends with a most unlikely candidate, but this can hardly have been done unintentionally. The reader is once more reminded of the fact that this collection was not undertaken voluntarily and that the author may have his own ideas about what he is sentenced to do. If the God of Love was ignorant enough to offer 'Jerome agayns Jovynyan' (G, 281) as an authority on the perfection of women, he might also fail to notice that Cleopatra, whose story he explicitly wants to come first, had a far from exemplary career. Or, to put it another way, the poet knows that stories can create a new reality that exists in its own right, a reality that can be very far from the historical truth and yet valid and convincing in itself. Cleopatra is a particularly interesting instance of the poet's power to recreate a character, to transform a crafty and notorious seductress into an innocent martyr. The vigorous and disproportionately extended description of the sea-battle, which has often puzzled critics, may be another sly pointer to the narrator's rather different interests and his admitted reluctance to perform the penitential task.[13] Chaucer the poet stands at some distance from his narrator, encouraging the reader to do the same.

Even if he is not making subtle fun of his penitential labour – and the question has to be decided by every reader for himself – he is certainly making a provocative statement about the nature of 'storyal soth' (G, 702), the truth of literary tradition and the authority of written evidence. As he asserts in the Prologue, we all have to take on trust many things which we only know from reading about them. Might not the same be true of Cleopatra and the other women whose lives the poet is going to describe? Who knows what the 'real' Cleopatra was like? And if the God of Love wants to hear stories of exemplary women, why not mould any famous biography into the prescribed form? It is certainly a very new concept of 'storyal soth', but one that – far from turning the *Legend* into a huge joke – raises fundamental questions and opens an intriguing discussion on the nature and function of poetry. The 'Legend of Cleopatra' may be read as a demonstration of poetic fairness, of the poet's ability to wring pathos even out of the story of a royal whore, or of the independent authority of a poet's personal vision. In any case, it seems a far from inappropriate beginning to a series of legends, as long as we recognize that Chaucer was not just naively reproducing an old story. Cleopatra's 'infinite variety' is reduced to pitiful weakness, and simple truth to her 'wyfhod': 'Was nevere unto hire love a trewer quene' (G, 695). It is perfectly consistent and in keeping with Cupid's demand, as long as we do not remember that the original story was quite different. Are we meant to be deceived or should we notice the provocative discrepancy? The poet, I think, leaves the decision to the reader, but he knows what he knows.

Cleopatra's death is more theatrical than in any previous version of the story and it is possible to see it within an iconographic and homiletic tradition that adds another dimension to her character: 'Cleopatra in her death dramatizes, and accepts with a fiercely stoic courage, the medieval commonplace that man's flesh was eaten by worms and serpents in the grave.'[14] For 'those who wish to respond to Chaucer's narrative most fully', this makes the legend of Cleopatra even more remarkable, and it may well be that Chaucer had in mind the final, apparently never written legend of Alceste, another, less gloomy comment on death and decay. In the present state of our knowledge and of the text it is difficult to judge what Chaucer ultimately meant by this impressively original version of Cleopatra's demonstrative end. There is nothing courtly about her love; it is only in her suffering and 'trouthe' that the poet seems to be interested, and he holds her up as an example to men who habitually swear that they will die if their love is angry but never do so. Cleopatra's death is thus presented as the opposite to merely rhetorical postures, but even here we cannot be absolutely certain of the narrator's sincerity and seriousness:

> But herkeneth, ye that speken of kyndenesse,
> Ye men that falsly sweren many an oth
> That ye wol deye, if that youre love be wroth,
> Here may ye sen of wemen which a trouthe! (F, 665–8)

Is he really speaking from his heart, or is he just paying lip-service to the God of Love's doctrine? Is Cleopatra's love of such high value that her sacrifice is justified? If she is criticized at all it is only indirectly, by the implied contrast to her 'real' story and by the narrator's fulsome praise. This does not, however, question the ideal of 'trouthe' or invalidate the story's claim that even a pagan woman can demonstrate some of the highest virtues and serve as a model for all lovers.

The 'Legend of Thisbe' retells another well-known classical story, one of the most popular episodes from Ovid's *Metamorphoses* and one that, on the face of it, is much better suited for the poet's purpose in hand. Ovid's version is a model of concise and effective narration, and Chaucer, following him pretty closely, must have realized that here was an author from whom he could learn a great deal; even by simple translation he could perfect his own mastery of the art of brief narrative, and Robert Frank, who gives a helpful account of the two versions, is quite right to insist on the importance and novelty of such compressed storytelling.[15]

Chaucer does not really reinterpret the old plot, but he introduces a number of small yet significant changes that, taken together, alter the tone and the emphasis of the original considerably. At first sight, Chaucer's legend seems to be nothing but a particularly successful and close translation, preserving the proportions and many brilliant details of the Latin text. There are hardly any substantial additions or surprising alterations, only a noticeable difference in vocabulary and style. It is perhaps inevitable that Chaucer's account of the lovers and their environment should suggest an English town rather than an exotic distant past. More important is the general effect of the relaxed and often colloquial tone, which makes it much easier for the reader to enter into the story and to sympathize with these young people. The narrator even adds a little word of explanation when he feels he is relating something his audience might find strange. This creates a link between the poet and his readers and introduces an element of everyday experience and familiar reality which is important for our reaction to the story:

> For in that contre yit, withouten doute,
> Maydenes been ykept, for jelosye,
> Ful streyte, lest they diden som folye. (F, 721–3)

This is emphasized by the addition of some simple popular wisdom, evidently confirmed by the events of the tale – another appeal to our common knowledge of the world:

> As, wry the glede, and hotter is the fyr;
> Forbede a love, and it is ten so wod. (F, 735–6)

This reminds us a little of the style of *Troilus and Criseyde*, except that love is portrayed here in far plainer and less sophisticated terms. There is no courtly ritual of falling in love or of extended wooing, but a straightforward process of mutual desire and uncomplicated purpose:

> Unto this clyft, as it was wont to be,
> Com Piramus, and after com Thysbe,
> And plyghten trouthe fully in here fey
> That ilke same nyght to stele awey,
> And to begile here wardeyns everichon,
> And forth out of the cite for to goon; (F, 776–81)

This directness is indeed new in Chaucer's love-poetry. He has not made the slightest attempt to turn Pyramus and Thisbe into courtly lovers, and this marks an important step towards the unconventional diversity of *The Canterbury Tales*.

Chaucer evidently wants to colour Ovid's tale in such a way that it fits
into his scheme and becomes the legend of a good woman. This is why
early in the story he draws our attention to Thisbe's 'trouthe' as to the
most important motive of her actions. She is almost presented as the
innocent victim of a moral ideal that can only be upheld at the expense of
the lady:

> For alle hire frendes – for to save hire trouthe –
> She hath forsake; allas! and that is routhe
> That evere woman wolde ben so trewe
> To truste man, but she the bet hym knewe!   (F, 798–801)

The tragic ending, too, is in Chaucer's version, a demonstration of
Thisbe's 'trouthe'. Pyramus is not directly blamed for his part in the
catastrophe, but he blames himself (as he does in Ovid) for asking the girl
to meet him in such a dangerous place, and it is clear that Thisbe is the
real heroine. Her death is the climax of the story and it is described by her
as proof of a woman's ability to be as faithful as any lover:

> But God forbede but a woman can
> Ben as trewe in lovynge as a man!
> And for my part, I shal anon it kythe.   (F, 910–12)

By her suicide she is united with Pyramus, even without Ovid's final
apotheosis, and the narrator draws the moral, confirming Thisbe's
exemplary 'trouthe' and women's equality to men in this respect. He does
not omit to mention however, that Pyramus too, unlike most of the male
lovers in this collection, is 'trewe and kynde' and that this is pleasing to
'us men'. This is a pointed reminder of the fact that *The Legend of Good
Women* is the work of a man who is forced to admit, more or less
grudgingly, that women are generally superior to men when it comes to
'trouthe' in love. We are not allowed to forget that these stories, quite
apart from their intrinsic value, are also a personal statement and must be
read in the context of this particular narrative situation:

> And thus are Tisbe and Piramus ygo.
> Of trewe men I fynde but fewe mo
> In alle my bokes, save this Piramus,
> And therfore have I spoken of hym thus.
> For it is deynte to us men to fynde
> A man that can in love been trewe and kynde.
> Here may ye se, what lovere so he be,
> A woman dar and can as wel as he.   (F, 916–23)

There is no marked contradiction between this conclusion and the
original story; it is not a case of an established reading being turned

upside down, as in the legend of Cleopatra, but we are, surely, allowed to wonder whether the events of the tale necessarily suggest the narrator's presentation of it as the legend of a martyr of love. Chaucer's friend Gower, at least, interpreted the lovers' tragedy in a very different way,[16] and the personal tone of Chaucer's version may be understood as an invitation to the reader to draw his own conclusions. The narrator's attitude to the story has to be seen in relation to his penance and to the royal command, but it is not the only possible interpretation and not an authoritative statement by Chaucer the poet, but rather a challenge to our own imagination and judgement. In this respect, the legend of Thisbe is not so very different from that of Cleopatra. The narrator's seemingly naive and literal obedience to the wishes of Alceste would strike us as provokingly simple-minded were it not for some clear signs of the author's own sceptical detachment. He never, by subversive irony or implied criticism, flatly contradicts the moral of his stories as stated by the narrator, but injects into his account enough teasingly controversial detail to make a perfectly simple reading unsatisfactory. As always in Chaucer, a good deal is left to the audience; this is not just an easy way out for the critic reluctant to commit himself, but an essential aspect of his art, an art that, above all, goes much deeper than 'simpleminded moral clarity'.[17]

This applies, in varying degrees, to all the other legends. Some of them give surprising versions of well-known stories, like the legend of Dido or of Medea, others seem more like faithful translations or deal with less familiar material. In some cases, the story did not have to be radically altered to make it fit into the general scheme of the collection, but in all of them we are reminded, explicitly or by implication, of the narrator who is doing his best to pile instance upon instance of betrayed women and treacherous men. There are several places where he lays it on so thick that even the God of Love might have found it a little too much of a good thing. A striking example is the double legend of Hypsipyle and Medea. It begins with a vigorous denunciation of Jason, who seduced and forsook not just one woman but two:

> Thow rote of false lovers, Duc Jasoun,
> Thow sly devourere and confusioun
> Of gentil wemen, tendre creatures,
> Thow madest thy recleymyng and thy lures
> To ladyes of thy statly aparaunce,
> And of thy wordes, farced with plesaunce,
> And of thy feyned trouthe and thy manere,
> With thyn obeÿsaunce and humble cheere,
> And with thy contrefeted peyne and wo.
> There othere falsen oon, thow falsest two! (F, 1368–77)

Jason sounds like a parody of the courtly lover in *The Book of the Duchess* or a sinister version of Troilus. The main purpose of the legend seems to be the unmasking of such a villain:

> O, often swore thow that thow woldest dye
> For love, whan thow ne feltest maladye
> Save foul delyt, which that thow callest love!
> Yif that I live, thy name shal be shove
> In English that thy sekte shal be knowe!
> Have at thee, Jason! now thyn horn is blowe!   (F, 1378–83)

Obviously, Jason's great sins are false swearing and 'foul delyt', but the poet omits to mention the heroic feats of his famous expedition and deliberately reduces a most colourful, complicated and justly celebrated story to a simple tale of betrayed love. In the sources, both Hypsipyle and Medea are far more spirited and interesting women. Medea, in particular, is the worst possible candidate for the pathetic legend of a guiltless martyr, and her awesome career does not by any stretch of the imagination confirm Cupid's or Alceste's views on the innocence of women. Chaucer offers a pointedly tendentious reading that flies in the face of most previous accounts and again makes us suspect that the poet and his narrator are greatly at variance here. One need not be a twentieth-century feminist to react to the story as one modern critic does: 'the juxtaposition of two women so easily taken in by one man makes it seem, again, common and inevitable that men betray and women beg for more'.[18] The long introduction to Hypsipyle's story, rather irrelevant to the ostensible purpose of the legend, suggests that the narrator is aware of the true nature of Jason's exploits and checks himself just in time before giving a too favourable picture. When he comes to the actual betrayal he only relates the barest facts and even hints that he does not want to give any encouragement to false lovers among his audience (F, 1554–8). The excessive brevity turns Hypsipyle into a completely insignificant figure; it is difficult to feel any sympathy for a character who is so easily taken in by a most transparent plot. Most of the wooing is done by proxy, and there is no attempt to make her 'fall' credible. All the narrator does, after the briefest of summaries, is to add an outline of Hypsipyle's letter from Ovid's *Heroides*, but there is no real attempt to make the most of the pathos of the situation or to rouse the reader's compassion.

Medea's story is given equally short shrift. Jason, 'That is of love devourer and dragoun' (F, 1581), is turned into a kind of Don Juan whose chief interest is the seducing of women, and Medea falls for him within ten lines. Her colourful career as a sorceress is reduced to 'the sleyghte of hire enchauntement' (F, 1650), and the gruesome murder of Jason's wife and children (Medea's own children) is omitted altogether.

'It is difficult not to think Chaucer had his tongue in his cheek as he scratched away at Medea's story', says Robert Frank, who comes to the conclusion that Chaucer has failed to create a convincing unity of tone.[19] Whether the legend is a 'failure' or not must be decided by every reader for himself, but it is important to recognize that deliberate violence has been done to a well-known story to bring it in line with the professed design of the whole collection. Whatever the poet's intention may have been, there is rather too much summary here and not enough dramatic narration to make the characters come alive, and the reader cannot be deeply involved in a story of which he is only given a bare outline.

The 'Legend of Dido' is a far more successful abridgement, although it is again a very one-sided version of a classical story. In this case, Chaucer was not the first to condemn Vergil's hero Aeneas and to make us see the whole episode from Dido's point of view. It had already been done, though in a very different way, in Ovid's *Heroides*, one of Chaucer's chief sources. Chaucer claims to follow Vergil's account as closely as space will permit him, but he is obviously more interested in the pathos of Dido's situation than in Aeneas' great mission as founder of Rome. He does not, however, reduce the story to a simple instance of betrayed love, but brings out the specific character and atmosphere of the whole situation; and there is, at least in the first part, a strong sense that this love is the result of exceptional circumstances. Dido's pity for Aeneas' unprecedented suffering is a sign of her noble character and is carefully prepared by the way the hero is presented from her point of view (F, 1061–81). Of all the heroines of *The Legend of Good Women*, she is presented with most sympathy, without any admixture of patronizing sentimentality:

> Anon hire herte hath pite of his wo,
> And with that pite love com in also;
> And thus, for pite and for gentillesse,
> Refreshed moste he been of his distresse.   (F, 1078–81)

Aeneas, too, is described in such a way that we can enter into his state of mind. After what he has gone through, the reception is so overwhelming that it is no wonder he becomes more than susceptible to his hostess's charm:

> He nevere beter at ese was in his lyve.
> Ful was the feste of deyntees and rychesse,
> Of instruments, of song, and of gladnesse,
> Of many an amorous lokyng and devys.
> This Eneas is come to paradys
> Out of the swolow of helle, and thus in joye
> Remembreth hym of his estat in Troye.   (F, 1099–1105)[20]

It is Dido, though, who falls in love first and is tormented by this new passion; thus she seems to be doubly a victim – to a power nobody can resist and to a 'fals lovere' (F, 1236). There is no suggestion that Aeneas is really in love; he only takes what he can get. It is a complete reversal of the conventional wooing (F, 1192), and Aeneas only goes through the motions of protesting his love and promising eternal faith. The narrator interrupts the story to make his own position clear:

> O sely wemen, ful of innocence,
> Ful of pite, of trouthe, and conscience,
> What maketh yow to men to truste so?
> Have ye swych routhe upon hyre feyned wo,
> And han swich olde ensaumples yow beforn?
> Se ye nat alle how they ben forsworn?
> Where sen ye oon, that he ne hath laft his leef,
> Or ben unkynde, or don hire some myscheef,
> Or piled hire, or bosted of his dede?
> Ye may as wel it sen, as ye may rede.   (F, 1254–63)

This is borne out by the following events, but only because the poet turns Aeneas into a cad who becomes tired of his conquest and has never really been in earnest. The dream in which he receives the divine command to pursue his mission and follow his destiny is an invention concocted on the spot to excuse himself, and there is no sense of a real conflict. Aeneas is simply a traitor who leaves his lady, to seek new adventures and to marry someone else. It is a complete distortion of Vergil's account, but it is done with so much genuine pathos and conviction that it is impossible to decide whether the narrator is completely in earnest or whether he knows that he has done injustice to the hero in the interest of his general theme.[21] There is no doubt that Dido is domesticated and has lost some of her heroic stature. She begs Aeneas to make an honest woman of her by at least marrying her before killing her, and her suicide seems to be motivated by shame as much as by love. She even claims that she is with child, another pathetic detail Chaucer added to the story. It could, of course, like some other little hints, be interpreted in a less favourable way. Chaucer's female martyrs often seem to care for their status and their good name more than for more hidden values. Lucrece very primly covers her feet before expiring, and although this detail is taken over from Ovid it seems a little more obtrusive and deliberate here:

> And as she fel adoun, she kaste hir lok,
> And of hir clothes yet she hede tok.
> For in hir fallynge yet she had a care,
> Lest that hir fet or suche thyng lay bare;
> So wel she loved clennesse and eke trouthe.   (F, 1856–60)

Ariadne looks forward to becoming a duchess or even a queen when she is taken in by Theseus (F, 2123–35). Her legend is another instance of Chaucer reducing a potentially complex story to a simple tale of betrayal. Theseus is false from beginning to end, and the narrator seems to fling the story in his face in order to expose him, rather than to extol the truth and steadfastness of the lady:

> Juge infernal, Mynos, of Crete kyng,
> Now cometh thy lot, now comestow on the ryng.
> Nat for thy sake oonly write I this storye,
> But for to clepe ageyn unto memorye
> Of Theseus the grete untrouthe of love;
> For which the goddes of the heven above
> Ben wrothe, and wreche han take for thy synne.
> Be red for shame! now I thy lyf begynne. (F, 1886–93)

The legend ends with a hearty curse: 'the devel quyte hym his while!' (F, 2227). The 'Legend of Phyllis' shows that his son is no better: he is another ungrateful cad, come ashore in great distress and received hospitably by a trusting woman whom he leaves ignominiously to her lone fate in the end. The narrator cannot keep back his indignation for long: he confesses that it wearies him to write about faithless lovers. The tone of this legend is not, it seems to me, consciously mocking or ironic, but rather naively trite. If 'Chaucer is concerned to keep her [Phyllis] from our sympathies',[22] he does it indirectly, by adopting a deliberately simple manner and a righteous anger not really justified by any real pathos. Phyllis is only one of a whole series of unsuspecting women, and her fate is too common to be really tragic. The narrator's efforts to arouse our pity sound a little perfunctory; he is not really moved by Phyllis' plight, because her folly seems almost as glaring as the man's falsehood. There is no sustained attempt to turn her into a tragic figure, although we are very far from fabliau territory.[23]

At the end the narrator mockingly presents himself as the only trustworthy lover: 'trusteth, as in love, no man but me' (F, 2561). It is clear that he cannot take the tale or the telling of it entirely seriously, but by this very attitude he raises a number of interesting poetological questions. The uncertainty of tone is, at any rate, no sign of incompetence, but rather a sophisticated reflection on the relation between the poet and his subject-matter, a provocation or at least an invitation to think about traditional stories and outworn clichés. Mere repetition of the same story-patterns is not enough; by variations in tone, rhetorical artifice and point of view the reader is alerted to the arbitrary nature of literary tradition and fame.

Similarly abrupt changes in tone and seriousness can be found in several legends. At the end of the 'Legend of Philomela' the narrator tells us that all men are wicked, even if they have not the courage to be as blatantly abhorrent as Tereus:

> Ye may be war of men, if that yow liste.
> For al be it that he wol nat, for shame,
> Don as Tereus, to lese his name,
> Ne serve yow as a morderour or a knave,
> Ful lytel while shal ye trewe hym have –
> That wol I seyn, al were he now my brother –
> But it so be that he may have non other. (F, 2387–93)

These last lines mark a sudden decline from elevated pathos to a rather trite piece of everyday experience and to a world of petty rather than heroic wickedness. If we assume that Chaucer meant his readers to recognize the deliberate pruning of the Ovidian story, this would again suggest that we are intended to see through the touching naivety or exasperation of the narrator who turns every women whose story he comes across into a colourless martyr, at the cost even of half her vitality and spirit.

The last legend, and indeed the whole collection, ends without a proper conclusion. The transmission of texts is a precarious process, and there are many possible reasons why the versions that have come down to us should end at this particular point,[24] yet it seems rather appropriate that a story that is so particularly empty of genuine pathos and leaves so little room for any interesting development should be left without an elaborate ending. It is, of course, tempting to assume that Chaucer stopped his narrator deliberately to make clear that there was really no more to say. He can hardly have been unaware of the fact that in its present form the 'Legend of Hypermnestra' will not move many readers to genuine compassion and sympathy; the poor heroine is so weak and her dilemma so artificial that it would be difficult to make a real tragedy out of it. By reducing the situation to its bare outlines and toning down the whole narrative, Chaucer leaves the reader with fragments of a potential legend rather than with the complete story, so that he might well suspect that the narrator has lost interest. What conclusion should we expect?

Several generations of scholars after W. W. Skeat were convinced that Chaucer grew bored with the monotony of his legends and plodded on for nine tales with growing dissatisfaction until he gave up altogether. This is to take a rather simple and anachronistic view of the medieval poet and to introduce modern prejudices that do not seem to have occurred to any reader between the fifteenth and the nineteenth century. We are, to be sure, faced with the fact that Chaucer did not finish his collection of stories as he originally planned it, unless all the manuscripts of the completed work have been lost, which is at least a possibility: 'The fact that the end has not survived is no proof that it was never written.'[25]

John Lydgate's famous statement about Chaucer's collection seems to suggest, however, that he, only a generation or so after Chaucer, thought of the collection as unfinished:

> This poete wrot, at request off the queen,
> A legende off parfit hoolynesse,
> Off Goode Women to fynde out nynteen
> That dede excelle in bounte and fairnesse;
> But for his labour and (his) bisynesse
> Was inportable his wittis to encoumbre,
> In al this world to fynde so gret a noumbre.
>
> (Prologue to *The Fall of Princes*, 330–6)

The reason given by Lydgate is clearly facetious and may well be an indication that he did not quite know what to make of the collection, but there is no insinuation whatever to the effect that Chaucer got tired of his subject. It is clear from the text, I think, that Chaucer was aware of the narrow scope of his theme, and the fact that he emphasizes rather than modifies this narrowness proves that he wants to make the reader conscious of it. There is no noticeable attempt to diversify these stories on a uniform subject; on the contrary, the theme of female martyrdom and male treachery is repeated and insisted on to such an extent that the sameness must be part of the whole plan.[26] One single look at *The Canterbury Tales* should be enough to make clear that Chaucer was very much alive to the possibility of various, even mutually contradictory, tales and narrative stances, and it is hardly possible that the poet who invented the Canterbury pilgrims should have failed to notice the glaring limitations of the *Legend* in this respect. This does not mean, however, that he got bored or did not think the whole project worth his while. He must have known many similar collections of rather uniform tales – such as saints' legends, animal fables, exempla, or even Ovid's *Heroides* themselves. If the text reveals signs of a certain exasperation, or at least a mild suggestion that all these legends of suffering women might be too much of a good thing, this is not Chaucer the poet getting bored, but rather Chaucer's narrator finding himself unable to fulfill his imposed task. Lydgate's not very original joke should not be taken too seriously, but at least the first reader whose reaction has come down to us comments on the fragmentary character of the collection and invites the question whether anything was wrong with the subject or the treatment of it. In other words, Chaucer, as he does so often, passes the problem of the poet on to the reader and leaves him to reflect on the difficulties of literary composition.

There is no doubt that Chaucer was deeply impressed and influenced by Ovid's narrative brilliance, and the story-material provided by the *Metamorphoses*, the *Heroides* and the *Fasti*, among others, had a strong appeal for him. He may well have felt that the challenge to retell these classical stories adequately in English was too much for him, and his narrator, evidently not quite capable of coping with the royal command, may be seen as an expression of his diffidence and modesty.[27] Even if he has not quite done justice to the time-honoured classical myths, there is no impression of pretentious failure, because the narrative method makes us share in the poet's struggle with his subject and appreciate his genuine achievement. The ancient stories are retold in such a personal and unexpected way that they come to life by the very process of presentation and interpretation.

8

Pilgrims and narrators:
The Canterbury Tales

FOR MANY GENERATIONS, *TROILUS AND CRISEYDE* WAS THE MOST highly esteemed and most frequently quoted of Chaucer's works; in our century, however, the interest of scholars and general readers has turned more and more to the fragmentary collection of *The Canterbury Tales*, which has generally come to be regarded as the most original and significant achievement of Chaucer's narrative art. *Troilus and Criseyde* has, on the whole, remained a work appreciated chiefly by connoisseurs and enthusiasts, whereas the *Canterbury Tales*, if only selections from them, enjoy a popularity not at all confined to an academic public. Nevill Coghill's verse translation, first published in 1952, has sold well over a million copies, which strongly suggests that the poem still has a very vital appeal. The *Canterbury Tales* seem to be especially in tune with a modern preference for formal variety, unorthodox experiment, 'realism' and ironic distancing; and even though these qualities were, in all probability, not the chief reason why these tales were written, or why they were read, at least for several centuries, they do make it easier for us to approach this many-shaped poem, and they seem to appeal immediately even to those readers who are not normally prepared to appreciate medieval conventions.

That *The Canterbury Tales* is, in fact, hardly less informed by such conventions than Chaucer's early poems will soon become clear to the reader in search of a more precise understanding of Chaucer's alleged realism and the stylistic variety of the text. The whole work is a clear demonstration of the futility of trying to play off originality and tradition, realism and rhetoric against each other. Nearly everything appears, at a first glance, to be new, even modern, and yet the work is firmly rooted in medieval conventions, from which it draws its life and without which there would be no originality.

THE FRAME

The whole design of *The Canterbury Tales* is puzzling in more than one way, not only so far as the work's genesis or the formal arrangement of the tales is concerned, but also with regard to the ultimate artistic intention behind the whole collection. It is not that the problems of interpretation are so very different from those we encountered in the case of Chaucer's earlier poems, but that they are more complex and evasive.

Judging by its transmission, *The Canterbury Tales* seems to have been among the most popular works of medieval literature. More than eighty manuscripts, though not all of them complete, have survived, and this is more than we have of any other Middle English text, except for the homiletic treatise *The Prick of Conscience*.[1] The astonishing number of copies, some of them quite lavish and elaborate, clearly demonstrates that the fragmentary character of the work did not in any way detract from its wide appeal; it also suggests that the completion of the poem was not necessarily prevented by external circumstances, such as the author's death. There is much to be said for the view that Chaucer relinquished his work on the collection some time before he died and that, moreover, he did not put those parts he had actually finished into anything like a final shape, because the surviving versions differ considerably in the way the individual tales are ordered and linked together – without, however, clearly recognizable stages of revision, as in the case of Langland's *Piers Plowman* or the Prologue to *The Legend of Good Women*. This makes it impossible to arrive at a final verdict as to the form the finished work would have taken, the way Chaucer would have 'closed' the frame, the relationship of the individual tales to each other and to the completed frame. Any interpretation, therefore, has to start from the simple fact that all we have to go by are a number of more or less unrelated constituent elements whose eventual positions and functions within the completed structure had not been definitely decided on, any more than the eventual shape of the structure itself had been. It is only with this proviso at the back of our minds that we can discuss the problem of the unity of this collection of tales.

What we can know for certain is that Chaucer adapted the popular tradition of the 'frame-story' in a most original way and that he seems to have found here a particularly suitable literary device for his personal narrative style and its experimental possibilities. A brief glance at some other varieties of the 'frame-story' may help us to see the characteristic features of Chaucer's collection more clearly.[2]

Framed collections of stories were very much in vogue during the Middle Ages, and there are several possible reasons for this. One of them must have been the flexibility and inconclusiveness of the device, which allowed for a larger poetical structure made up from smaller narrative units and must, incidentally, have been of considerable advantage for oral delivery. Another reason was certainly the immense popularity of exemplary tales, whose didactic point could be driven home all the more impressively if they were presented in connection with a fictitious audience and its model response. It is quite evident that the frame-story is a particularly apt device for dramatizing the narrative situation as such, making the act of storytelling part of the fiction itself, thus confronting the audience with the complexity of different levels of illusion to invite their intellectual and imaginative participation.

As to the form of the frame, the role of the narrator, and the relationship between the individual narratives, frame-stories can differ considerably. A frequently used type is represented by the collection of *The Arabian Nights*; it consists of a framing dramatic plot into which the stories are inserted to delay the final solution and to increase the suspense. This type also includes the collection of *The Seven Sages of Rome* – very popular during the Middle Ages in different versions and often even with different tales – in which an execution is first adjourned and eventually prevented by the telling of a series of stories.[3] The dramatic tension here acts on two levels simultaneously; frame and tales are very closely interrelated, though not necessarily in terms of subject-matter, because the stories could very easily be regrouped or even replaced by others – as was actually done in several versions without affecting their connection with the framing story.

This connection is effected quite differently in some novella collections of the fourteenth century, of which the best known is Boccaccio's *Decameron*. The scholarly debate about whether or not Chaucer knew this work at all has calmed down in recent years without having produced any conclusive evidence for the assumption that he was directly influenced by it; it would be somewhat surprising, on the other hand, if Chaucer, who owed so much to Boccaccio, should not have known this one of all his works.[4] It did not, however, appear in England before the fifteenth century. In Boccaccio, the frame is more formalized and less dramatic than in *The Seven Sages*: a group of ten young people leave the plague-stricken city of Florence for some neighbouring country residence and pass their time telling each other stories. On each of ten days each member of the party tells a story, which is usually followed by a brief discussion. Not only the narrators but also their stories are fairly similar to each other; there is no sharp class distinction or any very noticeable stylistic variation. On the other hand, certain themes are usually illustrated from different points of view by several tales, so that a fascinating inner coherence is created in spite of the fact that the individual narrators remain in the background and the frame provides little more than a decorative peg on which to hang the stories.

In another novella cycle which Chaucer probably knew, Giovanni Sercambi's *Novelle* (1374), a pilgrimage provides the occasion for storytelling, as it does in *The Canterbury Tales*. Representatives from different walks of life come together, and a leader is chosen to preside over the entertainment. Some of the stories are aimed at certain fellow-travellers, as in Chaucer's collection, but the most obvious difference between the two works lies in the fact that the stories are all presented by one narrator, who is the author himself.

In spite of many conspicuous similarities with other frame-stories, some of the most characteristic features of *The Canterbury Tales* cannot be found elsewhere in this form – not, at any rate, before Chaucer. The most important, and one that most affects the plan of the whole collection, is the assignment of each story to a clearly identifiable individual narrator, the stylistic differentiation of the tales according to the social and moral standing of the narrator and, in addition, the direct confrontation between some of these narrators, as reflected in their contributions. On the other hand, Chaucer does without a self-contained framing story or a plot creating narrative suspense in its own right; nor does he explicitly make the tales illustrate recurring themes. The fact that time and again scholars have claimed to have discovered such unifying themes while, at the same time, disagreeing radically about their precise nature seems to be evidence enough to prove that all-embracing 'themes' are not really part of the explicit literary programme of the collection, but are, at the most, suggested incidentally, by implication, subtle correspondences or the obsessions of individual narrators. What alone seems to cast doubt on any too neat concept of unity is the fact that some of the tales had, in all probability, been completed before the frame was conceived or, at least, independently of it, and were only later assigned by the poet to particular narrators for whom they seemed appropriate. Besides, an attentive reader will easily recognize that Chaucer made several rearrangements and changes which suggest that the relationship between story and frame was not definitely fixed in each case from the outset, but remained fairly flexible for a longer period of time. Thus, for instance, the tale of the Shipman, as its first lines make clear, was originally intended for a woman, presumably the Wife of Bath; the Man of Law announces a tale in prose, but goes on to present a poem in stanzas, and there are a number of similar inconsistencies to be found in the text.[5] For Chaucer, the frame obviously provided a most welcome opportunity to string together a number of widely differing narratives and, at the same time, to present stories he had already written within a context that would bring out their particular qualities more sharply. This is, however, only the most peripheral aspect of the problem of unity, which is, most of all, a problem concerning the frame and its function.[6] The transmission of *The Canterbury Tales* offers such a bewildering picture that it is impossible to reconstruct a consistent plan from the manuscripts alone. The 'General Prologue', as starting-point and introduction, must have been fixed at an early stage, and the stories, too, remained on the whole more or less constant, but the order of the tales and the links between them undoubtedly kept creating new problems and difficulties for the author.

Looking at the manuscripts, the first thing we can say with any confidence is that, besides the 'General Prologue', there existed single groups of tales expressly linked to each other, whereas the groups themselves represented isolated and unconnected units; as a result even the most widely used modern editions differ as to the order in which these groups follow each other. In the last resort, this is not so much a matter of textual criticism as it involves a decision about the character and the importance of the frame in general.

One simple clue is provided by the indications of time and locality within the frame, especially in the links between the tales. Since they are all told during the pilgrimage to the shrine of St Thomas of Canterbury, an obvious thing to do seems to be to reconstruct the route by the various allusions to known places on the way and group the stories accordingly. The details we can extract from the text are, however, so vague and inconsistent that we are not even able to gather from them whether the tales left by Chaucer were all to be told on the way to Canterbury or whether they were meant to include the return journey as well.[7] If one groups them according to geographical clues only, the resulting order differs from that of the best manuscripts in some important particulars. It is, however, very likely that these manuscripts are only the work of later redactors and that the poet himself never came to a final decision about the plan of the work before he parted with it.

More important is the question, arising from this discussion, as to the importance we should attach to the 'realistic' background suggested by the frame. Was it really Chaucer's intention to give a verifiable, geographically accurate record of a pilgrimage from Southwark to Canterbury? Did he reckon with readers who would notice discrepancies in his account of the route and, what is more, be worried by them? Such questions would only, if at all, be relevant for the hypothetical work Chaucer at one time might have had in mind; but in *The Canterbury Tales* as he left it the fictitious pilgrimage is little more than a vaguely sketched setting, recalled from time to time to provide a solid background for the individual tales, without adding up to a self-contained or even coherent plot. The mention of familiar places on the way creates, at certain intervals, an illusion of reality, a definite link with a specific time and locality, but it is not intended to suggest a factual basis for a consistent framing plot, and we are on the whole not encouraged to pay too much attention to the actual journey of the storytellers. In view of the fragmentary character of the collection, any detailed reconstruction of such a framing story is bound to be no more than an attractive hypothesis. We shall probably never know whether Chaucer ever really intended to satisfy all the expectations he aroused with his 'General Prologue'. There are good reasons to suspect that, during the process of composition, he himself was considering some major changes of his original plan. These would affect, first of all, the number of stories promised.

It is stipulated in the 'General Prologue' that each pilgrim should contribute four tales, two on the way to Canterbury and two on the way home. In the prologue to the 'Parson's Tale', however, it is assumed that every pilgrim has already met the requirements of the agreement by having told just one story. The whole entertainment is now to be rounded off by the story of the Parson who promises to 'knytte up al this feeste, and make an ende' (x.47). Most readers have taken this to mean that Chaucer found his original plan too ambitious and demanding and modified it accordingly to reduce the number of tales. The unexpected intrusion of the Canon and his Yeoman shows that the frame still left room for surprising developments.[8] The fact, moreover, that neither the party's arrival at Canterbury nor the verdict as to the best tale is ever described is, as long as we keep to the surviving texts, another indication that the original plan has undergone some modification; because whatever Chaucer's conception of the whole work might have been when he started, the text as we have it confines the function of the frame almost entirely to the announcement or some motivation of the individual tales. There is no plot worth mentioning to divert the reader's attention from these tales, and there is no additional suspense outside the tales to detract from our interest in them. Chaucer's intention to create a series of narrative situations as diversified as possible, in order to justify and make us aware of the stylistic differentiation of the tales all the more clearly, seems to me so obvious that I do not think many readers will feel this fading-out of the frame-story as a serious loss. From the outset, no real interest in the fate of the pilgrims as characters within a story has been aroused: we care for them only in their capacity as narrators. This accounts for the frame's easy hospitality to all kinds of tales and narrative situations and makes it, at the same time, an essential part of the poetical experiment, with the stylistic diversity of the tales as its very centre.

What limited amount of action and drama the frame-story, nevertheless, does contain in no way contradicts this view, but actually confirms it, because all the lively activity described in the 'General Prologue', as well as in the links – in particular, too, the confrontations and quarrels between individual pilgrims – keep directing our attention firmly towards the stories themselves, their contrasts in subject-matter, form and style and the possible reactions provoked by them. In this respect, it is rather misleading when critics keep concentrating on the vitality of the frame, at the expense of the tales, as if their main function were to create the lively 'roadside drama', which was often seen as the real core of the whole work.[9] The somewhat naive question, frequently discussed by earlier critics, whether the frame was created for the sake of the tales or the tales for the sake of the frame seems, in view of their actual proportions alone, to be quite absurd: the frame makes up less than one-fifth of the whole text and virtually never becomes a really independent narrative in its own right.[10] There is no action hastening towards some definitely expected conclusion; the crowning dinner promised to the best storyteller is more and more lost sight of after the 'General Prologue'. The dramatic action, like the place-names, is there only for local effects within the whole collection. It creates a colourful and memorable assembly of storytellers whose individual destinies are of interest only insofar as they throw into relief their intellectual and moral dispositions as well as their place within the social hierarchy. The fact that Chaucer-critics have, time and again, treated the frame as a self-contained work of art or even as the central focus of the whole story-cycle, testifies to its vivid originality, but such misplaced emphasis can easily lead to an inadequate idea of the work as a whole.

To be sure, the fascination exercised by this frame is as old as the work itself. Two particularly interesting continuations of *The Canterbury Tales* suggest that some of Chaucer's contemporaries at least responded to the work not very differently from Kittredge and Lowes. John Lydgate, a consciously imitative admirer of Chaucer and his junior by only a few years, introduces his extensive narrative poem *The Siege of Thebes* by the fiction that he himself joined the pilgrims on their way back from Canterbury and proceeds to put his own work into the mouth of the Knight.

Even more illuminating is an apocryphal continuation in alliterative verse, written, presumably, at the beginning of the fifteenth century, in a dialect very different from Chaucer's own language. Here, the arrival of the pilgrims at Canterbury, their visit to the cathedral, and their burlesque adventures at the inn where they have put up for the night are described with much gusto.[11] After their homage to the shrine, the Miller and the Pardoner speculate about the meaning of the stained-glass windows and steal from a stall a handful of brooches of which the Summoner, who has caught them red-handed, demands his share as hush-money.

This farcical continuation, written in a completely un-Chaucerian idiom, suggests that the characters of the frame impressed themselves even on some of the earliest readers as individual personalities to whom they felt tempted to ascribe typical adventures; this, not surprisingly, applies most of all to the more comically and satirically portrayed representatives of the lower estates. It is just this kind of imaginative embroidery, however, that should make us aware of what Chaucer himself did *not* do: there is nothing to suggest that he himself ever intended this kind of dramatization or that he would ever have made the frame an independent part of the whole work, which would have distracted the reader's attention from the tales themselves. The fact that in each case the continuators used their own expansion of the frame to introduce only a single story also suggests that they proceeded from an entirely different conception of the work and did not care simply to adopt Chaucer's plan. On the other hand, Lydgate, in his introduction to *The Siege of Thebes*, gives an account of *The Canterbury Tales* that, as the interpretation of a near-contemporary, is particularly instructive and illumines a crucial aspect of Chaucer's collection:

> The tyme in soth whan Canterbury talys
> Complet and told at many sondry stage
> Of estatis in the pilgrimage,
> Euerich man lik to his degrè,
> Some of desport some of moralitè,
> Some of knyghthode loue and gentillesse,
> And some also of parfit holynesse,
> And some also in soth of Ribaudye
> To make laughter in the companye,
> (Ech admitted for non wold other greve)
> Lich as the Cook the millere and the Reve
> Aquytte hem-silf ...[12]

What Lydgate here picks out as a characteristic element of the *Tales* points in a direction any interpretation should take as a starting-point. The diversity of the tellers and of their tales is the most striking common feature of this collection, and to it all the action within the frame is strictly subordinated. The individual links and, in particular, their variants in the manuscripts, confirm such an interpretation: what they all have in common is not so much the illusion of a real pilgrimage as the attempt to establish connections between particular tales, to underline contrasts between them, and, by describing personal animosities and clashes among the narrators, to create a wide spectrum of expectations and narrative stances. Chaucer himself and, perhaps even more, some of his subsequent editors, were continually experimenting with different

links between the individual tales and with personal reactions to them, so
that any modern editor has to make his own decisions and to ignore
certain links, because not all of the fragments of the frame that have come
down to us are compatible with one another.

A particularly illuminating example is the so-called 'epilogue' to the
tale of the Man of Law, printed in some editions as the 'Shipman's
Prologue'. It nicely illustrates how textual problems often raise, at the
same time, fundamental questions of interpretation:

> Owre Hoost upon his stiropes stood anon,
> And seyde, 'Goode men, herkeneth everych on!
> This was a thrifty tale for the nones!
> Sir Parisshe Prest,' quod he, 'for Goddes bones,
> Telle us a tale, as was thi forward yore.
> I se wel that ye lerned men in lore
> Can moche good, by Goddes dignitee!'
>   The Parson hem answerde, '*Benedicite!*
> What eyleth the man, so synfully to swere?'
> Oure Host answerde, 'O Jankin, be ye there?
> I smelle a Lollere in the wynd,' quod he.
> 'Now! goode men,' quod oure Hoste, 'herkeneth me;
> Abydeth, for Goddes digne passioun,
> For we schal han a predicacioun;
> This Lollere heer wil prechen us somwhat.'
>   'Nay, by my fader soule, that schal he nat!'
> Seyde the Shipman; 'heer schal he nat preche;
> He schal no gospel glosen here ne teche.
> We leven alle in the grete God,' quod he;
> 'He wolde sowen som difficulte,
> Or springen cokkel in our clene corn.
> And therfore, Hoost, I warne thee biforn,
> My joly body schal a tale telle,
> And I schal clynken you so mery a belle,
> That I schal waken al this compaignie.
> But it schal not ben of philosophie,
> Ne phislyas, ne termes queinte of lawe.
> Ther is but litel Latyn in my mawe!'   (II.1163–90)[13]

This whole section is not found in those manuscripts which, according to
the majority of textual critics, represent the most authentic order of the
tales, and it seems likely enough that Chaucer, having found it incompatible with his revised sequence of stories, dropped it and replaced it by
different links. For all that, it presents a particularly lively piece of
'frame-story' and – so it seems at first glance – of realistic character-
drawing. But this is exactly what the transmission of the passage makes
rather doubtful, because there is disagreement among the witnesses as to

who actually is the speaker who rejects so emphatically the announcement of a pious tale and thrusts himself forward as an entertainer instead. Most manuscripts put the speech into the mouth of the young Squire, with whose aristocratic character, however, it will not comfortably agree; other manuscripts name the Summoner, without, however, having his tale follow, and one single copy, not very reliable in other respects, has the Shipman speak the lines. In view of his character and his tale this seems to be the most suitable assignment, and this is why it is accepted by most editors.

This uncertainty suggests that the speech was not necessarily written for one particular character – that there was at least room for change – and that the importance of individualizing characterization in general should therefore not be overestimated. More relevant than any specific assignment were, obviously, the function of the whole scene as a lively transition from one tale to the next and the introduction of a dramatic contrast between conflicting attitudes toward edifying narration.

Which tales were actually supposed to be linked here is, however, just as uncertain as the identity of the speakers. Since, according to a widely accepted hypothesis, the Man of Law was originally meant to be the narrator of the 'Tale of Melibee', while the Wife of Bath was to relate what is now the 'Shipman's Tale', the passage could have been written as a link between these two tales. This would in no way conflict with the tone of this little scene, but it still remains a mere hypothesis. For the copyists and editors of *The Canterbury Tales*, the piece was obviously adaptable or even dispensable enough to be either left out altogether or inserted at any other point where it was felt to be suitable and where some sort of transition was needed. The actual contribution of this brief but effective sketch to the whole collection thus has little to do with individualizing character-portrayal. Nevertheless, it is a very lively scene which creates a very vivid impression of spiritual contrasts and a dramatic narrative situation. The Host is spontaneously moved by the moral force of the preceding tale, even though his rough tone seems to suggest that its spirit has not left any lasting impression on his mind, and his pleasure is of a rather superficial kind. The introduction of a topical religious dispute creates a provocative climate of intellectual controversy and a teasing context for the next tale. More important than the actual pilgrimage (of which, however, we are reminded by the Host's stirrups and his allusion to the initial agreement) is the illusion of a colourful gathering of people who are anything but of one mind when it comes to moral or aesthetic principles. At the same time, the intervention of the Shipman (or some other 'low' character) upsets the expected order of the tales: instead of the sermon demanded by the Host, we are treated to a fabliau which obviously appeals to quite a different mentality from the preceding 'thrifty tale'. The theological controversy is trivialized by the simple truism 'We leven alle in the grete God', and thus any kind of sophistication is excluded from the start.

Here, again, the frame is entirely subordinated to the narrative situation; the actual function of the passage is almost completely independent of its specific assignment. This flexibility and indefiniteness of the narrative situation explains the substantial discrepancies within the transmission of the text and confirms the impression that the order of the tales and the consistency of the frame in general are of secondary importance. The somewhat chaotic state of textual criticism on this point has neither done harm to the popularity of the work nor, in the long run, stood in the way of our understanding it. This is not to suggest that the function of the frame of *The Canterbury Tales* is altogether negligible or that the tales should be regarded only for themselves, but it proves that the frame is a different kind of literary fiction from the tales and that, most of all, it is intended to guide and enrich our response to these tales and not to distract from them. It is, I am sure, from this general assumption that we have to approach some other problems which have, time and again, claimed the attention of Chaucer-critics: the realistic aspects of the 'General Prologue', the interrelation between narrators and tales, and the unity of the whole work.

THE 'GENERAL PROLOGUE'

The impression, shared by many readers, that *The Canterbury Tales* is somehow more 'realistic' than Chaucer's earlier works is probably, most of all, based on the 'General Prologue' which introduces the collection and outlines the narrative situation. It ranks, as an almost autonomous work of art, among the most popular and best-loved passages in the whole of English literature. This alone proves that it has always been felt to be much more than a mere excuse for the following tales or an introduction of minor importance.

The very first lines are a wonderful example of the effortless virtuosity with which Chaucer combines learning and the seemingly artless, a genuine faith in tradition and creative originality, rhetorical artifice and colloquial ease. The seasonal opening – a highly conventional form of introduction, to be found, in countless variations, as an almost indispensable item in dream-allegories and love-lyrics as well as in poems relating religious visions – is employed here in a form which is, at the same time, strikingly personal and decoratively stylized. It invites us to expect something like a revelation, be it secular or religious, and the general tone of Chaucer's description at first leaves us prepared for either of the two. Spring is seen as a manifestation of the re-awakening of nature, of a vitality, bursting with the urge to make itself felt, expressed most pregnantly in the line 'So priketh hem nature in hir corages' (I.11). 'Nature' is presented as an active force, inspiring new life, and the whole account is informed by an unusual energy, not at all typical of all such conventional openings. The vivid and concrete detail is integrated in the wider context of the unfolding year, and this in itself is a metaphor for the healing and creative powers of life. It also serves as the reason for the introduction of the subject of pilgrimages, which may seem a little surprising at first: 'Thanne longen folk to goon on pilgrimages' (I.12).[14] Like all created things, man too feels the impulse to go out and participate in the general animation and the renewing of nature. The pilgrimage is presented as an activity related to the re-awakening of the year, which includes religious experience, because even the beneficial intervention ascribed to the Holy Martyr is part of the restorative powers of nature. Canterbury, as the actual destination of the grateful pilgrims, is immediately included in the account, which thus moves quickly from the general to the particular. Within eighteen lines, the poet has established an intellectual and spiritual starting-point, suggesting secular as well as religious concerns, arousing a variety of expectations in the reader, and preparing him for a wealth of possible impressions. This inclusiveness, no doubt, reflects the practice of many medieval pilgrimages, which must have combined penitential exercise and sociable tourism in a way that by no means excluded a religious motivation or personal sincerity.

The beautifully controlled naturalness of the transition should not, however, make us overlook that Chaucer is here clearly drawing on well-established rhetorical devices, not only in the traditional seasonal 'headpiece', but also, for instance, in the astrological method of dating the story – a decorative way of specifying the time of year, linking the signs of the zodiac with appropriate human activities, as, for example, in the splendid manuscript of the 'Bedford Hours', where small vignettes show the signs of the zodiac together with typical seasonal occupations, such as sowing, hunting, reaping and feasting.[15] This conventional induction serves on the one hand to emphasize the representative character of the particular pilgrimage recorded here, in which the poet himself takes part, and on the other to mark it as a piece of literary fiction. The point is not that we are treated to an autobiographical anecdote, but that a universal experience is presented here which is no more dependent on the 'credibility' of outward circumstances than Chaucer's early dream–visions. The poet adopts a pose which is sanctioned by tradition and defined by a particular set of associations, to give authority to his poem and to invest his experience with a significance beyond the merely personal. In this respect, there is certainly a marked affinity between the introduction to *The Canterbury Tales* and many didactic poems, whether presented as straightforward allegories or as dream–visions.[16]

Like the spring, the pilgrimage was a well-established metaphor; it was seen as an image of human life, and the party of pilgrims thus becomes an analogy of society. This vaguely allegorical reference to a more general layer of meaning does not in the least detract from Chaucer's realism and the vividness of his description. What Chaucer achieves here is far more than just a reproduction of a well-tried literary cliché; on the contrary, a conventional device is taken up and reshaped in a way that invests it with the spontaneity of immediate observation, without affecting the traditional associations. It is an essential part of Chaucer's poetic art that the concrete detail keeps pointing towards a more universal meaning, while the representation of general truths draws its authority from the very vividness of the particular detail. True enough, it is, more often than not, the illusion of a reality personally observed rather than a simple reflection of it. The facets of reality selected by the poet are on the whole much more general and conventional than is often realized; but Chaucer's way of presenting them makes us respond as if it were reality, something we can recognize as part of our own experience and observation.

This applies, in particular, to the account of the party of pilgrims which immediately follows the general introduction. Its basic setting seems realistic enough: Chaucer, the pilgrim, joins the party assembled at the Tabard and talks to all of them to make their acquaintance. He is anxious to give the impression that his description of the fellow-travellers is founded on personal observation and knowledge; at the same time, this description is announced with rhetorical artifice, as a skilfully ordered piece of literature governed by its own fixed rules:

> But nathelees, whil I have tyme and space,
> Er that I ferther in this tale pace,
> Me thynketh it acordaunt to resoun
> To telle yow al the condicioun
> Of ech of hem, so as it semed me,
> And whiche they weren, and of what degree,
> And eek in what array that they were inne;
> And at a knyght than wol I first bigynne. (1.35–42)

It is obviously not just the pilgrim, relating a personal experience, who is speaking here, but the poet, who, at the same time, explains the principles of his art to the reader, and who subordinates the details to an ingenious artistic pattern. True enough, the order promised here is not observed in every detail – the characters are not arranged strictly according to their rank and their estate; but such discrepancies very often serve to disclose deeper similarities and contrasts and to draw our attention to the more general characteristics of the individual estate-representatives.[17] It is rather obvious, for instance, that the bracketing together of the Parson and the Ploughman has hardly anything to do with their position within the feudal hierarchy but is meant to illumine their exemplary perfection as models of a modest and active Christianity within the religious and secular professions respectively. The fact that they are brothers, too, is interesting less as a personal biographical detail, than as a visible sign of their moral affinity.

By his deliberate introduction, the poet has already prepared the reader not to expect a group of people lumped together by blind chance, but a kind of paradigmatic abstract of human society, and the gallery of estates presented here is conclusive evidence that this typical aspect is more important for a full understanding of the text than all the colourful detail. The well-known topos of the Dance of Death and, most of all, the medieval estates satire make it clear, too, that an array of several different estates was traditionally taken to represent the whole of mankind in their diversity of social function and degree. Nevertheless, the notorious question of the relationship between typical and individual features cannot be disposed of by a simple explanation. Every reader will probably arrive at a somewhat different answer, and a glance at the variety of literary conventions behind this part of the 'General Prologue' leaves us in no doubt that the reaction of a medieval reader must have been quite different from our own.[18] It is essential, however, to free oneself from the prejudice that the typical and the individual are bound to be mutually exclusive or contradictory. More often than not, these two aspects complement each other in their impact on the reader: responding to a 'character' spontaneously, as if he were a living fellow-man, we often become all the more sharply aware of his typical features. The one aspect brings out the other more clearly, and it is chiefly by his very original selection and arrangement of the details in his description of the individual pilgrims that Chaucer achieves this effect.

The portrait of the Knight, for instance, who is the first pilgrim to be described, combines so many concrete features that more than one critic has tried to prove that Chaucer meant to portray some particular contemporary of his. The battles and campaigns listed can indeed be fitted together to make up a possible biography of an active warrior of the fourteenth century, even though the campaigns named in the course of the description cover a period of more than forty years, so that the career would have been distinctly above the ordinary. It is, of course, possible to conclude from this that such a spectacular career has been suggested to the poet by some living model. But even if this were the case the portrait of the Knight is hardly likely to have had the status of a *roman à clef*, or to have been limited to personal allusions which only a small part of Chaucer's audience would have fully understood. The whole description is obviously intended to give a vivid idea of all that is most admirable in courtly chivalry within a single biography, credible and idealized at the same time. The Knight is 'a verray, parfit gentil knyght' (I.72), a knight *par excellence*, the exemplary embodiment of a particular form of life stylized to the point of flawless perfection and yet within the limits of plausibility. This impression is created not just by the individual details themselves, but, most of all, by their concentration in one single character.[19]

The same applies to the Squire. Whereas in the case of the Knight Chaucer felt that a concise biography, the listing of military activities and exploits, would be the most effective form of characterization, what we have here is more a compilation of typical attributes and accomplishments which add up to an exemplary picture of hopeful youth. The Squire is a sort of knight-to-be, and the description of his youth recalls the freshness of spring celebrated at the beginning of the poem. Hope and fulfilment are juxtaposed in these two portraits: the youthful aspect of courtly knighthood is embodied, most of all, in stylized love-service, its mature achievement in the active service of the church militant. There is nothing in the figure of the Squire that might strictly be called 'individual'; everything is perfectly in keeping with the stereotype of the youthful aspirant to knighthood. And yet we get the impression that he is a living person; it is Chaucer's rhetorical art that convinces us of the solid reality of the type. A comparison with the Knight's portrait, however, makes it equally clear that it is a somewhat lower ideal and that the Squire's 'curteisye' is of a rather different kind.[20]

At the beginning of the portrait gallery, it is the consideration of social rank that serves as an organizing principle. Soon, however, the description is determined by different criteria. The first group is followed by a series of religious figures who are so different from each other that we get a most colourful picture of practices and abuses within the medieval Church.

The first portrait of this group, that of the Prioress, is a particularly complex example of Chaucer's technique of characterization. Faced with the simplicity and, at the same time, the ambiguities of the description, any confident interpretation is in danger of missing the specific form of discourse. The ostentatious innocence of the narrator arouses the reader's suspicion by disappointing his expectations. Is there, perhaps, a first hint of irony in the fact that this portrait follows immediately after that of the Squire? Does not the lady, in spite of her spiritual calling, belong to the courtly world as much as to the clergy? The teasing ambiguity of the characterization results mainly from the way in which the words used by the poet to describe and praise her would be much more appropriate for an aristocratic lady eager to be considered perfect in the social graces of a secular society.[21] The Prioress, obviously, strives after the fine polish of courtly conduct no less than after spiritual perfection. The very words of praise by which, in view of her office, quite unexpected and by no means indispensable qualities are picked out are puzzling and invite the reader to wonder whether the poet has not left out some rather more essential qualities. The Prioress has not been in want of defenders who have tried to prove that her portrait was perfectly in keeping with what a medieval audience would have expected here. On the other hand, the good lady has been charged with hypocrisy, snobbishness and violation of basic monastic rules, which, for instance, forbade the keeping of pets and participation in pilgrimages. Such differences of opinion only underline the simple fact that Chaucer does not express any final judgement but leaves much in suspense. The reader's uncertainty, surely intended by the poet, is produced, above all, by the fact that, like almost all character sketches in the 'General Prologue', this portrait is not presented from a superior moral position, even though the very details selected seem to challenge the reader to form his own judgement. Chaucer the pilgrim describes what he observes without clearly taking sides, but the provocative selection of characteristic details is evidence enough to suggest that Chaucer the poet knows what he is doing. In other words, the ostentatious absence of moral evaluation, especially in places where we would expect it, is bound to be felt as a teasing invitation or even an act of defiance. To portray an exemplary prioress one would surely not devote the better part of her praise to a description of her irreproachable manners. Her spiritual virtues are hardly mentioned at all; only the beauty of her liturgical singing is singled out, but it is a detail that allows for as great a diversity of interpretation as does the inscription on her brooch: *Amor vincit omnia*. Whatever the reader's reaction towards this portrait may be, the tone of the description is that neither of an indignant moralist nor of a malicious satirist, but that of a dispassionate observer unwilling to anticipate our own judgement and, moreover, not even prepared to provide us with a sufficient factual basis for a confident verdict. What emerges instead is a provoking tension between the reader's expectations, the terminology employed and the traditional attributes of ideal womanhood secular and spiritual. To what extent the reader will be disturbed by the Prioress's worldly aspirations depends largely on his own standards and his moral temperament. Chaucer, however, challenges him to re-examine these standards critically, and thus elicits a very personal reaction towards the whole portrait. The 'reality' of the Prioress therefore depends much more on our own reaction towards her than on any remarkably individualized traits of her character.

The tension created by the text between our reaction and the neutral tenor of the individual portraits rises in proportion as the facts reported about the pilgrims clash with our own expectations and with traditional models. This becomes particularly clear in the two portraits of religious figures following that of the Prioress. They are largely made up from commonplaces of traditional satire. Thus, in the case of the Monk, what surprises us is not so much the selection of details and the terminology employed, as the explicit repudiation of the accepted vocational ideal and the enthusiastic praise of a form of life which, under different circumstances, would hardly seem objectionable, but must, in this context, look like grotesque misdemeanour. But Chaucer does not fall back on the simple satirical technique of overstatement or unmistakable irony. By leaving the precise nature of the offences and the Monk's motives unspecified, by avoiding a tone of outraged condemnation, by even putting himself in the Monk's place and admiring his virtuosity in enjoying a life of indulgence, he makes the reader distrust his own judgement. Only the prejudiced moralist, insensitive to Chaucer's tone, will find in the text an unambiguous condemnation of the Monk. Few readers will honestly be able to resist this figure's attraction, created by the exuberant vitality of the description, and this clearly challenges us to re-examine our true standards. Although the satire against ecclesiastical abuses is only too conspicuous, its effect is more like an intellectual provocation than a straightforward attack. The innocent tone of the narrator seems to take for granted that everybody shares the Monk's views on his vocation, that abuse has almost become the rule and that, in consequence, the charge of irresponsible perversion is not really directed at the individual trespasser but at the whole of society, the reader included.

This technique of indirect satire, which takes for granted and, at the same time, calls in question traditional estate ideals, becomes even more pointed in the portrait of the Friar. Not even the most naive reader can fail to recognize that this man is the embodiment of almost every kind of abuse of which the mendicant orders were accused. Here again, however, by contrast to most similar descriptions, the dispassionate neutrality of the account, the approving, indeed admiring tone and the ambiguity of many details are striking. To a large extent the narrator records what he sees without any personal intervention; for part of his account he seems to present the Friar in his own words, or at least from the point of view of an observer who shares his moral standpoint:

> Ful swetely herde he confessioun,
> And plesaunt was his absolucioun:
> He was an esy man to yeve penaunce,
> Ther as he wiste to have a good pitaunce.
> For unto a povre ordre for to yive
> Is signe that a man is wel yshryve;
> For if he yaf, he dorste make avaunt,
> He wiste that a man was repentaunt;
> For many a man so hard is of his herte,
> He may nat wepe, althogh hym soore smerte.
> Therfore in stede of wepynge and preyeres
> Men moote yeve silver to the povre freres. (1.221–32)

Here again the foremost effect is that the reader feels a little confused. Is the Friar not really an admirable figure – would we not, in real life, admire him ourselves? The attraction of vice practised with consummate artistry works against a simple condemnation – all the more so since Chaucer's choice of words very often does not allow for a precise definition of the Friar's offences, nor is always in harmony with our traditional expectations regarding the validity of certain concepts and standards. When the narrator states

> Ther nas no man nowher so vertuous.
> He was the beste beggere in his hous (1.251–2)

the second line obviously modifies the accepted meaning of 'vertuous', and the superlative 'beste', too, is restricted in its meaning by the context, insofar as it does not, evidently, define a moral quality but rather the perfection of one of the vices of this profession. This technique of ironic simplicity and malicious insinuation does not finally have the effect of an all-the-more devastating satire, but leads to a conflict between our sympathies and our moral values, thus intensifying our critical participation.

Going through the portraits one after the other we find that in spite of many differences, as to their sources as well as the estates they describe, they have much in common. They are to a large extent presented in the voice of an almost indiscriminate reporter who avoids any moral evaluation and always picks out what is most typical of the respective estate. However much our intellectual and moral involvement may foster the impression of realistically portrayed personalities, the crucial fact remains that they are held up primarily as representatives of certain estates or professions. Each pilgrim excels in those arts and crafts that are particularly necessary or profitable for his profession. Almost every portrait lists details that create the image of a brilliant expert; this applies equally to the Monk and the Friar, to the Merchant and the Summoner, as well as to the Wife of Bath, whose estate is defined by her being a woman and a wife.[22] The failings, abuses and perversions, too, that are so often referred to have to be seen in the context of the respective estates; they are not meant to illustrate personal idiosyncrasies or individual moral corruption. In most cases they correspond to what other literary sources, mostly estates satires, attack as the vices and crimes of certain professions and estates. This is particularly true for the clergy: here Chaucer could draw on a long tradition of satire, mostly Latin, though Langland's *Piers Plowman*, too, contains a great number of themes that reappear in Chaucer.[23] The Monk as a hunting enthusiast, the brilliant Friar, as well as the exemplary country Parson – all of them are to a large extent traditional figures, just as the estate gallery itself is a traditional literary form.

In addition, each estate-representative is portrayed as a supreme master of his trade. Nearly every portrait revels in superlatives and assures us that the subject of the description is an unrivalled model of skill and second to none among those who follow the same occupation, be it for good or evil. This again makes us view these pilgrims as an exemplary and representative sample of human society. This is no less true of those professions that had, as far as we know, no long tradition of estates satire behind them, such as the Cook, the Shipman and the Manciple. Even an unobtrusive portrait like that of the Cook, for instance, can illustrate the way Chaucer, even without a concrete model, concentrates on professional accomplishments rather than any personal attributes:

> A COOK they hadde with hem for the nones
> To boille the chiknes with the marybones,
> And poudre-marchant tart and galyngale.
> Wel koude he knowe a draughte of Londoun ale.
> He koude rooste, and sethe, and broille, and frye,
> Maken mortreux, and wel bake a pye.
> But greet harm was it, as it thoughte me,
> That on his shyne a mormal hadde he.
> For blankmanger, that made he with the beste.   (1.379–87)

Almost everything we get to know about this figure is connected in some way or other with his occupation. If he nevertheless strikes us as an 'individual', this is, again, as with all the other figures, a result of Chaucer's specific descriptive method, which always provokes us to a personal reaction towards the character in question. This is partly achieved by the selection of the skills mentioned. It does not permit a confident verdict as to whether or not the Cook abuses his trade; but the reference to his familiarity with London ale might be understood as a sly hint that he is addicted to drink, and this would suggest associations with satirical descriptions of gluttony.

The casual and regretful allusion to his 'mormal', too, could have a satirical background and suggest professional corruption.[24] More important, however, than possible insinuations of a moral or satirical nature seems to me again the complete absence of any unambiguous explanation and, thus, of calculated satire. It is left to the reader to interpret the facts and to bring them into harmony with one another; any too definite conclusion can only be reached without the author's sanction. The 'mormal' does not make the Cook a highly individualized character, but our reaction has something of the indefiniteness and emotional intensity we experience in our own daily social intercourse. On the other hand, it is this very personal mark that directs our attention to the social role of the Cook, so that his portrait, too, turns out to be a contribution to the gallery of estates, which is a reflection of human society split up into a diversity of functions. The fact that – for obvious reasons – the higher spiritual and secular dignitaries are left out does not really contradict this impression, because Chaucer does not attempt to make a complete sociological inventory or to draw an accurate picture of fourteenth-century life, but rather to give a representative selection of the different estates, their skills and tricks, their temptations and vices. It seems almost like a collection of abstract clichés which, nevertheless, evokes for the reader a much more vivid picture of social forces and contradictions than a mere compilation of facts aiming at completeness could do.

At the same time – and this is no less important for the tone of the work – the superlative singularity of each of the estate-representatives creates a persistent impression of restless activity and wholehearted commitment on many different levels. All the pilgrims are bound together but, at the same time, isolated from one another by their single-minded devotion to the demands and temptations of their professions. Each of them concentrates all his energy on what he has chosen as his ultimate goal, and this enthusiasm which they all have in common informs the 'General Prologue' with its characteristic forward-looking vitality, which combines with the awakening of spring and the theme of the pilgrimage to create a colourful picture of man's aspirations and desires. And as each of the pilgrims seems to be enclosed in his own world of particular needs and standards of value, so, too, each of them has apparently his own reasons for taking part in the pilgrimage, even though on this point the narrator does not go into particulars.

The diversity of descriptive methods and the absence of reliable authorial evaluation might justify the question whether any claim to moral order has been abandoned altogether – whether, indeed, competence and vitality are the only standards recognized by the author. Such an impression could arise if one took note only of the explicit comments by the narrator, thus ignoring the persistent involvement of the reader, which is one of the author's main objectives. Every single portrait demands our intellectual and moral partcipation and encourages us to read between the lines. At the same time, those pilgrims who are described as really ideal representatives of their estates provide a standard to guide our judgement. The Parson and the Ploughman are obviously exemplary and blameless embodiments of the pastoral and the practical ideals of Christianity, and this suggests the reflection that the selfless devotion to their calling they demonstrate might well be practised within the other professions too.

True enough, Chaucer's portrait gallery remains static inasmuch as the individual estate-representatives are not shown in their mutual interdependence. All of them – even the idealized figures of the Knight, the Parson, the Ploughman and the Clerk – are unmatchable and lonely experts, and although each of them, within his estate, embodies a deliberately chosen ideal, the relevance of these ideals to society as a whole is left in some doubt, if only because the poet is remarkably silent on this point. The reader may well wonder whether the brilliant achievements or the values of the individual estates can really be generally applied. The social criticism of the 'General Prologue', therefore, hardly goes beyond exposing singular abuses within those estates which traditionally had the reputation of being particularly susceptible to them.[25]

Our attitude towards the individual estate-representatives depends, as my observations so far have tried to make clear, to a much larger extent on the narrative method than on any precise information the poet gives. Each description, as a close analysis of any one of the portraits would show, has a highly personal colouring; and, not unlike our reaction to Chaucer's earlier poems, we see the characters through the eyes of a very distinct personality. There was a time when the role of the narrator was discussed by critics with a thoroughness that gave a somewhat exaggerated impression of its relevance. In spite of his very personal tone, Chaucer the pilgrim remains a rather shadowy figure who does not by any means thrust himself forward. The narrative method of the 'General Prologue' is completely subordinated to its subject, and this is sometimes lost sight of when the narrator is analysed as a particularly remarkable and interesting character – for instance, as a naive and unworldly simpleton who is taken in by the brilliant intelligence of villains because he can see only the façade where the reader perceives what is behind it.[26]

The more closely we look at Chaucer's narrative method, the clearer it becomes that it is too complex to be reduced to the simple opposition of a naive narrator and an omniscient author. The narrator himself is often ironic, and his refusal to pass authoritative judgement is not a sign of obtuseness at all, but rather an aspect of his efforts to present a faithful account, an expression of modest politeness and detachment, as well as of the wish to let the characters described speak for themselves, as becomes particularly noticeable in the portraits of the Monk and the Friar.

The main function of the teasingly ambiguous and often indefinite narrative method is to focus all the reader's attention on the portrayed figures and to invite his own judgement. The narrator's personality is only of secondary importance in this, unlike the situation in the dream-allegories, where the obtuseness of the first-person narrator is an essential device for the reader's instruction and mental participation. Although the Prologue to *The Canterbury Tales* is evidently influenced by the tradition of such visions, this aspect of revelation and instruction remains marginal here, and a definitely individualized figure of a naive narrator would easily distract our attention from the actual subject-matter of the poem. There are, moreover, only a few portraits in the 'General Prologue' where such an approach might really be justified, because the tone of the description is by no means consistent but varies considerably according to the requirements of the individual portraits. This, again, reinforces the impression that we see the pilgrims almost entirely as they see themselves, not as a prejudging observer committed to fixed moral principles would see them. The narrator repeatedly uses reported speech as a means of suggesting uncensured self-portrayal, particularly in those cases where the character's own opinion of himself is bound to clash with the reader's expectations, but also in the description of the exemplary clergyman. This point of view is not, however, consistently kept up: time and again we recognize the voice of the omniscient author who views the party of pilgrims as a whole, imposes his own kind of order on the series of portraits and does not always speak in the tones of an immediately involved fellow-traveller. Thus the narrative method of the 'General Prologue' is anything but consistent in terms of recent narrative theories; but it is the very indefiniteness of the first-person narrator that is so conducive to the reader's intellectual participation, because it challenges him to make deeper sense out of many uncommented facts by his own observation and moral standards.[27]

At the same time, the reader is kept aware of the fact that he is confronted by the poet with a fictitious reality to which other rules must be applied than to everyday reality when, for instance, at the end of the series of portraits, the poet apologizes for having presented them in an arbitrary order, this is primarily a reminder of the literary and rhetorical character of his description. At the same time, the principle of order according to estate, rank or artistic decorum is made a subject for discussion. This is indirectly supported by our impression that within the individual portraits, too, there does not seem to be an immediately recognizable order.

The static description of the individual pilgrims, Chaucer's version of the traditional estates satire, is evidently not completely integrated within the framework of *The Canterbury Tales*, at least not in terms of a consistent or uniform piece of fiction. The series of self-contained character-vignettes is to some extent separated from the frame-story proper – at least there is no inevitable continuity – and we are confronted with quite different concepts of what constitutes a character, particularly in those cases where the pilgrims presented here reappear later in action. It would really be naive to expect perfect psychological consistency, because, from the point of view of the narrative technique alone, the purely descriptive portraits in the tradition of the estates satire differ categorically from the narrators and speakers who enter the stage in the links. The close affinity to the estates satire underlines the status of the 'General Prologue' as a self-contained work of fiction. The portrait of the Host, made up of direct utterance and action to a much larger extent than of static description, can make the differences more immediately obvious. His position is outside the portrait gallery, and, as the first character to speak, he stands opposite to the pilgrims as a whole, who at first remain silent or, at most, express a collective opinion.

Chaucer's apology for the particular form of his collection of tales, however, establishes a brilliant connection between estates satire and the ensuing narratives:

> But first I pray yow, of youre curteisye,
> That ye n'arette it nat my vileynye,
> Thogh that I pleynly speke in this mateere,
> To telle yow hir wordes and hir cheere,
> Ne thogh I speke hir wordes proprely.
> For this ye knowen al so wel as I,
> Whoso shal telle a tale after a man,
> He moot reherce as ny as evere he kan
> Everich a word, if it be in his charge,
> Al speke he never so rudeliche and large,
> Or ellis he moot telle his tale untrewe,
> Or feyne thyng, or fynde wordes newe.
> He may nat spare, althogh he were his brother;
> He moot as wel seye o word as another. (1.725–38)

The passage is particularly illuminating as a description of Chaucer's narrative method, as a very explicit defence of stylistic diversity. His claim that he has to reproduce the words of each character faithfully must not be understood in the sense of a theory of poetical naturalism, but it does formulate a rhetorical principle: the presentation of a diversity of narrators justifies, indeed demands, a corresponding diversity of stylistic register: 'The wordes moote be cosyn to the dede' (1.742). It is the justification of such stylistic diversity and freedom, not a naturalistic imitation of reality, that the poet is here concerned with, although the observation of the rhetorical principle may well result in an illusion of astonishing realism.

Moreover, by using the device of a frame-story in this way, Chaucer has created for himself an opportunity of reflecting the whole diversity of human activities, experiences and insights in the form of different narrative genres and levels of style, while, at the same time, shifting the responsibility to the individual narrators. Thus the 'General Prologue' is not just a self-contained estates satire on its own, but at the same time a particularly fitting introduction to a heterogeneous collection of stories. As the individual estate-representatives demonstrate the simultaneity of different modes of life and codes of behaviour as well as 'the coexistence of different methods of judging people',[28] so in their tales, too, they reflect a colourful diversity of literary traditions and techniques to represent reality, a coexistence of contradictory perspectives and stylistic ideals. This, in my view, is the most important principle of composition to give unity to the collection of *The Canterbury Tales*, if, in view of this deliberately diversified design, the concept of unity has any meaning at all.

THE UNITY OF THE COLLECTION

Leaving aside the particular form of the 'General Prologue', there are two other general problems that have been discussed by critic after critic: the first concerns the relationship between the narrators and their tales and the second the formal or thematic unity of the whole cycle. Both problems are closely related to more recent developments in literary theory and practice during the last decades and hardly seem to have troubled earlier readers.

Thus, the dramatic interrelation between tales and tellers, first described by Kittredge and often praised since, may well be based on a concept of character that has little relevance for Chaucer's poetry. In the 'General Prologue', as we have seen, the pilgrims are described as typical representatives of their respective estates rather than as unique individuals; similarly the links that have been preserved create typical situations and do not, for example, dramatize personal conflicts or psychologically motivated tensions. For this reason alone it is rather unlikely that the individual tales were conceived as an expression of complex personalities – a claim which could at any rate be made for only a very small number of them – or that they were primarily intended to contribute to the portraits of their respective narrators. Moreover, it is not quite clear in what way precisely such a close interrelation between portrait and tale would really make sense. Whereas the portrait gallery presents a largely unconnected series of descriptions of estates, it is in the links that we see some of these representatives as characters in action; they come to life in their speech and in a number of personal confrontations, although, again, it is easy to demonstrate that it is above all the social and professional aspects that are thrown into relief. The animosities which flare up, for instance, between Miller and Reeve or between Friar and Summoner, arise entirely out of the characters' obsessions as members of a particular estate and are not at all due to personal differences or conflicts among incompatible individuals. The enmities are largely traditional ones, and accordingly we cannot expect more from the tales than a further illustration of such professional antagonisms. It is only appropriate, therefore, that these four characters should treat their audience to stories that make fun of the opponent's estate by introducing a particularly nasty or ridiculous representative of it. In these cases we may indeed note a close relationship between narrators and tales, if only in a very limited sense. The tales, in a way, continue the social tensions implicit in the estates satire.

In other cases, however, this interrelation is much more vague, and only by a rather forced interpretation of the text could one really establish a convincing connection between teller and tale. The series of gloomy tragedies related by the Monk is not particularly in keeping with his portrait in the 'General Prologue' – much less so, at any rate, than the Host's unheeded invitation to contribute a hunting story. In many cases, such as those of the Nun's Priest, the Second Nun and the Physician, the portraits of the narrators are really too vaguely outlined to make a particularly fitting story possible; in other cases, there are, at most, similarities in the social context, as in the case of the Knight and his tale. Even the 'Canon's Yeoman's Tale', introduced in a more dramatic manner, is motivated by the narrator's estate and social position, not by any personal attributes. Thus with the majority of tales the most we can say is that there is no striking incongruity between the person of the narrator and the tale he chooses to contribute.

On the other hand, the assignment of the tales is by no means arbitrary;

though we have to keep in mind that it is not based on personal idiosyncrasies or complexities of character but either on the practices of certain estates or on stylistic decorum. Just as the individual estate-representatives embody different degrees of insight, so the stylistic levels of their tales are clearly graded and correspond, more or less, to the social positions of the speakers, even though these correspondences cannot be defined too narrowly and should, therefore, not be overemphasized. Although at first glance every reader will gain the impression, no doubt encouraged by Chaucer, that the tale of the Miller, for example, is very appropriate to his estate, it would on closer inspection be difficult to show that more than a merely superficial fittingness, confined to a few typical features, was intended here. The coarse man of brawn and muscle, with some talent as a popular entertainer, as 'a janglere and a goliardeys' (1.560), who is, moreover, more than half-drunk, is hardly a figure of whom we would expect such a sophisticated narrative, making brilliant play of popular and learned traditions and showing an easy familiarity with all the arts of rhetoric. From the point of view of a reasonably consistent characterization the relationship between this narrator and his tale could hardly be described as particularly close. Nevertheless, there is no real inconsistency here, since it is obviously Chaucer's main object to exploit the pointed contrast between Knight and Miller as it manifests itself in their respective tales, and in this he is entirely successful. The narrators' characters are of interest only insofar as they motivate and underline these contrasts of style, setting and perspective. The only facts necessary to an understanding of the 'Miller's Tale' derive from his social position: he is a 'cherl' (1.3182), and he hates the Reeve. The motivation of the 'Reeve's Tale' is quite similar. There is hardly any instance where the character of a narrator becomes strikingly differentiated by his tale; if this occurs at all, it is a mere side-effect resulting from the very personal tone of some of the tales.

In any case, a narrator-figure abstracted from the tone and style of a tale is a completely different kind of fictional character from a rhetorical portrait, and the personal traits that might impress themselves on the reader's attention are of a different nature. If we tried to describe the narrator of the 'Knight's Tale' or the 'Miller's Tale' in more detail, the terms we would use would be not at all like the data given in the 'General Prologue'. And this applies to practically all the tales, with the exception, perhaps, of the soliloquies of the Wife of Bath and the Pardoner. The tales of these two figures are so closely intertwined with their 'confessions' that they are clearly meant to complement their self-portraits and to contribute to a vivid sketch of a certain intellectual and spiritual physiognomy. With the Wife of Bath, however, the correspondences between soliloquy and tale are on a more thematic level: her tale illustrates a problem which is closely related to the traditional issue of anti-feminist satire discussed in her prologue, whereas her narrative style in itself can hardly be described as particularly typical of the narrator. The tale of the Pardoner, however, is a demonstration of his brilliant demagogy, though it would be appropriate for any pardoner or popular preacher, so that again it would be misleading to talk of a complex revelation of a sharply individualized character.[29]

The extensive self-portraits of the Wife of Bath and the Pardoner are largely independent of the actual frame-story, and they represent a particularly lively link between the pilgrimage and the tales. Yet they are, like the highly original appearance on the scene of the Canon's Yeoman, singular effects which hardly allow the conclusion that, after all, Chaucer *did* really intend to present the pilgrims as individual characters. More appropriately, we might say that the diversity of literary forms displayed in *The Canterbury Tales* is further enriched by another genre: the uninhibited soliloquy of an anything but exemplary figure. The confession, unchecked by any diplomatic considerations or extenuating dissimulation, is a traditional form, particularly suitable for the profession of the Pardoner as Chaucer presents it. It cannot be measured by the ordinary standards of psychology, but turns out to be a particularly impressive and pointed form of estates satire; it serves, at the same time, as a demonstration of brilliant rhetoric used for an evil purpose.

When the unscrupulous Pardoner, having just bluntly and boastingly confessed his fraudulent avarice, at the conclusion of his drastically edifying story, makes an impudent attempt to talk his fellow-pilgrims into buying some of his worthless indulgences and relics, this should not be interpreted as the drama of an individual whose psychological background we have to uncover, but, more probably, as an aspect of the poet's attempt to expose his profession from as many different angles as possible, to show his extortionate practices in action in order to complete the impression of the self-portrait. The question whether the speaker here is carried away by his own eloquence or whether he seriously expects his appeal to be successful seems to me quite irrelevant and will only worry a reader who comes to the text expecting the kind of psychological consistency we have become used to demanding of fictional characters – mainly owing to the practice of the realistic novels of the last two centuries.[30] Much more important is the fact that we are confronted with a very lively sketch of an estate-representative which on the one hand elaborates on his portrait in the 'General Prologue', and on the other provides an ideal frame for his tale, whose brilliant rhetoric may only be understood adequately if we see it as part of an edifying as well as deceitful and calculating sermon. No other tale is tailored so neatly to the person of its narrator; in fact it is only a subordinate part of the whole performance, which appears as a self-contained literary achievement within the collection of *The Canterbury Tales*. The tale can hardly be separated from it without losing much of its edge and of its function as an important part of the Pardoner's self-portrait.

The breathless monologue of the Wife of Bath may, at first, appear to the reader more realistic and personal than it actually is. This is in no way meant as adverse criticism, but a closer inspection of the text will make us realize that here again we are confronted with a particularly original version of traditional estates satire, not with a psychologically consistent portrait. The unrestrained defence of sexuality and of female domination turns out to be a concise anthology of the anti-feminist literature of the Middle Ages and should not be misinterpreted as the individualized confessions of a complex personality.[31]

The first part of her one-woman act consists of a pseudo-learned refutation of the Christian ideals of celibacy and chastity; it is a brilliant demonstration of wilful distortion and misapplication of ecclesiastical authorities – the vindication, carried to the extreme, of a point of view which, in this reduced form, can only appear as comical and absurd.

The second part of her soliloquy, however, presents the speaker as a shrew of the first order, obsessed by her lust for absolute power, as the proverbially quarrelsome, domineering and extravagant female who not only suppresses, demoralizes and ruins her husbands, but even demands to be spoilt by them in return. The highly original way in which she is made to report her own words, pouring forth once again her devastating verbal torrent, gives a lively impression of a tempestuous domestic scene. With great gusto she goes retrospectively through her vituperative performance, in which, with unconscious irony, she puts all those traditional complaints and imputations of anti-feminist satire into the mouths of her intimidated spouses – not a particularly effective way of refuting them. The crowning stroke is her admission that the poor husbands never did in fact say any of these things: she made them all up, presumably from her reading, from experience, or from the fifth husband's book. Never was anti-feminist satire delivered in such a round-about way, and the effect of this oblique method is rather complex. At least we are prevented from taking all these traditional charges at their face value. They are part of a dynamic situation; and, though some readers may feel that nothing demonstrates their essential truth more than the Wife's own behaviour, it is by no means as simple as that, because we are not really told in so many words that her own actions justify all these accusations or that the husbands' motives are really above reproach. The reader has to think twice before he can come to a comfortable verdict, and there is no question of Chaucer simply embracing the cause of traditional anti-feminism.

The third part of her monologue, with its repeatedly anticipated dramatic crisis, is almost in the nature of a satirical fabliau. It describes a very practical kind of victory of 'experience' over the authority of anti-feminist literature as represented by her learned husband's book, from which she quotes with great relish. The classical exempla and diatribes against women are, however, hardly invalidated by her act of violence, but rather confirmed or at least made more relevant. Burning a book is not the most effective way of dealing with its unpleasant contents, and the wife's physical triumph only adds to the reader's suspicion that those misogynist 'clerkes' knew quite well what they were writing about. Again, however, the poet does not simply subscribe to their views, but rather shows how inadequate they are in the face of a very complex reality. They are distanced from us by several quotation marks and by a dramatic situation that does not allow us to put all the blame on one person.

In spite of the Wife of Bath's lively solo performance and some very brilliant characterization, which includes her quite unmistakable idiom, it would still be misleading to present her as a consistently individualized personality; rather, she is a dramatization of anti-feminist commonplaces, combined in this irrepressible person, the very nightmare of moral and (as she insinuates) impotent scholars and the complete opposite of the courtly ideal of womanly behaviour, especially in her relations with men. If the individual parts of this confession cannot, perhaps, be brought quite into harmony with one another because they draw on different literary traditions, this will worry only those readers whose ideas of a consistent character in fiction have been formed by realistic novels.

Both these monologues thus attempt to reproduce certain effects of the estates satire, and both of them employ a well-tried narrative device which was traditionally used for the description of swindlers and comical figures and would have been quite inappropriate for the majority of pilgrims. They remain, in the last resort, isolated set-pieces within the frame-story; they do not, at least, refute my impression that the purpose of the frame is primarily functional: its chief point is to establish a diversity of narrators who are sufficiently differentiated in social and moral terms, not a colourful party of individuals for its own sake. The inclusion of these 'confessions' is yet another demonstration of Chaucer's unorthodox delight in experimental diversity, extending to the field of literary genres and narrative methods. The comic and, at the same time, encyclopaedic juxtaposition of the most heterogeneous narrative and rhetorical conventions suggested by the mixed society of pilgrims is much more important for an understanding of the collection than any speculations about a 'roadside drama'.

The poet's apology, quoted above and repeated in the introduction to the 'Miller's Tale', shows how crucial Chaucer himself considered this particular aspect of his work to be and may suggest that his audience had yet to get used to this kind of experiment:

> And therfore every gentil wight I preye,
> For Goddes love, demeth nat that I seye
> Of yvel entente, but for I moot reherce
> Hir tales alle, be they bettre or werse,
> Or elles falsen som of my mateere.
> And therfore, whoso list it nat yheere,
> Turne over the leef and chese another tale;
> For he shal fynde ynowe, grete and smale,
> Of storial thyng that toucheth gentillesse,
> And eek moralitee and hoolynesse.
> Blameth nat me if that ye chese amys.
> The Millere is a cherl, ye knowe wel this.   (1.3171–82)

Not only is the diversity of tales emphasized here with almost programmatic clarity, but there is at the same time an appeal to the reader's own judgement, and the responsibility for the actual effect of the tales is firmly transferred to him. It is the reader himself who has to draw the correct conclusions from the relationship between narrator and tale and to assess the relative validity of the individual utterances. It is only if we ignore this distancing function of the frame that we can make the mistake of confusing comedy with seriousness and entertainment with edification.

This again supports the conclusion that the frame does not provide the work with the unity of a coherent plot and that, indeed, all attempts to define the unity of the work on the basis of characterization seem to be rather questionable. More plausibly, the collection, incomplete though it is, may be understood as a brilliantly inclusive compendium of literary forms – ranging from the estate portraits of the 'General Prologue' to the penitential sermon of the Parson – not in the sense of a mere compilation, but as a grand debate in which one utterance complements the other, or calls it in question to illumine the relativity of any isolated point of view.[32] In Chaucer's earlier works, most of all in *Troilus*, it has already been striking enough that the poet hardly ever commits himself to an unambiguously professed point of view; every fundamental attitude is put in perspective by being contrasted with its opposite: the idealism of the eagles in *The Parliament of Fowls* with the animalism of the lower birds, Troilus' seemingly disinterested love with Pandarus' 'olde daunce'. The poet seems to mistrust any rigorous and exclusive restriction to one single point of view or one particular form of expression, and it is this obvious delight in diversity and debate that is at the root of the encyclopaedic wealth of *The Canterbury Tales* and accounts for the particular type of frame-story Chaucer has devised here. Each of the tales is put in quotation marks, as it were, each has to be seen as the expression of a particular stylistic and intellectual stance; but none of them stands completely on its own, since each derives part of its meaning by the context of contradictory attitudes. This always leaves the author free to retreat and hide behind his fictional characters, like the Nun's Priest: 'Thise been the cokkes wordes, and nat myne' (VII.3265). This close interrelationship, created by the programmatic diversity of tellers and tales, suggests a much more satisfactory explanation of the whole structure of the collection than many attempts to produce a theory of thematic unity, be it on the basis of the concept of the Seven Deadly Sins or by proposing the idea of a 'marriage group'.[33] Wherever thematic correspondences and associations between individual tales are established – and no attentive reader can really miss them – they are still subordinated to the more comprehensive principle of provocative diversity; they are not the central concern of the whole debate, but rather illustrations of the possibility of widely differing points of view and their coexistence within one close-knit community.

Of course, the frame does create a strong sense of unity, first of all by emphasizing the narrative situation, of which we are regularly reminded in the 'links', and secondly by the idea of the pilgrimage, which, in the course of the work, seems to lose more and more of its realistic and literal substance and to turn by degrees into a metaphor.[34]

The colourful assembly of narrators naturally implies a corresponding diversity of listeners; the heterogeneous and even contradictory variety of tales is answered by a great range of conflicting reactions on the part of the audience. This may not be apparent in every single case, but it is usually sufficiently present to stimulate the reader continually to reconsider his own reaction and to direct his attention to the important function of the audience. What appeals to one reader may well be boring or offensive to another; but, again, it is most of all the differences in social rank, occupation and spiritual or aesthetic insight that are reflected in the pilgrims' reactions to the individual performances. When, for example, the Knight interrupts the monotonous series of tragedies recited by the Monk, he does it for reasons quite different from those of the Host, who supports his intervention. The Knight finds it too depressing to be so insistently reminded of the inconstancy of fortune by this superabundance of examples, whereas the Host only gives vent to his boredom and lack of interest and clearly would have preferred a hunting-story. It is very often a one-sided or plainly wrong-headed reaction that can direct the reader's attention to the real qualities of a tale. When, for instance, the Host applies the lesson of the didactic tract on patience, presented by Chaucer himself, merely to his domestic situation and understands it as a remedy against shrews, this obviously limited interpretation should provoke the reader to ask where the real significance of the tales lies. Similar situations recur, particularly instructive in this respect being the admiration of the Franklin, who is himself striving for 'gentillesse', for the decorative tale contributed by the Squire; its artificial courtliness is made all the more conspicuous by such one-sided praise. The rather superficial emotion of the Host after the story of the Physician, too, is a comic, even though perhaps more ambiguous, comment.

The diversity of reactions towards the tales corresponds to the diversity of expectations. While the 'gentils' take exception to the Pardoner preparing himself for his narrative by a mouthful of ale and do not want to hear any 'ribaudye' (VI.323–6), the Shipman rudely refuses to listen to a sermon (II.1178–83). This, again, creates the impression of a diversity of tastes and, at the same time, of a lively interrelation between narrator and audience which is important for an appreciation of Chaucer's intentions and by the same token includes the present audience or reader.

The figure of the Host is also a very important factor in this respect: he functions as a judge and a chairman and by his interventions keeps the narrative situation continually before us. He has been compared with the eagle in *The House of Fame* and described as a comic version of the traditional guide figure, comparable, for instance, to Vergil in Dante's *Divina Commedia*. His often irreverent but, as a rule, good-humoured directness in his dealing with the pilgrims contributes much to the impression of cheerful conviviality which is so characteristic of the frame of *The Canterbury Tales*; but his verbal skirmishes with some of the narrators and his inability to grasp more than the surface meaning of many of their tales draw the reader's attention again and again to all those areas that remain inaccessible to this sociable guide. At the same time, they keep alive the fiction of the original agreement, and thereby too they contribute to the outward unity of the cycle.

The frame is thus solid enough to throw into relief the exhilarating variations on the theme of narrative attitudes, but in its present form it leaves the pilgrimage itself rather vague. It is true that occasional place-names and similar details keep up the illusion of a real journey, but as to its actual progress and its ultimate goal, the information we receive is rather scanty; and, as we have seen, the state of the text precludes any confident assertion as to whether Chaucer himself had any definite ideas or plans in this respect. The prologue to the 'Parson's Tale' and the tale itself, however, prove that he or his literary heirs had decided on a rather unexpected and unprepared for reinterpretation of the motif of the pilgrimage, replacing the fiction of a real journey to Canterbury by the metaphor of a pilgrimage to the Heavenly Jerusalem. The effect is that, retrospectively, the whole frame is invested with a deeper significance, and the group of representatives of different estates thus begins to appear in a new light, as an image of mankind on its way toward the Last Judgement. Whether this interpretation was intended from the outset or whether it is but an afterthought, due to the impracticability of the original plan, is a question we cannot decide at this stage – nor does it seem to be really crucial for an understanding of the work. In *The Canterbury Tales* as preserved in the majority of reliable manuscripts, the sermon of the Parson appears as the crowning climax and conclusion of the encyclopaedic structure: the tolerant diversity of individual points of view is followed by a penitential sermon in which all ambiguities, rhetorical brilliance and playful irony are given up in favour of straight-forward, unmitigated and unpretentious didacticism. The systematic account of the Deadly Sins includes all the individual offences of the erring pilgrims and the estates they represent and it seems to refute everything that has gone before, as did the conclusion of *Troilus*, though even more uncompromisingly. And yet, as in *Troilus*, the colourful diversity is not revoked by one stroke, but only radically challenged. Some over-zealous interpretations of *The Canterbury Tales* read as if it had been Chaucer's real intention to write nothing but the Parson's sermon or as if, at least, all the rest was nothing but supporting material for the list of sins denounced in this tract. However much Chaucer personally might have agreed with the Parson's point of view, it is clearly impossible to reduce *The Canterbury Tales* to an exercise in moral systematics. All attempts to find parallels between certain pilgrims (and their tales) and the sins described in the sermon only confirm, if anything, that Chaucer himself did not present such simple equations. Nowhere in *The Canterbury Tales* – if, for a moment, we discount the 'Retraction' – are we encouraged to read the whole work from this single angle. In the context of the whole collection, the Parson's sermon is, in one sense at least, just one form, among several others, of instruction and of the rhetorical presentation of moral principles. The variety of literary forms and genres does, on the other hand, make us realize that the prose sermon represents a mode of discourse different from that of the poetical fictions of most of the other tales.[35]

If many modern readers find this homiletic tract rather boring (assuming they are interested enough to get much beyond the first paragraph or two), this is certainly not at all what Chaucer expected his audience to feel – nor is it in the least likely that they would have reacted in this way. The discrepancy should remind us of the historical distance between Chaucer's poetry and our own literary standards, a distance that can never be completely bridged. It would be wrong, however, to leave it at that or to be content with our first superficial impression and impute our modern impatience with undiluted instruction to Chaucer.[36] It is also important to note that the rather astonishing change in subject-matter and style does not come entirely without preparation. The 'Tale of Melibee', which is received very approvingly by the Host, and with which Chaucer introduces himself as a very didactic narrator conversant with homiletic treatises, has already made us aware of the contrast between an entertaining plot and theoretical instruction. The Parson's sermon belongs to the same kind of writing and seems like a deliberate counter-stroke, formally as well as in substance, to all the 'ribaudye' of the burlesque tales. It remains, however, an isolated instance, and the reader is by no means convinced that such an abstract insistence on absolute values is really meant to be the final answer to the many troubling questions raised in the rest of the collection. The radical change in form and mode of discourse seems almost like an explicit renunciation of any claim to find such an answer within a series of fictional narratives, however diversified. Imaginative abundance and unadorned instruction are boldly placed side by side without any transition and, in spite of very persuasive attempts to demonstrate the significance of the 'Parson's Tale' as a unifying conclusion to the whole cycle,[37] most readers will probably find some incongruity here and remain sceptical towards any interpretation that boils down to a simple subordination of all the entertaining stories to the uncompromising sermon. The Parson is, after all, one character among others, and his interpretation of the pilgrimage as 'thilke parfit glorious pilgrymage/That highte Jerusalem celestial' (X.50–1), as well as his sermon, is a personal statement of a particular point of view and not necessarily identical with the views of the author, who might well, even with reference to this part of *The Canterbury Tales*, have retorted: 'Thise been the cokkes wordes, and nat myne.'

The plain homiletic prose of the 'Parson's Tale' and, even more so, Chaucer's 'Retraction' nevertheless raise the uncomfortable question whether all fictional and entertaining art is not bound to fail us when it comes to the salvation of man's soul: to this question, however, there is no confident answer within *The Canterbury Tales*. All really responsible poetry will, from time to time, feel the need to justify itself,[38] but the collection of stories as a whole demonstrates by the very vitality and range of its presentation that the appeals of art and of mere instruction are very different from each other and that the exhilarating abundance of narrative and stylistic performances cannot simply be replaced by a penitential treatise. The *Canterbury Tales* do not add up to a satisfactory solution of these problems; rather, they make us more sharply aware of contradictions that have troubled poets and readers for centuries and have to be faced again by every generation. No interpretation of Chaucer's poem should try to simplify this fundamental discussion or explain away the tensions within the collection of conflicting points of view. Rather, we have to recognize that the poet presents basic contra- dictions for which his own art is unable to offer anything like a comfortable reconciliation. For all that, the position of the sermon, right at the end of the series of tales, strongly suggests that, within the hierarchy of literary forms, Chaucer wanted to invest it with special authority, and we are surely justified in recognizing a deeper analogy between the stylized description of a courtly way of life at the beginning and the strictly biblical view of human experience at the close. As there is no question of subversive irony here, we cannot escape the conclusion that Chaucer indeed meant his collection of tales to lead up to this unmitigated religious account of human society. One can hardly say that this is inappropriate for a poem that describes a pilgrimage, a traditional image of man's need of salvation and his more or less sincere efforts to achieve it:

> The hooly blisful martir for to seke,
> That hem hath holpen whan that they were seeke. (I.17–18)

The precise function of the 'Retraction' is even more difficult to describe than that of the 'Parson's Tale'. As the manuscript tradition is unanimous in placing it at the end of *The Canterbury Tales*, we have to take it as a fact that it was part of Chaucer's own plan to conclude his poetical compendium with a kind of literary testament. It is, I feel, pointless to speculate whether the poet is expressing his deepest personal convictions here. There can be no doubt about the seriousness and sincerity of this statement within the context of the work to which it is attached. One might, however, conceivably wonder whether it is a loosely appended personal declaration or a deliberately integrated part of the pilgrimage. As to this question, not all readers will respond to the text in the same way. If we look at the whole collection as a coherent literary perform- ance, the 'Retraction' will be seen as an integral part of its composition: the poet's repentance is his own immediate response to the sermon of the Parson. The author joins the group of pilgrims called upon to repent and includes himself in the number of sinners in need of forgiveness. By his own contrition he sets an example which, within the fictional context, is aimed at his fellow-pilgrims, but, at the same time, he makes an appeal to the reader to feel that his own salvation is at stake, too. The pilgrimage metaphor is extended to embrace the personal existence of each individual listener or reader.

When the poet publicly professes to revoke several of his works, in particular some of those that immediately precede the 'Retraction', this can hardly, in the context of the complete collection, be interpreted as a sudden fit of puritan iconoclasm; it is, rather, a final appeal to the audience not to take his work in the wrong spirit, still less to confuse entertaining playfulness and serious message. The poet's repentance for those tales 'that sownen into synne' (x.1085) challenges the reader either to turn away from these tales altogether or else to take care he is not corrupted by their irresponsible lewdness. It is probable, however, that he does not suggest a simple distinction between edifying and possibly corrupting stories, but wants to set up a standard applicable to every single tale.

For most twentieth-century readers, however, it will be difficult to avoid the impression that the untroubled homily at the conclusion presupposes a far more simple view of human nature than is presented by *The Canterbury Tales* as a whole, and no scholarly assurance that medieval readers would have responded quite differently will set their doubts at rest. Even if we grant that Chaucer deliberately exchanged the role of the artist for that of the preacher, the obvious fact remains that both roles appear side by side within the same work. The portrait of the Parson in the 'General Prologue' does not automatically turn all the other pilgrims into incorrigible sinners or point out an easy way of leading all this failing society to glorious perfection; nor would it be at all like Chaucer's characteristic style to impose an authoritative interpretation on his work by a dogmatic conclusion, repudiating and indeed denying all the ambiguities that have gone before. The uncompromising morality of the Parson, like the single-minded *contemptus mundi* at the end of *Troilus and Criseyde*, is a challenge to all of us, but Chaucer's art as a whole is informed by a different spirit: wise and undogmatic sympathy with man's complex and contradictory nature is the essential prerequisite for any real instruction and guidance.

The Parson's sermon and the poet's contrition no doubt provide an impressive conclusion to the whole work, but they impose an interpretation not necessarily implied in the text that has gone before, and one can hardly claim that they really give a kind of retrospective unity to the whole cycle, a unity we were not perceptive enough to notice before. At any rate, it does not greatly help our understanding of the collection if, in our reasonable desire to discover some all-embracing principle of order, we ignore the experimental diversity or count it as a fault that the individual parts resist our attempts to subsume them under some neat label, be it formal or thematic. Chaucer did not press his encyclopaedic compendium of stories into a harmonious or strictly hierarchic system, even though he discusses the possibility of such a system. There is no simplifying general principle that will save the reader the trouble of a personal decision.[39]

9

Stories and storytellers:
The Canterbury Tales

IN RECENT CRITICISM, AS WE HAVE SEEN, MORE EMPHASIS HAS often been put on the unity of *The Canterbury Tales* than on the autonomy of the individual narratives. Earlier readers, however, saw the work mainly as a collection of self-contained stories, loosely strung together by the frame, but perfectly intelligible and enjoyable without it. The idea that the tales have to be read as dramatic monologues, as parts of a many-voiced debate, is a comparatively new one and one that would probably not have become so fashionable without the development of sophisticated narrative techniques long after Chaucer. From a more historically orientated point of view, such an idea should only be adopted if we take into consideration Chaucer's personal narrative style, which works against any too thorough individualization of the different narrators and serves as an effective link between them.[1]

Leaving aside the problems of unity and the function of the frame discussed in the preceding chapter, *The Canterbury Tales* presents a highly heterogeneous assortment of nearly all the narrative genres known in the Middle Ages. It has often been observed that from these stories alone one could draw up a more or less complete list of medieval types of narrative and that this quality of a representative cross-section in form, style and theme, is perhaps Chaucer's most remarkable achievement.[2]

On closer inspection it becomes clear, however, that Chaucer hardly ever takes over any of the traditional genres uncritically or without some characteristic modification. Practically none of the *Canterbury Tales* really represents a 'pure' type of narrative: the courtly romance of the 'Knight's Tale' includes unmistakable reminiscences of more burlesque attitudes, and even the most uninhibited fabliaux are, in their turn, brought closer to courtly poetry by ostentatious rhetoric or learned debate – without, however, blurring the essential differences between the established genres. The contrast between the first two tales is a particularly obvious and surely deliberate example: the 'Knight's Tale' is not simply a conventional courtly romance, nor is the story told by the Miller

157

adequately described by the label fabliau usually applied to it. Each of the two tales includes stylistic features of the other, but the fundamental contrast between them is brought out even more sharply by such mutual allusions than it would be by a mere opposition of two totally unrelated stories. It is the same consummate artist who is behind both these contrasting versions of the rivalry between two lovers, and it is his evident delight in narrative experiments that links them effectively in the reader's mind. Something similar might be said of nearly all the stories in this collection, with the possible exception of those tales in which Chaucer confines himself to one unambiguous form or level of style, as in 'Sir Thopas', in the 'Tale of Melibee' and in the Parson's sermon. The conspicuous, even demonstrative one-sidedness clearly marks these performances as special cases and, at the same time, as deliberately accentuated narrative stances. More interesting for our purpose are those stories where the model of a certain genre is clearly recognizable while many of its conventions are critically examined or reinterpreted by some surprising variation. This applies, most of all, to those large genres that are so difficult to define and therefore particularly open to experimental innovation, such as the romance, the burlesque tale and the moral exemplum. This will now be illustrated by a few examples. After discussing, in the preceding chapter, the problems of the frame and the arrangement of the tales, it seems more appropriate for the present purpose to take the tales in the order suggested by genre and theme rather than sticking to the tentative and in many cases provisional plan of the early manuscripts.

VARIATIONS OF THE ROMANCE

The 'Knight's Tale' with which Chaucer opens his collection, has been described as his most successful version of medieval romance. The fact that the Knight, who in the 'General Prologue' has been introduced as the perfect embodiment of courtly chivalry and its military achievements, enters the stage with such an extensive tale invests it, from the start, with an aristocratic glamour, and we get the impression of an appropriate correspondence between narrator and tale. This is further underlined by the general applause the story is greeted with, especially by the 'gentils' (1.3113). Its dignified balance and rhetorical splendour, as well as the conventionality of the plot, has often been pointed out and will be apparent to most readers. The story makes use of so many traditional romance motifs that their concentration seems almost ostentatious, like a deliberate demonstration of literary clichés on the theme of courtly love and the art of tournament.

And yet, the work presents so many other aspects besides that it seems, again and again, to go beyond the confines of the genre. This can be partly explained by a glance at Chaucer's source. Boccaccio's *Teseida*, Chaucer's principal model, is four times as long as the 'Knight's Tale' and in its ambitious design seems to aim more at the grandeur of the classical epic than the conventions of medieval romance.[4] Chaucer took over some of the traditional epic devices, such as the division into books and the invocations, in his *Troilus*, whereas in the 'Knight's Tale' it seems to be the dramatic action, condensed and more sharply accentuated, that is the poet's main concern. He concentrates this action on the rivalry of the two lovers and subordinates all other aspects of the story to this central conflict. The stylistic variations, with a frequently comic undertone, the philosophical debate and the mythological superstructure, all contribute to a sharper accentuation and differentiation of the contrast between the two knights. The implications of the romance situation are examined from all sides, and the reader's attention is continually directed at the fundamental questions raised by the plot. The characters themselves are of secondary importance in this context. Neither Theseus nor Emily really appeals to our sympathy as an interesting individual, and not even the two heroes are sufficiently individualized to be easily distinguishable as unique human beings, so that the question as to which of the two is more deserving of the girl remains rather academic at first. Since love in this poem appears to be an all but exclusively one-sided passion, not a mutual relationship, and since the lady remains an entirely passive object of the young men's consuming desire, a large number of questions are automatically left out of account that would almost inevitably arise if the characters were more clearly individualized. Neither of the two knights appears more suited to be Emily's husband by any personal attributes than his rival, nor does she herself seem to be capable of a distinct opinion in the matter; her assent to any possible outcome is taken for granted. 'Compared to Boccaccio's, Chaucer's characters are dramatic forces rather than human beings.'[5]

Chaucer's reduction of the characters' individuality makes the story appear almost like a puzzle or prize question set before the reader: the two knights are placed in an extreme situation, which is deliberately stage-managed in such a way that a solution which would satisfy everyone concerned seems well-nigh impossible. This becomes particularly obvious at the end of the first part and before the crucial tournament. Arcite's release from prison and his ensuing banishment give rise to the somewhat casuistically formulated question of which of the two lovers has more reason to despair. The question is passed on to the readers experienced in these matters:

> Yow loveres axe I now this questioun:
> Who hath the worse, Arcite or Palamoun?
> That oon may seen his lady day by day,
> But in prison he moot dwelle alway;
> That oother wher hym list may ride or go,
> But seen his lady shal he nevere mo.
> Now demeth as yow liste, ye that kan,
> For I wol telle forth as I bigan. (1.1347–54)

The contrast that has led to this impasse is elaborated by the long complaints of the two knights.

A new situation is created by Theseus' idea of judgement by personal combat. Now, the reader will justly expect, an unequivocal decision in favour of one of the two rivals can no longer be avoided, but the dilemma is suddenly brushed aside by the surprising separation of the two aspects of courtly love (i.e. amorous desire and military achievement) embodied in the two classical deities Venus and Mars, who are here subsumed within the more inclusive concept of planetary influences. The fact that each of the two knights firmly commits himself to one of these two principal forces opens up the possibility that each of them will gain a victory, and thus a solution is prepared which, for all the suffering and grief it involves, has the neatness of a comic denouement. The tournament combines the notion of ingenious trickery with genuine tragedy and humane wisdom. By the elegant sophism proposed by Saturn, the claims of both the rivals are satisfied; Arcite's request for a victory and Palamon's prayer for the lady's hand are made compatible with one another and the ground is prepared for a happy ending. Arcite's death is not just the pitiful end of a victor cheated by fate, but the fulfilment of what he has asked for. The 'consolation' proclaimed by Theseus exactly describes the nature of Arcite's victory:

> And certeinly a man hath moost honour
> To dyen in his excellence and flour,
> Whan he is siker of his goode name; (1.3047–9)

Palamon is, for the time being, excluded from this fame, and it is clear, although it is not told us in so many words, that he is not the gods' only favourite. He is the one who is defeated, and at any rate no more worthy of the lady than the victorious Arcite.

In Boccaccio's poem, Arcite's death is followed by his apotheosis; from a celestial vantage-point he is able to smile at those who grieve for him. The mournful survivors are but a comic spectacle to him. Chaucer, as we have seen, transferred this passage to the last book of his *Troilus* and left the 'Knight's Tale' without this extra perspective. This also means that the poet does not in any way take sides. The conclusion is left in the balance, and it is up to the reader to decide which of the two has really met the more enviable fate; but not before Theseus has raised the philosophical question of the ordering principle behind this seemingly arbitrary direction of man's destiny. His advice to submit to the ultimately incomprehensible and unalterable state of things is not a conclusive answer, but rather (on the author's part) a deliberate simplification to make us even more conscious of the complexity of the issue.[6]

This combination of insistent questioning and serene helplessness is quite typical of Chaucer's narrative art. The deeper contradictions of the story are in no way smoothed over, but rather deliberately accentuated, by the decorative expansion of the action on the one hand and ironic understatement on the other. Every reader will notice the emphasis put on the ceremonial aspects of the story by decorative description and circumstantial accounts of external details; here, however, Chaucer was obviously following Boccaccio. More characteristic are all those passages where rhetorical pathos is undercut in an almost parodic manner and the more trivial aspects of the action are sharply and – from the point of view of stylistic decorum – unnecessarily brought to our attention. When Arcite's hopeless state after the accident is commented upon by the intervening narrator, 'Fare wel phisik! go ber the man to chirche!' (I.2760), and, after his death, the grief of the survivors is described from an ironic distance as mere routine (I.2817–36), the reader may well ask to what extent he is supposed to take the whole story seriously. This, of course, would be an all too simple response, because it is evident that the 'Knight's Tale' is far more than just an amused parody of chivalric conventions. The stylistic exuberance, the conscious display of rhetorical virtuosity, and, indeed, the whole tone of most of the narration suggest that Chaucer has made a deliberate effort to find an adequate poetical form for his courtly subject-matter. Ironic half-tones effectively work against an all too one-sided emphasis on rhetorical pathos and stylized emotion and provoke the reader to reflect upon the fundamental questions raised by the story – questions that the poet does not want to get buried under decorative design and theatrical ceremony.

The elaborate discussion of cosmic harmony and human helplessness shows that Chaucer was well aware of the larger moral and religious problems implicit in the traditional romance and wanted to make the reader aware of them too. Thus he created a poem of most impressive intellectual scope, a work not confined to a single point of view like so many traditional romances, but open in many different directions and therefore not adequately described by the rather loose term 'romance'. It is a brilliant experiment in courtly style, a bold attempt to illumine side by side the philosophical and the potentially ridiculous aspects of chivalry without tying himself to just one level of style.[7]

In view of the stylistic and thematic diversity of the 'Knight's Tale', it seems rather pointless to argue about the question whether it presents, in the last resort, a pessimistic or a hopeful view of life. The story does not claim to give a satisfactory answer to the problems raised by the events: order and disharmony continue to coexist and the solution proposed by Theseus, 'To maken vertu of necessitee' (1.3042), for all its humane wisdom, remains an all too simple theory when put to the test by a far more complex reality. We are left with an unresolved tension between a beautifully balanced structure, suggesting universal order and harmony, and the arbitrariness of fate, personified in the capricious and unpredictable planet-gods. This tension certainly clouds the seemingly untroubled serenity of the happy ending, but it would be anachronistic to assume that the chivalric mode of life as a whole is made fun of.

Most readers will probably soon have lost sight of the Knight as narrator of this engrossing poem, and it is only when we try to define the relationship between teller and tale more precisely and consistently than Chaucer has done that we begin to wonder whether such a sophisticated view of the courtly world can really be credited to the person introduced to us in the 'General Prologue'. The poet obviously thought it sufficient to emphasize the narrative situation and to put the whole poem, which may well have been in existence as an independent work before the *Canterbury Tales* were put together, in quotation marks. This clearly helps to make it appear a stylistic experiment – as one possible form, among others, of presenting and varying traditional romance material.[8] Beyond that, it is hardly possible to discover a very subtle correspondence between the narrator and his performance; nor is it really relevant to our appreciation of the poem whether we ascribe the ironies of the tale to the Knight or to Chaucer himself. It is just one of the teasing ambiguities of Chaucer's style that a neat separation is impossible here.[9]

The tale of the Miller, following immediately after the 'Knight's Tale', shows clearly enough that the Knight does not have the last word and that Chaucer deliberately exploits the mutual affinities and interdependences between different narrative genres. No less instructive than this evident contrast between the decorative romance and the, for all its rhetorical artifice, rather outspoken fabliau is a comparison between the different narratives based on romance motifs. As the Knight and his son the Squire are presented in the 'General Prologue', as two aspects of traditional chivalry, so their tales, which could both superficially be described as courtly romances, are quite unlike each other and illustrate very different concepts of 'romance'.

The 'Squire's Tale' might be characterized as an ostentatious, not particularly sophisticated display of romance clichés, expressing the youthful enthusiasm of the narrator for a particular way of life to which he aspires, but also exposing his inexperience and worldly innocence. The demonstratively exotic fable and the accumulation of rhetorical embellishments, hardly justified by the weight of the subject-matter, create the impression of competent immaturity; at any rate, there can hardly be any doubt that Chaucer would not have written this story, like many others in the collection, if he had not, by means of the frame, contrived to put it in the mouth of a narrator whose limitations we will recognize and take into account when assessing the poem. The 'Squire's Tale' is a perfect specimen of what many naive listeners probably expected of a romance: an indiscriminate collection of fairy-tale material, miraculous adventure and clear-cut emotions, without the serious moral or religious claims of the best romances. The scintillating brilliance of its exotic and mysterious atmosphere has no doubt contributed to its popularity with later poets, and the tendency of some recent critics to put all the emphasis on the tale's ironies, as if its only purpose were to hold up for ridicule the Squire's incompetence and immaturity, seems to me founded on a misunderstanding of the text.[10] It is certainly true that the performance betrays his youth and idealistic confidence, but this is not the main purpose of the tale. If it reflects satirically on its narrator, it does so only in a very gentle and unobtrusive way, certainly not enough to spoil the genuine magic of the story.

The Franklin's praise for the courtier-to-be ('thow hast thee wel yquit / And gentilly', v.673–4) is evidently quite sincere and without mockery; it is another indication that we are to see the Squire's narrative as an expression of ingenuous hopefulness not yet disillusioned but eager to learn and to acquire the accomplishments of his estate. At the same time, the words of the Franklin make clear that the young Squire has satisfactorily fulfilled his obligation as far as the storytelling competition is concerned and that he is released from the duty of continuing the tale to its conclusion. I do not think the text allows us to be quite certain whether the Franklin really means to cut the Squire short or whether Chaucer left the tale unfinished for other reasons; but, even if he himself lost interest in the story, he followed the example of the formel (and of Theseus) and 'made vertu of necessitee' (v.593), because the performance does not seem to lose much by the absence of a conclusion which, to judge by the Squire's promising preview, might have turned out more lengthy than he had anticipated.[11] The most important sections of the tale, the description of the strange visitor and the complaint of the deserted formel, do not really call for an elaborate continuation, especially since the reader's suspense as to the ending is satisfied by the narrator's brief hints. It does not seem unlikely, therefore, that Chaucer really intended a dramatic interruption which would leave the tale half-told, as he did in the case of the 'Monk's Tale' and his own tale of Sir Thopas. The 'Squire's Tale' is all but complete in that it adequately characterizes the teller and the narrative situation and, at the same time, presents all the important elements of a particular type of romance.

The first part of the tale is designed to meet the listeners' traditional expectations of surprising incidents and exotic places and almost seems like a parodic imitation of *Sir Gawain and the Green Knight*,[12] whereas the second part presents a stylized account of a courtly love-tragedy in the guise of an animal fable, which surely prevents us from taking it as seriously as its rhetorical pathos seems to demand. A glance at *The Parliament of Fowls*, or, still more obviously, the 'Nun's Priest's Tale', shows that this kind of literary disguise is hardly possible without some comic intention, even though the narrator may not be fully conscious of it. The lady's complaint, lamenting her betrayal by a lover, shows her to be in the same situation as the deserted Troilus, but her vehement accusations recall, at the same time, the less gentle possessiveness of the Wife of Bath and are not in perfect harmony with the conventional ideal of a courtly beloved. The lover's complaint hardly transcends the elegant but empty formulas, because the slightly absurd artificiality of the situation and the hysterical excitement of the bird–lady rather weaken the tragic impact and make us conscious of the story's deliberate conventionality. The narrator's idea of courtly love appears only to go as far as its superficial symptoms, and there is no suggestion of genuine partnership or the kind of total personal commitment that is characteristic of courtly love in its deeper sense. The faithless hawk remains a rather shadowy figure; one need not go so far as to sympathize with him,[13] yet the reader will scarcely endorse the formel's wholesale condemnation uncritically, nor will he believe that the lover's intentions were evil from the very first. The lady's version of past events seems to be dictated more by her present indignation than by reliable truthfulness.

As in some other of Chaucer's poems, we find here some indirect quotation from Boethius, without, however, the philosopher's superior insight and wisdom. The impulse of all animated creatures to follow their inborn natures and to break out of their artificial cage is here misrepresented as a culpable desire for diversion and novelty.[14] This almost looks like an involuntary admission on the part of the lady that her lover felt his devotion to be a kind of imprisonment and that his escape really sprang from a natural longing for a freer existence. But even a less critical reader who fails to recognize the Boethian implications will notice that the comparison of the lover to a caged bird does not quite fit in with the reproachful complaint of the lady and that its tone rather contradicts the attitude of betrayed innocence. There is no sufficiently moving human situation to correspond to the passionate lamentation, but a slightly comic disproportion between convention and reality – a disproportion we will not find, for instance, in *The Book of the Duchess*, certainly not with the same deflating effect.

The narrator, however, does not seem to be aware of this less serious aspect of his tale, and he promises a happy ending, with the repentant return of the faithless lover. There are other points in the story where it is suggested that there are limits to the narrator's insight and that he often makes rather indiscriminate and uncritical use of the conventions he so much admires. Still, it would be a mistake and an anachronism to confuse this subtle form of characterization with deliberate satirical parody or to make a rigorous distinction between poet and narrator. There is no really consistent characterization of the narrator as a naive young man throughout the whole tale, and I do not think that in this case we are encouraged to read it as the dramatic monologue of a sharply drawn individual. If we are all the time conscious of the Squire as one who aspires to the highest form of courtly knighthood, this is not meant to detract our attention from the tale itself. Its peculiar charm lies in the never quite defined or resolved tension between the rhetorical bravura and the much less sophisticated subject-matter. Chaucer is not concerned here with pointed mockery of courtly conventions, but rather with a review of different traditions and possibilities of courtly narrative. The enchanting fantasy is not discredited by the subdued suggestions of comedy, and the tale remains, in spite of its immaturity, a brilliant and attractive demonstration of the irresistible glamour of courtly romance.

The Franklin's reaction to the Squire's performance shows that one listener at least is sincerely impressed by the surface splendour of the story. His wistful comparison of this young representative of the courtly world with his own son is surely not meant in an ironical sense; it rather suggests that for the Franklin, too, himself outside the courtly circle, there is no material difference between its superficial conventions and their ethical and religious basis. For him, at any rate, the Squire's youthful idealism is full of promise, and he seems a little too easily impressed by a form of life from which he feels himself and his son excluded.[15]

His own contribution to the storytelling contest is another specimen of romance narrative, and here again we have a subtle combination of a fascinating literary masterpiece and the impression of the narrator's limitations; as with the 'Squire's Tale', many readers will be a little uneasy or doubtful in places where the Franklin himself obviously does not recognize any problem at all. The splendour of an exotic fairy-tale world is contrasted with a rather simple morality whose underlying idealism seems hardly less naive. Again there is an ambiguous discrepancy between courtly conventions and real experience; it extends, however, to the substance of conventional notions of value, probing much deeper than the Squire's demonstration of accomplished rhetoric. Like the Squire, the Franklin aims at an ideal of courtly style and behaviour, but, by contrast to the young knight-to-be, he is himself excluded from this world by his social standing and his whole mentality. This is made fairly clear by the curious juxtaposition of courtly terminology and a somewhat simple-minded use of it. This teasing discrepancy is ignored by those critics who see in the Franklin's attitude Chaucer's own solution for all the marriage problems raised by the preceding stories. The idea of a 'marriage group' as a coherent debate in the form of narrative contributions within *The Canterbury Tales*, brought to a satisfactory conclusion by the Franklin, is, in my view, the product of a kind of literary criticism eager to impose neat patterns and has little to do with the experience of an unbiased reader, who will certainly keep discovering new thematical connections and interrelations with every fresh reading, but will hardly come away with the impression of a debate that could be described as systematic or even clearly structured.[16] There is even less in the text to suggest that the Franklin is meant to be anything like the poet's mouthpiece, even though there are some characteristic attitudes the two narrators have in common, such as their somewhat humorous modesty and the evident desire to reconcile extreme positions. Many readers will associate these with Chaucer himself, and they recur in the Franklin's performance; it is surely not quite wrong to discover an element of peace-offering in it, after some of the earlier skirmishes and more antagonistic extremes presented by the Wife of Bath, the Clerk or the Merchant.

Looking at the tale's narrative style, it seems hardly practicable, or indeed profitable, to draw a clear line between Chaucer and his Franklin. The introductory professions of incompetence and inadequate rhetorical training are constantly belied by the highly decorative style, but this is a comic effect by no means confined to this story and it tells us much more about Chaucer than about this particular narrator. Thus the playful use of established narrative formulas which we find from time to time, and which give the tale its unmistakable Chaucerian tone, is not so much a subtle means of individual characterization as an instance of Chaucer's own stylistic virtuosity, although, at the same time, they fit in very well with the Franklin's not always quite successful endeavours to achieve an appropriate courtly idiom.

The narrator's mentality emerges more clearly if we look at the tale's moral programme. His glorification of marriage as an ideal partnership which includes all the virtues and joys of a courtly love-union and in which each partner is at the same time master and servant sounds, after the extreme positions illustrated by earlier tales, like the very solution we have instinctively hoped for, and many critics have understood it as such. But the elegant reconciliation of all contradictions, celebrated in elaborate rhetorical paradoxes, sounds a little too glib to do justice to the complexity of the problems under discussion, and it has rightly been questioned whether the elimination of 'maistrye' from the concept of marriage would really have been so easily compatible with medieval convictions about the relative positions of husband and wife, however convincing it may appear to the modern reader.[17] But, even apart from this consideration, the somewhat theoretical and sophistic neatness of the definition is all too obvious, and its realization on this earth hardly seems a real possibility; this is why, like all pat solutions, it is not particularly helpful in practice. It is difficult to avoid the impression that the following story demonstrates, if anything, the impracticability of such a concept of marriage free from all conflict, not its simple attainability, as obviously intended by the Franklin. This is not so much a question of criticizing the individual characters as of the slightly absurd nature of some of the situations described.

The whole design of the tale suggests that the actors themselves are less important than the test-situations in which they are placed by the story; it would not be very relevant for instance, to blame Arveragus for leaving his wife on her own for two years, or to blame her for parting with her thoughtless promise in a momentary outburst of despair and pity. The story makes it psychologically plausible enough that the rocks for her become an image of all that threatens to jeopardize her happiness, and her rash promise is not altogether improbable. The real purpose of this introductory part of the story, however, is to create the agonizing dilemma to which the lady is brought by the actual fulfilment of her seemingly impossible condition. It is a situation that seems equally appropriate for a fabliau or for a romance. The lover who speaks almost like a blackmailer is obviously not concerned with disinterested love-service or the lady's happiness, but with plain sexual gratification; this is the only possible explanation for his, in spite of all verbal modesty, brutal and heartless demand. The potentially comic aspects of the situation – a person cornered by her own rash promise – soften the tragedy of her dilemma and add a slightly playful note. This is not simply a conflict between two incompatible concepts of love – the truth and integrity of Christian marriage and the obligations of courtly love-service – because the emotions exhibited by Aurelius are symptoms of a rather superficial form of *fin amour*, reduced to empty conventions. His desperate attempt to defeat the laws of nature by means of deceiving magic helps to make the situation somewhat unreal. The dilemma is an artificially contrived one and Dorigen's despair must appear a little like a pose, although there can be no doubt as to her personal sincerity.

The rhetoric of her lament also seems to be in excess of the real issues involved, and this prevents the reader from any too personal commitment.[18] Dorigen is no tragic Lucretia who chooses death rather than shame. The idea of heroic suicide remains an abstract, almost formulaic, thought without any serious threat; the reader is not really made to fear for her life, and this keeps alive our confident hope for a happy outcome. The narrator himself is anxious to encourage such confidence: in one of the few passages where he tries to anticipate possible objections by the reader, he reminds us that we have to await the conclusion before we are in a position to pass judgement on the characters in the story:

> Paraventure an heep of yow, ywis,
> Wol holden hym a lewed man in this
> That he wol putte his wyf in jupartie.
> Herkneth the tale er ye upon hire crie.
> She may have bettre fortune than yow semeth;
> And whan that ye han herd the tale, demeth. (v.1493–8)

At first, this looks like an ironic excuse which only very simple readers will take seriously. Arveragus' actions are not made any more honourable by the reflection that some surprising turn of events, certainly not reckoned with by him, may suddenly resolve her dilemma and put her out of her misery. His act of selfless loyalty would be completely invalidated if he were not genuinely convinced that Dorigen would become Aurelius' mistress. Thus we may easily get the impression that, for all his apparent integrity, he violates the principle of conjugal faith by asking his wife to commit adultery. The modern reader, at any rate, will not have the faintest doubt that the obligation to honour an absurd promise, given half in jest and in a moment of despair, is clearly overruled by the circumstances of the story and by the priority of the marriage bond, and it is difficult to believe that Chaucer's contemporaries should have thought very differently in the matter. The Franklin's inserted comment, quoted above, suggests that the situation may have given rise to such doubts from the beginning.[19]

It is obvious, though, that the narrator wants to present Arveragus' decision as exemplary, and he is partly justified by the clearly unrealistic character of the story, which is in many ways more akin to a parable than to a psychologically consistent narrative. Its logic is rather like that of the

Old Testament account of Abraham and Isaac: Abraham's unquestioning obedience is put to the test, proved and rewarded even though the strict observance of the divine command would have meant killing his own child. The happy outcome is by no means to be counted on from the beginning, but nevertheless justifies, in retrospect, the exemplary reaction of Abraham, who was seriously prepared to sacrifice his own son to the divine will. Similarly, Arveragus, according to the premises of the story, acts quite correctly by choosing the more difficult path and by refusing to resolve the moral dilemma with a simple sophism. He is proved right by the course of the action because his ungrudging demonstration of human loyalty and generous integrity produces two further acts of 'gentillesse' and thus sets off a veritable competition of disinterested magnanimity.

It seems evident, however, that at this point the story allows for divergent responses; the great number of readers who have understood the 'Franklin's Tale' as an example of truly perfect human behaviour proves that there is no question of unambiguous subversive irony or superior scorn for the naive Franklin. It is, on the other hand, quite possible to discover, behind the stylized polish and detachment of the tale, the gentle scepticism of the poet who does not entirely share the narrator's confidence in such a neat solution. The Franklin evidently wants to make a point of demonstrating that true 'gentillesse' is not the privilege of one particular estate, but is within reach of any man who is willing to act according to its principles; it is clear, at the same time, that the narrator has but a faint idea of the complexity of the problems he has raised, and his optimistic conviction that an act of exemplary generosity must immediately inspire others to the same kind of moral conduct will not necessarily communicate itself to every reader. Nevertheless, within the context of *The Canterbury Tales* the Franklin's story is an original and positive attempt to present a synthesis of simple morality and courtly sophistication, of matrimonial loyalty and the conventions of *fin amour*; nor is the reader encouraged to sneer at the narrator, even though he recognizes his limitations.

As far as the range and the depth of its themes are concerned the 'Franklin's Tale' goes much beyond the superficial glamour of the Squire's performance. As in the 'Knight's Tale' the lovers' suffering gives rise to philosophical reflections that are very close to Boethius. For Dorigen, the threatening cliffs are reason enough to question the harmony of God's creation; like Boethius before her, she wants to know the meaning and purpose of a universe that includes such destructive elements, of no use to anyone. She knows well enough that orthodox theology provides explanations that assign even to evil and misery a meaningful place within the harmonious system of creation. Boethius adduces a number of traditional arguments to this effect – but they do not alleviate her helpless despair. For Aurelius, too, the rocks present a threat to personal happiness, and his long prayer to the heathen god Apollo is another expression of an all too human desire for a simple transformation of the created world, a magical elimination of all obstacles to the gratification of human wishes. The help he receives from the magician, in consequence, turns out to be of the same quality as the illusory vision of an ideal landscape provided for his entertainment before dinner. Both Dorigen and Aurelius only take their dilemma as proof of the world's imperfection, not as an occasion for reflecting on their own obligations. Their elaborate soliloquies occupy a central position within the structure of the whole story and they make clear that Chaucer was anxious to invest the tale with a depth of moral and philosophical insight that contradicts an ironic interpretation. Even though we may not find the solution offered quite adequate, there is no doubt that the sincerity and the intensity of the effort to find a satisfactory answer provides a pointed contrast to the romances of the Squire and the Wife of Bath or to the more cynical treatment of the marriage question by the Merchant. When earlier critics kept associating the Franklin with Chaucer himself – an idea which would be quite absurd in the case of most of the other narrators – they did at least realize the profound seriousness of the tale, even though they may have failed to recognize its complexities and ambiguities of tone. The whole story, especially its conclusion, which almost reminds us of a prize question, is an invitation to the reader to think about the premisses of courtly love-poetry from a fresh point of view and to see its problematic character in the light of the Christian concept of marriage.

This concentration on an almost casuistically constructed problem links the 'Franklin's Tale' with the genre of the French lay, very aptly described by Leo Spitzer as 'Problem-Märchen'.[20] In many of them there is, at the centre, a carefully contrived situation confronting one or more characters with a specific problem, usually connected with a particular point of courtly love. In other respects, however, Chaucer's poem is quite different from the usually much shorter and more concise lays of Marie de France, and it does not become quite clear where the relevance of the long introduction, with the careful description of the Breton lays, is supposed to lie. It is worth noting, however, that there are quite a number of narrative poems from about the same period that call themselves lays; the term obviously implied a distinct quality and perhaps authority, although it is difficult to define what all these poems have in common. It is possible that for Chaucer's audience the word 'lay' was associated with a slightly old-fashioned patina and that thus the moral of the story, too, would have the aura of an idealized picture of times long past.

Although the Franklin's story is concerned with moral and aristocratic values different from those treated in the 'Knight's Tale' and seems to be much less class-conscious in its ethical assumptions, the two tales have this in common that they both use the conventions of medieval romance as vehicles of a debate on moral and philosophical issues – not in terms of an uncritical presentation of exemplary ways of conduct, but as a provocative dramatization of situations designed to invite sceptical questioning. Some of the basic principles behind many of the traditional courtly narratives are subjected to critical scrutiny more radically than in most of the Middle English romances before Chaucer.

The tale of the Wife of Bath, similarly, begins as a romance explicitly associated with the world of King Arthur and his knights, but ends as a 'Problem-Märchen', though in a more burlesque and less philosophical manner. Here, too, fundamental moral and social issues are raised and most skilfully integrated in the plot, though at the same time the whole tone of the story as well as the situation of the characters involved prevents the reader from taking them too seriously.

Right at the beginning, the world inhabited by King Arthur and his knights is, by a lighthearted satirical gesture, removed into the faraway distance of a fairy-tale past, exempt from the harsh laws of the present, and in consequence the dilemma of the condemned knight does not touch us as nearly as the suffering of Palamon and Arcite or even, perhaps, the grief of the forsaken formel in the 'Squire's Tale'. In tone and spirit, though not in every detail, the tale is made quite consistent with the character of the speaker, for whom all the conventions of courtly romance are clearly subordinated to the one question that is really relevant to her, the predominance of women in marriage.[21] The farcical elements of the story show how closely this kind of romance can approach those tales we would generally count among the fabliaux. At the same time, however, the extensive curtain lecture to which the poor knight is treated, teaching the moral irrelevance of traditional class distinctions, is a piece of serious moral instruction whose substance is in no way devalued by the slightly comic situation, though it ends in two not very courtly alternatives put before the knight – lovely but unfaithful or ugly and loyal: a choice which the knight, in a state of perplexity we can well sympathize with, hands back to the old woman. Whether we can still call the tale a romance, is, in the last resort, an academic question. It is more illuminating to watch Chaucer experimenting once again with a comparatively well-defined narrative genre, twisting it into a highly original shape and adapting it to a particular thematic and dramatic purpose. The same applies, though in varying degrees, to the comic as well as to the didactic types of narrative.

When, after the Knight's performance, the order of tales proposed by the Host is rudely upset by the drunken Miller's boisterous interruption, we are being treated not just to an amusing episode within the frame-story, but to a particularly original form of linking stories and preparing us for what is to follow. It is made quite clear that the 'Miller's Tale' is introduced as a direct response to the romance of Palamon and Arcite, of which the Miller has evidently grasped not much more than a rough outline of the plot and the idealizing tone, not at all congenial to him. The sharp contrast in style and moral outlook is further underlined by another authorial apology (1.3171–82, quoted above); by refusing to accept any responsibility for possible offences against the reader's ideas of good taste and decorum the narrator effectively anticipates and answers our possible objections without really heeding them. The tale about to begin is classed unmistakably as that of a 'cherl', and this categorical classification is much more important for its general effect than a more detailed and altogether consistent correspondence between narrator and tale, which, on the level of psychological credibility, would be very hard to demonstrate. It is easy enough to see that the 'Miller's Tale' gives evidence of a stylistic virtuosity and a familiarity with literary traditions far beyond the scope of a drunken churl. After his noisy intrusion we would expect a rather more boorish performance, but this does not really affect the impression that the fundamental contrast between the Knight and the Miller is reflected in their tales. Romance and fabliau are directly juxtaposed in a way quite unprecedented in Middle English literature.

On closer inspection, though, the parallels between the two tales are almost more striking than the differences so obvious to every reader. It is above all on the level of style that the similarities are conspicuous enough to invite repeated comparison. Decorative rhetoric, familiarity with classical myths and a particularly flexible use of the rhyming couplet are common to both poems. Both begin, though with characteristic differences, with the typical formula of the popular entertainer, 'Whilom, ... ther was...', and both are about the rivalry in love of two young men for the same lady, ending in a Salomonic solution.[22] To be sure, the tale of the Knight leads up to a happy marriage while the 'Miller's Tale' centres round the classic fabliau situation of the old husband whose young and beautiful wife really represents a silently eloquent invitation to cuckold him. The learned allusion to Cato, whose sage advice recommending parity (of age, in this case) in husband and wife the carpenter has failed to follow, only makes the comedy more obvious and, at the same time, more sophisticated. Classical wisdom, perfectly appropriate in the context of a romance, seems ridiculously out of place here and draws our attention to the stylistic incongruities of the story.

Beyond that, it is perhaps not very profitable to pursue the parallels in greater detail. They remain largely within the area of veiled associations and do not combine to make up a consistent and continuous parody. It is, however, striking to note how the two narrators, according to their very different lights, lard their stories with general reflections, sometimes surprisingly similar in content. Thus the Miller, even in his prologue, takes up the problem of the unfathomable ways of divine providence which plays such an important part in the 'Knight's Tale'. What there is accepted, with philosophical resignation, as man's inborn helplessness and ignorance, here becomes the subject of humorous instruction, extending to the most private sphere:

> An housbonde shal nat been inquisityf
> Of Goddes pryvetee, nor of his wyf.
> So he may fynde Goddes foyson there,
> Of the remenant nedeth nat enquere. (1.3163–6)

Later, in the course of the narrative, the theme is taken up again:

> Men sholde nat knowe of Goddes pryvetee. (1.3454)[23]

There are several other places in the 'Miller's Tale' where the plot gives rise to general reflections; although they are, as a rule, much briefer and more superficial than those in the 'Knight's Tale', they are still a little unusual in a comic tale of this kind and go to show that Chaucer deliberately takes a very close look at the moral and philosophical implications of the fabliau, thus bringing it much closer to the romance.[24] The idea, expressed very often in medieval literature and theology, that any aspect of reality is potentially rich in instruction and edification for those able to see and to read is constantly illustrated by the diversity of scenes presented in *The Canterbury Tales*.

The Miller's performance hardly confirms the view, once generally accepted, that the fabliau was a kind of bourgeois and realistic counterpart to the idealizing romance.[25] It is basically not much less 'courtly' than the tale of the Knight – at least in the sense that it draws on conventional concepts of courtly poetry, though in most cases comically distorted, and is evidently meant to appeal to the same audience. The much-quoted description of Alison is a particularly striking example. Its

wording unmistakably suggests the traditional praise of female beauty,
and at first sight there seems little to distinguish it from the portrait of any
courtly lady. There are, however, subtle modifications of the conventional vocabulary, and the lady's attractions are held up to our view in a
much more tangible manner than is usual within the conventions of
amour courtois. This may well produce a certain amount of confusion in
the reader who compares the solid and alluring charms of Alison with the
ideal, much less concrete virtues of Emily and begins to realize how
differently the same subject can be presented by slight shifts of emphasis
and tone of voice. The comic effect of the description obviously has to do
with the way the conventions of stylized description are applied to a
person and within a context where the reader does not expect them, so
that there is a provocative discrepancy between the elaborate rhetoric
and its rather down-to-earth subject. There are many other places where
Chaucer achieves such comical surprises by the use of courtly terminology for unexpected purposes.[26]

The most glaring contrast between courtly love-conventions and the
world of the fabliau comes out in the behaviour of the two lovers. While
Absolon tries to impress the lady by a comically elaborate aping of
courtly love-service and wooing, Nicholas takes the initiative without
ado and knows from the start what he really wants. His very first advance
is in flagrant contrast to any form of love imaginable, for instance, in the
romance told by the Knight:

> so bifel the cas,
> That on a day this hende Nicholas
> Fil with this yonge wyf to rage and pleye,
> Whil that hir housbonde was at Oseneye,
> As clerkes ben ful subtile and ful queynte;
> And prively he caughte hire by the queynte,
> And seyde, 'Ywis, but if ich have my wille,
> For deerne love of thee, lemman, I spille.'
> And heeld hire harde by the haunchebones. (1.3271–9)

It would be wrong to see all this as an unambiguous mockery of courtly
ideas of love; by presenting these two diametrically opposed tales side by
side, however, the poet evidently wants to demonstrate contrasting
attitudes towards traditional forms and ideas. Each of them represents
only a section of reality, clearly limited by the stylistic level chosen by the
narrator.

Nor would it be appropriate to talk about Chaucer's realism in this
connection (at least not in the modern sense), since it would be rather too
simple to assume that the tale of the Miller gives us a truer picture of life
in the Middle Ages than the romance of Palamon and Arcite. What really

happens is that idealizing romance is confronted with a mode one might describe as negative idealization; rhetorical worship of the beloved is countered by a farcical and short-lived dream of a world in which the woman is little more than a delightful delicacy to be conquered by cunning and where it is the resourceful adventurer who is most likely to win the prize. Absolon looks at Alison with the eyes of a hungry beast of prey:

> To looke on hire hym thoughte a myrie lyf,
> She was so propre and sweete and likerous.
> I dar wel seyn, if she hadde been a mous,
> And he a cat, he wolde hire hente anon. (1.3344–7)

This is hardly more 'realistic' than the courtly ideal of the inaccessible lady to be won only by patient and disinterested service, and the whole sequence of farcical situations, from the hilarious gullibility of the carpenter to the grotesque chastisement of the all too confident Nicholas, is not in any way more 'probable' than its courtly counterpart. It is by no means a celebration of natural instincts, as some modern interpreters will have it, or a positive alternative to more abstract concepts of love, but rather an unrestrained and exuberant reversal of all the clichés of elevated love-poetry. Nicholas, the learned bookworm, is anything but a representative of the lower orders: his theoretical studies have made him an expert in matters of love ('Of deerne love he koude and of solas', 1.3200). His straightforward suit is therefore in no way an expression of an artless attachment, but only the conscious application of superior intelligence and practical knowledge for the sole purpose of easy pleasure without any obligation.

It is true, of course, that this picture of a world reduced to crude sensuality and selfish cunning does indeed create, on the part of the reader, an illusion of concrete reality. It is achieved, above all, by the precise details of observed everyday life. This does not turn the actors into credibly individualized characters, but we do get a sense of watching a more familiar world, a world that does not demand abstract reflection but only an immediate human fellow-feeling, made easier by the precise localization of the action in the midst of Chaucer's England.[27]

The description of Nicholas' feigned ecstasy and his landlord's consternation is a good example of this particular kind of realism. The brief scene gives us a lively sketch of a simple household where a hole in the door has been provided to let in the cat and also turns out to be handy for spying, and where you smash in the door, if need be, to rush to your tenant's help. At the same time, the reflections of the carpenter recall the theme of the 'Knight's Tale' and again raise, with comic urgency, the problem of the true object and use of all science, and of astrology in particular. The unsuspecting carpenter finds confirmation for his prejudiced opinion that nothing good can come from such intensive study of abstract matters. The reader knows full well, however, that what Nicholas really has in mind is a much more concrete scheme and that it is the carpenter's blind faith in a science beyond his grasp, more than anything else, that will be his undoing.

Other details, too, such as the strong drink procured by the bewildered carpenter, contribute to the 'realistic' character of the scene, strengthening the impression that the narrative is founded on close observation of ordinary life – without, however, engaging too much of our sympathy on behalf of the actors. On the contrary, the highly stylized and rather more abstract romance of the Knight appeals much more intensely to the reader's emotions and conveys a far more differentiated idea of mental processes. In the fabliau, even in Chaucer's sophisticated and rhetorically elaborate form, what really matters are the amusing twists of the plot, the comedy of the situations, the pattern of deft outwitting and retaliation. Thus, for instance, we need no Freudian analysis to see the drastic justice of the individual punishments; and any interpretation which investigates the numerous allusions to courtly and religious conventions and forms of instruction too seriously is in danger of ignoring Chaucer's warning that 'eek men shal nat maken ernest of game' (1.3186).

Finally, the contrast to the 'Knight's Tale' is again brought home to us by the reaction of the pilgrims. Unlike the prudish reader warned off by the poet at the outset, they obviously see no reason to take exception to the drastic tale, whose only aim is to provide uninhibited entertainment; and, although the audience's approval does not seem to be completely unanimous, the prevailing attitude is good humour and laughter. We should never forget, therefore, when discussing the tale's subtleties, that it is deliberately more light-weight than the Knight's contribution and meant to meet the Host's demand for 'solaas' rather than 'sentence'.[28] For all its technical and rhetorical finesse it remains within the narrower range of 'harlotrie' (1.3184). At the same time, it is sufficiently pointed and suggestive to make its impact on our attitude towards the more serious tales.

It is an essential feature of the burlesque tale and its presentation in a sociable context that it provokes rejoinder and the wish to go one better. The comically boisterous and at the same time personal nature of the 'Miller's Tale' is thus even further emphasized by the fact that the Reeve, himself a carpenter, takes it as an affront and tries to get his own back by telling a story in which a miller falls victim to an even coarser joke. Again the frame establishes a direct link between the two tales, in this case

bringing out their generic affinity and arousing our expectations. After
the unrestrained merriment produced by the Miller the reader now looks
forward to a retaliation of the same calibre.

The 'Reeve's Tale' seems, at first, to be mainly an attempt to outdo the
Miller in coarseness. Again, a foolish 'cherl' is outwitted by the superior
intelligence of 'clerkes' (this time from the University of Cambridge) and
sheer delight in defeating the crafty scoundrel is the predominant motif.
Sexual pleasure is not gilded over by even the merest pretence of genuine
affection, but remains firmly on the level of a crude joke, with no thought
of any consequences whatever.[29] Whereas in the 'Miller's Tale' the
narrator makes playful use of the clichés of courtly love, there is, in the
Reeve's story, very little rhetorical embellishment to detract from the
coarseness of the plot, and the well-tried comedy turns of mistaken
identities, bed-swapping and cuckolding are presented much more
directly. The Northern dialect – a singular instance of linguistic naturalism in Chaucer – underlines the impression of a narrative art based on
close observation; but, again, this is not so much an artless imitation of
reality as a demonstration of Chaucer's stylistic versatility and consummate rhetorical art.

The deliberately vulgar tone of the story should not be interpreted as
naked cynicism, but is due mainly to the dramatic situation. The tale is
part of an angry dialogue; one 'cherl' seeks to outdo the other, and as a
result we have two stories, both closely related to the fabliau tradition
and yet so different from each other that we do not get the impression of
Chaucer having tried to do the same thing twice over. The fragment of the
'Cook's Tale' seems to suggest that it was precisely this kind of repetition
Chaucer wanted to avoid and that, for this reason, he lost interest in the
further continuation of the comic exchange (always supposing that he did
not, in fact, finish the tale).[30] The other comic tales, too, contributed by
various narrators in the course of the pilgrimage, show Chaucer's evident
preference for variation. None of them is exactly like the other as far as
narrative genre is concerned, and this is perhaps the most striking
difference between *The Canterbury Tales* and Boccaccio's *Decameron*
with its hundred practically uniform novellas.

The 'Shipman's Tale' comes, perhaps, nearest to the type of the
original fabliau. Here we have neither a great deal of rhetorical amplification nor a marked preponderance of realistic detail. The interest of the
reader is concentrated mainly on the plot, which turns round a witty
equation of different modes of payment at the disposal of the rich
merchant and his liberal wife – liberal, that is, in her favours – and
culminates in the unashamed pun on 'taillynge'. There is much to be said
for the assumption that the story was originally meant for the Wife of

Bath; the present 'Wife of Bath's Tale' is evidently better suited to her spirited plea for female rule; nevertheless, the whole tone of the 'Shipman's Tale' is in conspicuous harmony with the first part of the 'Wife of Bath's Prologue', with its brilliant apology for the gifts and weapons given by nature to the Wife's sex. The Shipman, on the other hand, remains a rather shadowy character in the 'General Prologue' as well as in the links.[31]

The story told by the Merchant, almost unbearably cynical at a first reading, is a rather more complex performance. Here, Chaucer departed from the traditional fabliau more radically than in all the other comic tales, not only by rhetorical amplification and borrowings from other genres, but by a more provocative and disturbing use of ironies and such a pyrotechnic display of ambiguous literary allusions that the reader may well feel, at first, that no authorial guidance can be relied on; any glib interpretation seems hopelessly inadequate.[32]

Here, again, theme and tone are prepared for within the frame: by his self-pitying complaint about his own marital martyrdom, the Merchant not only reveals that he has completely misunderstood the Clerk's tale; he also, unintentionally, introduces himself as the traditionally comic figure of the hen-pecked husband, and this places him unmistakably with the 'lower' characters among the pilgrims – characters whose authority in moral and spiritual matters is not to be taken too seriously – although his story makes rather higher demands on the reader's mental cooperation than the other fabliaux in the collection. Again, however, there is no question of a detailed correspondence between the character of the narrator as portrayed in the 'General Prologue' and the links, and in the tale itself; rather, the tale's theme and spirited tone are intensified by the dramatic preparation, and the obvious bias of the narrator, whose embittered disillusionment seems to colour much of his narrative, makes for additional irony.

This is most evident in the long passage in praise of marriage, inserted right at the beginning of the tale (IV.1267–1392). At first sight it seems to be the narrator's derisive comment on the deluded old man, a rhetorical disgression inspired by the subject and the Merchant's emotional involvement. On the other hand, the passage appears to be such a close account of Januarie's foolish illusions that we could almost read it as an interior monologue.[33] As not infrequently in Chaucer's narrative poetry, it is not really possible to make out the speaker with absolute certainty, although there is nothing vague or imprecise about this diatribe. The confusion of the two so very different actors by means of this grammatical ambiguity rather emphasizes the merciless irony of the enthusiastic encomium on the blessings of marriage, which in another context might well have to be taken seriously as an example of sincere didacticism; here, however, our suspicions are aroused by the fabliau situation sketched right at the outset and by the bitter experience of the Merchant. The disillusioned cynicism of the Merchant and the old knight's blind folly are present in the passage side by side, and we can no longer make a clear distinction between the two victims in our minds.

To be sure, the irony is laid on rather thick in places and the Merchant's real attitude shines through the dazzling ironies when, for instance, the wife is viciously contrasted with other, more transient goods:

> A wyf wol laste, and in thyn hous endure,
> Wel lenger than thee list, paraventure. (IV.1317–18)

Here, we are obviously not listening to the deluded fantasies of the old knight, but to a mocking aside of the narrator. Less direct, and yet not in doubt when seen in the light of the fabliau convention and traditional anti-feminist satire, is the barbed scorn expressed in the following lines:

> A wyf! a, Seinte Marie, *benedicite!*
> How myghte a man han any adversitee
> That hath a wyf? Certes, I kan nat seye.
> The blisse which that is bitwixe hem tweye
> Ther may no tonge telle, or herte thynke.
> If he be povre, she helpeth hym to swynke;
> She kepeth his good, and wasteth never a deel;
> Al that hire housbonde lust, hire liketh weel;
> She seith nat ones 'nay,' whan he seith 'ye'.
> 'Do this,' seith he; 'Al redy, sire,' seith she. (IV.1337–46)

Here, again, the context is enough to invest this otherwise innocuous passage with rich irony.

From the beginning of the tale, two very different and normally quite incompatible modes of discourse are juxtaposed. From a burlesque tale, such as the opening seems to promise, we do not expect a serious discussion of the problems of Christian marriage; on the other hand, the reader is bound to be puzzled when, side by side with the beautiful theory, he is pointedly confronted with a totally different reality – a contradiction first articulated in the Merchant's reproachful comparison between Griseldis and his own wife. Such provocative juxtaposition of contradictory stylistic and moral attitudes is typical of the whole tale and has led critics to deny that there is an artistic unity.[34] This is only to say, however, that Chaucer's idea of unity is different from that of many modern readers; it is the very coexistence of discrepant forms of expression that constitutes the tale's unity (if we must speak of unity).

The long rhetorical digression serves not only as an ironic commentary, but also as an extension of the story's thematic and intellectual scope. By bringing in the whole range of problems traditionally associated with marriage, the poet invests the simple farce with a depth of meaning quite alien to it, and this teases the reader into discovering all sorts of unexpected associations and connections between the tales.

Thus, right at the beginning, marriage is described as an earthly paradise (1265) and its institution by God Himself in the Garden of Eden is emphasized (1325–9); the wife is her husband's 'paradys terrestre' (1332). This repeated reminder of the Christian ideal of the marriage union is not simply invalidated by the farcical reality described in the fabliau; it suggests an ethical standard which the reader is encouraged to keep in mind and by which he will unconsciously assess the characters even while he is laughing at them. When, in the second half of the story, the old knight makes the absurd and (for him) disastrous attempt to create for himself a literal replica of the original Garden of Eden, a discrepancy of which we have already been made conscious by the poem's imagery is translated into concrete action.

The theoretical debate about the blessings and the dangers of marriage is taken further in the dispute between Placebo and Justinus, the basic idea of which Chaucer probably took from Deschamps' *Miroir de Mariage*. Its meaning is enriched and complicated by the context because it is placed in direct relation to the character of the old knight, obsessed by his blind desire, whose reaction to all the learned counsel only shows again how completely besotted he is.[35] It is a comic version of the traditional morality situation in which a man is placed between the good and the bad counsellor and fails to recognize which of the two has his best interests at heart. The names of the counsellors alone make clear that they are not presented as individualized characters, but as static personifications of contrary points of view, which unexpectedly brings another literary genre into direct relation with the farce. While Placebo, the flatterer, only repeats the illusions the knight deceives himself with and wants to hear confirmed, Justinus is the warning spokesman of clear-sighted experience and traditional satire on marriage, whose authority is even strengthened by the fact that he preaches to deaf ears. Since the knight's decision is fixed from the outset and he has no intention of being influenced by any adverse counsel, there is no chance of a real debate and the scene never gets beyond a declamatory repetition of well-tried arguments; these do not, however, remain merely theoretical, but are soon to be measured against the knight's own experience.

After such extensive preparation there can be little doubt about the old suitor's real motives: the traditional commonplaces of the Christian marriage-debate are only a decorative accompaniment to what this marriage in fact means to him: the legally sanctioned, permanent availability of the young wife as an object of sexual pleasure. This is made explicit enough by the metaphors of the gourmet:

> She shal nat passe twenty yeer, certayn;
> Oold fissh and yong flessh wolde I have ful fayn.
> Bet is,' quod he, 'a pyk than a pykerel,
> And bet than old boef is the tendre veel.
> I wol no womman thritty yeer of age;
> It is but bene-straw and greet forage. (IV.1417–22)

The description of the wedding, too, shows very clearly, that he views May as a possession; she is turned into his property with all due form and there is never any question of a genuine love-relationship, let alone partnership.[36]

As the old knight himself keeps harping on the great disparity in age the reader is repeatedly prepared for the almost inevitable consequences of the familiar fabliau situation. At the same time, the poet, by the allegorical names of the two main characters, suggests a wealth of wider associations to which no learned commentary can really do justice. Januarie is not just the ridiculous sexagenarian and potential cuckold of the traditional burlesque, but in his union with May we see something of the perennial incompatibility of old age and youth, mirrored in the periodic succession of the seasons, which are represented in irreconcilable conflict in folklore as well as in literature. Januarie and May are two timeless aspects of created life, in permanent opposition to each other, not just two actors in a frivolous anecdote. There is no end to the surprising interpretations suggested by this seemingly unpretentious comic entertainment.[37]

This inexhaustible wealth of thematic and literary associations is the 'Merchant's Tale''s most original feature and more important for its effect on the reader than any precise point of view we might extract from it. The brilliant and light-hearted virtuosity with which the most disparate conventions are playfully taken up and dropped again effectively works against the apparent cynicism of this picture of marriage and prevents the satire from becoming too venomous. This could be supported with reference to almost any part of the tale; to pick out three particularly successful instances, I mention the description of courtly love, the garden motif and the introduction of classical deities. They almost seem to weigh down the modest farce with an excess of learned reference, and they show how consistently Chaucer's rhetoric can turn even the most trivial subject into an exhilarating display of stylistic bravura and provocative didacticism.

Little as farce agrees with theoretical debate, there seems to be even less room in it for courtly idealization of woman. The burlesque drama of adultery works on the assumption that love is nothing but the desire for sexual satisfaction without any moral or psychological consequences. Thus it must come as a surprise to the reader when the knight's young squire suddenly shows all the symptoms of genuine love-longing and the narrator begins to make use of a vocabulary from a completely different literary sphere from that of the farcical situation in hand. It is a technique similar to that used in the 'Miller's Tale', but the discrepancy between the display of high rhetoric and the undignified events, between unblinkered realism and idealizing theory, is even more glaring. Thus the narrator on the one hand gives very precise and not exactly edifying details, such as the knight's repulsively pathetic behaviour during the wedding-night or the tearing of the love-letter in the only place May is still allowed to visit on her own; on the other hand, he praises in hymnic tones the compass- ion of the lady who does not wish her yearning lover to perish:

> Lo, pitee renneth soone in gentil herte! (IV.1986)

It is one of Chaucer's best-known lines, which recurs verbatim three times in his work and only here is given an unmistakably ironic meaning by the context.[38] The traditional idea of the faithful lover being granted the lady's favour out of 'pitee' after long and patient service is turned into a farce because after all that has gone before the reader will gather that May's motives are very different – especially since Damian, too, is evidently only interested in the physical charms of the young wife. It would be too simple, however, to see this only as a parody of courtly conventions and to assume that Chaucer's attitude to the whole concept of *fin amour* was as fiercely critical as the Merchant's.[39] As in many other tales, there is no simple mockery of empty conventions, but rather a deliberate provocation of the reader by the juxtaposition of such diver- gent ideas of love and such divergent stylistic attitudes. Most readers will, however, suspect that such an uninhibited mixture suggests at least a rather detached attitude towards any uncritically accepted and com- placent traditionalism. It is difficult to imagine Chaucer really believing in conventions he ridicules with such evident gusto, even though he engages just enough of our sympathy for the characters to make us feel that it is not all mockery and satire.

Chaucer's use of the garden motif is even more difficult to interpret. The image of the lovely garden protected against intrusions from the outside world had, in the course of the centuries, been invested with such a wealth of moral and spiritual associations by Christian poetry, homi- letic literature and iconography, as well as by courtly love-allegories, that here again our first impression is that of a most original and daring game with learned and popular traditions without the assumption of any unequivocal authorial position.[40] The reader is invited to compare the old knight with Adam and Solomon, to view him simultaneously as the image of impotent lust, as a pathetic lover and as a sinner whom God has struck with blindness. Allusions to the *Roman de la Rose*, the Old Testament and the liturgical tradition of the Song of Songs combine to present a dazzling firework display of variegated suggestions which might well produce a slightly different effect on every individual reader and cannot, at any rate, be adequately described as a parody.[41] Of course, the old knight, in his helpless lechery and impotent jealousy, remains a comic figure; but, however mercilessly his blindness is exposed to our laughter, his story does not appear as an isolated or exceptional anecdote, but includes an element of the hopeless longing for some imperishable possession and eternal youth common to all men. The manifold allusions to religious and secular concepts of paradise will make the reader reflect on the deeper reasons for all these comic contradictions and, perhaps, prevent him from remaining merely an amused and detached spectator of all these burlesque antics.

The conclusion of the tale, with the unexpected divine intervention and its hilarious outcome, leads us firmly back into the realms of farce. Whereas in earlier versions of the story it is God and Saint Peter who watch the knight's humiliation and decide to open his eyes, Chaucer introduces a pair of ancient deities whose well-known pre-history again recalls the motif of the old lecher and cruelly abused youth. The divine marriage turns out to be a mirror of the rivalry between mortal husbands and wives, with the husband getting the worst of it and the resourceful eloquence of the wife triumphing over actual experience and traditional wisdom. This last stroke once more underlines the anti-feminist elements of the story and suggests another extension of the farcical towards the universal. Chaucer's amplifications of the material he found before him thus serve the complex unity of the tale and are not just loosely added digressions. Fabliau, divine miracle and rhetorical debate are combined in a comic finale whose harmonious conclusion stands in ironic contrast to the mental blindness, drastically confirmed, of the knight who has regained his sight. The farce, like the romance in other instances, is but a starting-point for the poet, with which all the other literary modes of expression are placed in surprising relationships, so that the farcical action, with its basically rather narrow scope, eventually embraces all the wide thematic range of *The Canterbury Tales* as a whole, without, however, blurring the characteristic distinctions between the different genres.

The tale contributed (after an amusing skirmish with the drunken Cook and the Host's humorous pacifying) by the Manciple is related to the 'Merchant's Tale' by the theme of cuckoldry, divine miracle and obtrusively inappropriate moralization. In this case, however, the comedy is much more subdued and the didactic digressions are so extensive that it is not altogether easy to decide how seriously we are meant to take them.

The story begins almost exactly like the 'Miller's Tale', and the situation is also strongly reminiscent of the 'Merchant's Tale'. We begin to feel that we are in for another fabliau:

> Now hadde this Phebus in his hous a wyf
> Which that he lovede moore than his lyf,
> And nyght and day dide evere his diligence
> Hir for to plese, and doon hire reverence,
> Save oonly, if the sothe that I shal sayn,
> Jalous he was, and wolde have kept hire fayn.
> For hym were looth byjaped for to be,
> And so is every wight in swich degree;
> But al in ydel, for it availleth noght. (IX.139–47)

It hardly comes as a surprise after this introduction that Phoebus, for all his 'gentillesse' and 'worthynesse' (IX.123–4) is, by the laws of the genre, destined to have an unpleasant shock, but the fabliau situation is not exploited for comic effect: the husband's revenge is swift and deadly, and if there is comedy, it is in the wrath and superficial remorse aroused by the tell-tale bird and in its punishment, a comic metamorphosis duly commented on by the naively moralistic narrator:

> Lordynges, by this ensample I yow preye,
> Beth war, and taketh kep what that ye seye:
> Ne telleth nevere no man in your lyf
> How that another man hath dight his wyf;
> He wol yow haten mortally, certeyn.
> Daun Salomon, as wise clerkes seyn,
> Techeth a man to kepen his tonge weel. (IX.309–15)

If this is meant as a serious lesson to be learnt from the tale, it is ludicrously inadequate, but there is no suggestion in the text that the narrator is not perfectly serious, and any subversive irony must be at the expense of the Manciple, who is trying to turn an amusing anecdote into a moral exemplum. The discrepancy between the substance of the tale and the moral drawn from it is not as glaringly obvious as in the 'Merchant's Tale', but it is still very unlikely that we are meant to identify the speaker with the author himself or that we should class the story with the truly moral and homiletic tales. It is, again, an intriguing mixture of

traditional types, remarkable for its light-hearted use of classical mythology and conventional moralizing, and, possibly, placed in deliberate
contrast with the Parson's straightforward moral treatise.[42]

The comic tales contributed by or dealing with the clergy are, in
comparison with the 'Merchant's Tale', more limited in their stylistic and
thematic range, but even here we find a very similar tendency to enrich
the brevity of the anecdote by rhetorical digressions and associations
with other forms of religious literature.

The story of the Friar, as well as that of the Summoner, is basically a
satirical anecdote, directed against the profession of the main character,
and a lively expression of popular prejudice or experience. The venomous
aggressiveness of the satire is further sharpened by the highly dramatic
narrative situation: the Friar and the Summoner are not simply personal
enemies, like the Miller and the Reeve, but rivals by the very nature of
their occupation, since both of them thrive by diverting the money of
unsuspecting believers into their own pockets – the one by brilliant
penitential sermonizing, the other by simple blackmail and intimidation
– both shamelessly abusing their real duties. Consequently, the manifold
ironies of the two tales arise, above all, from the fact that each of the two
narrators wants to paint the vices of the other in the most lurid colours,
thus indirectly confirming all the accusations against his own profession.
In this way, stories and storytellers are particularly closely related to each
other by their very subject. This only concerns their occupation, however,
not the individual personalities – if such a distinction can sensibly be
made in the context of *The Canterbury Tales*. At any rate, the two tales
reflect on each other in more subtle ways than the stories told by the
Miller and the Reeve, which are related mainly by personal irritation and
revengeful spite.

The Friar obviously tells his tale with the intention of exposing once
and for all the corrupted nature of all summoners and their certain
punishment, but he does it with an unscrupulous eloquence that goes far
to explain and justify all the popular prejudices against the friars'
consummate art of preaching and thus adds a certain amount of
credibility to the Summoner's account.[43] The Summoner's depravity, as
we have already seen in the 'General Prologue', is of a more primitive
nature. He shamelessly abuses the authority and the privileges of his
office for his personal enrichment. Brutality and deceit are his chief
methods and there is little need for any subtle cunning. Accordingly, the
summoner's part in the 'Friar's Tale' is above all that of a malignant and,
at the same time, obtuse victim who falls into the trap set for him and
meets his well-deserved punishment. The dramatic irony of his encounter
with the Devil, who is his fellow in all respects except the Fiend's superior

craftiness, will not be lost on any reader. The summoner is, from the start, painted as such a repulsive character that the Devil, in comparison, seems to be almost too likeable, for he is sure of our sympathy when he puts down his nasty companion. The summoner very quickly recognizes the kindred spirit and, with cunning familiarity, enters into a compact with him, thus paving the way for his spectacular descent into hell of his own free will. The narrative leaves us in no doubt that the summoner does not fall victim to an arbitrary divine tribunal, but – in accordance with perfectly sound doctrine – chooses his own way to damnation, deliberately rejecting all opportunities offered to him to mend his ways and to repent. This is made particularly clear by the fact that the Devil does not even find it necessary to dissemble. The inquisitive summoner is freely granted all the theological information he wants about the nature of Hell and Satan's divine mission; but his greedy stupidity prevents him from applying any of this to himself, and thus he corroborates, in effect, the Devil's orders to put the sinner to the test, either, as in the case of Job, for his eventual salvation or, as here, for everlasting damnation. Quite apart from the tale's malicious undertone and personal venom, the competent instruction of the unsuspecting summoner by the affable and obliging Fiend is one of the most successful examples of lively religious instruction in Chaucer's poetry.

For the narrator, the ending of the story is a valid picture of what is in store for all summoners. This is in no way mitigated by the pious request to pray for all members of the profession, which is not only an offensive dig at the actual Summoner among the pilgrims, but also an instance of the popular style of preaching, venting personal interests and animosities under the guise of truly Christian concern for the salvation of other people's souls. The smoothness of the rhyming transition suggests the routine of the experienced preacher and accentuates the comic contradiction between pious homily and spiteful denunciation:

> And with that word this foule feend hym hente;
> Body and soule he with the devel wente
> Where as that somonours han hir heritage.
> And God, that maked after his ymage
> Mankynde, save and gyde us, alle and some,
> And leve thise somonours goode men bicome! (III.1639–44)

The blasphemous abuse of religious rhetoric could not be illustrated more poignantly than by this brilliant adaptation of familiar pulpit clichés.

The irony, however, is extended even further than that. Like the Devil and the summoner in the story, the crafty Friar acts as a divine instrument, for in spite of all his quite unbiblical maliciousness, his tale still remains, to some extent, an edifying sermon from which the reader may derive genuine spiritual instruction. Theological debate and estates satire here combine with a farcical exemplum by which the narrator condemns not only the summoner, but himself, thus confirming the satirical portrait in the 'General Prologue'. The whole tale effectively characterizes the Friar as the corrupt representative of a profession whose disinterested devotion to an unworldly ideal has been largely undermined by selfish avarice and unashamed hypocrisy; it has obviously become a favourite subject of popular satire.

The Summoner's story offers another instance: presenting an even more venomous portrait of a friar in action by which the Summoner attempts to take revenge on his hateful competitor. The friar's consummate skill as a preacher, with his blasphemous perversion of Christian terminology and pastoral didacticism, is parodied with devastating accuracy and rhetorical competence hardly credible in this vulgar narrator; similarly, the concluding part, with its pseudo-learned mock-debate is not exactly in tune with his coarse narrative style. The exuberant rhetoric of the satire is evidently more important here than strict psychological consistency and the whole performance most adequately expresses the speaker's intention, even though his literary weapons occasionally seem to be those rather of the learned poet than of the primitive Summoner.

The coarseness of the joke, however, clearly enough betrays the intellectual and social position of the narrator; the colossal fart presented to the friar and his whole order by the infuriated patient is a most eloquent demonstration of pent-up popular exasperation with the hypocritical homiletics which have become nothing but an instrument of avarice. After the friar's long admonition, with its brilliant crescendo of brazen impudence, the explosive point of the story comes as a hilarious dramatic effect; it is a particularly happy and convincingly motivated combination of uninhibited farce and discursive rhetoric. After the smooth homily on the sin of violent anger, the uncontrolled outburst of the duped victim finally unmasks the successful hypocrite, who is made to look even more ridiculous by the concluding part of the tale.

Here again, a burlesque anecdote which forms the basis of the story is almost smothered by rhetorical embroidery and digressions, and we end up with a tale which, like the majority of the comic *Canterbury Tales* will not easily fit into any systematic hierarchy of narrative genres, although it clearly employs established genre conventions. A wealth of theological thought and religious didacticism has been incorporated and put to the service of pointed satire whose domestic realism recalls the fabliaux of the Miller and the Reeve and whose timeless vitality needs very little explanation. At such points, even the modern reader will find the approach to Chaucer's narrative art easy enough.

The 'Canon's Yeoman's Tale', by contrast, is rather more difficult to enjoy because the subject seems so particularly 'medieval' and the narrator's attitude not only personally spiteful but inimical to scientific progress and without genuine humour. Again, it is hard to find a suitable label for the story. It begins, like some of the other comic tales, as a venomous satirical attack on particular abuses – as pure invective, with plenty of concrete detail and specialist jargon – a decidedly new voice in the polyphonic structure of *The Canterbury Tales*. The alchemist's obsession is presented as a breathlessly pursued activity and a craft as highly developed and exclusive as any of the professions described in the 'General Prologue'. It is a 'cursed craft' (VIII.830), but as hard to acquire as any less sinful accomplishment:

> Ascaunce that craft is so light to leere?
> Nay, nay, God woot, al be he monk or frere,
> Preest or chanoun, or any oother wyght,
> Though he sitte at his book bothe day and nyght
> In lernyng of this elvysshe nyce loore,
> Al is in veyn, and parde! muchel moore.
> To lerne a lewed man this subtiltee –
> Fy! spek nat therof, for it wol nat bee;
> And konne he letterure, or konne he noon,
> As in effect, he shal fynde it al oon. (VIII.838–47)

After the long introduction, the story proper is presented as an illustration of the alchemist's viciousness, an example of elaborate trickery that almost ceases to be funny and is punctuated by the indignant narrator's execrations and curses against the villain. The Canon's Yeoman sounds like the Pardoner preaching against drunkenness, and he is anxious to assure his audience that he only tells the tale as a warning exemplum:

> Al to symple is my tonge to pronounce,
> As ministre of my wit, the doublenesse
> Of this chanoun, roote of alle cursednesse!
> He semed freendly to hem that knewe hym noght,
> But he was feendly bothe in werk and thoght.
> It weerieth me to telle of his falsnesse,
> And nathelees yet wol I it expresse,
> To th'entente that men may be war therby,
> And for noon oother cause, trewely. (VIII.1299–1307)

The deluding of the credulous dupe is pathetic rather than comic and the narrator's derisive and at the same time pitying comparisons underline the ambiguous effect:

> This sotted preest, who was gladder than he?
> Was nevere brid gladder agayn the day,
> Ne nyghtyngale, in the sesoun of May,
> Was nevere noon that luste bet to synge;
> Ne lady lustier in carolynge,
> Or for to speke of love and wommanhede,
> Ne knyght in armes to doon an hardy dede,
> To stonden in grace of his lady deere,
> Than hadde this preest this soory craft to leere.   (VIII.1341–9)

The total impression, however, is that of a narrowly one-sided statement, and several critics have pointed out that the story by no means allows us to count Chaucer among the conservative enemies of scientific progress. The Canon's Yeoman is embittered and, like many others among the pilgrims, uses the opportunity offered by the Host's invitation to vent his long-suppressed animosities and hatreds. Like the Manciple, he loads a simple anecdote with more moral application than it will comfortably bear, but his bias is more specific and the story is a unique document of a controversial debate in which Chaucer seems to have been very interested, even though it may not be one of the most brilliant of the *Canterbury Tales*. Its satirical drive and the tricks it exposes may be a reason for reading it along with Chaucer's comic tales, but one might also describe it as a pointed exemplum that uses comic effects for the deeper purpose of wholesome instruction. Its vivid appeal to the audience is more important than its exact place in Chaucer's hierarchy of genres, and it is up to the individual listener whether he sees the Canon's Yeoman as a disappointed man, not to be taken all too seriously, or as a genuine convert who has become wiser by disillusionment and material loss.[44]

SAINTS, SINNERS, AND EXEMPLA

For the twentieth-century reader, it is perhaps even more difficult to come to terms with those tales in which the didactic intentions of the whole collection are openly admitted and the Host's demand of 'best sentence' (I.798) is more literally complied with. But these seemingly more conventional legends and moral exampla are no less remarkable as demonstrations of Chaucer's versatile art, though it manifests itself not so much in closely observed detail and brilliant rhetoric or dazzling irony as in the subtle and sophisticated transformations of familiar and traditional story-material and in the deliberate manipulation of the reader's reaction. This does not apply to all these tales in the same degree, but even those that seem, at a first glance, rather undistinguished routine performances very often turn out to be far more interesting on closer inspection, especially if they are read in the context of the other tales and of the frame-story.

Very few readers, for instance, will consider the simple tale told by the Physician a striking masterpiece of subtle narrative art. It seems possible, though there is no definite proof, that it belongs to the earlier tales of the collection and that it was not from the start tailored to suit one particular narrator. The subject of which there are many different versions, among them one by John Gower, is here presented with rather naive seriousness, and it would be quite anachronistic to assume that its harsh, even brutal, moral must always have appeared as unacceptable as it does today.

On the other hand, it is difficult to avoid the impression that here, again, Chaucer's evident delight in literary role-playing has led him to give a slightly provocative emphasis to the more puzzling or even repulsive aspects of the tale, such as the pathetic parting dialogue between father and daughter and the fussing admonition to all parents and teachers to shield young daughters from corrupting influences – both somewhat surprising in their context.[45] As we have seen in the case of some romances and comic tales, Chaucer deliberately raises questions and points out possible problems which this particular type of tale usually leaves well alone, and which often produce a disturbing complexity of emotions and reactions on the part of the reader. The story, one would think, can only work if we are not made to look at the girl's emotions too closely; Gower's version is rather more consistent in this respect, but at the same time less disquieting. Chaucer seems to be vaguely aware of the story's potential offensiveness, and though he does not make very much of this he introduces some tantalizing hints that make the exemplum a little less glib than an all too naive retelling would make it appear to be.[46]

The noisy emotional reaction of the Host does not suggest that he has been truly edified, but rather strengthens our suspicion that the Physician has presented a deliberately simplified specimen of popular moral instruction, as a pointed contrast to the instances of genuine homiletic narrative contributed by the more learned and spiritual pilgrims. At least, our critical sense is alerted when the sermon-like conclusion of the tale is immediately followed by the Host's outburst:

> Oure Hooste gan to swere as he were wood;
> 'Harrow!' quod he, 'by nayles and by blood!
> This was a fals cherl and a fals justise.
> As shameful deeth as herte may devyse
> Come to thise juges and hire advocatz!
> . . .
> But wel I woot thou doost myn herte to erme,
> That I almoost have caught a cardynacle.

> By corpus bones! but I have triacle,
> Or elles a draughte of moyste and corny ale,
> Or but I heere anon a myrie tale,
> Myn herte is lost for pitee of this mayde.'   (VI.287–91, 312–17)

One would hardly think that this is the most appropriate reaction to the story.

As to its metrical form, the 'Physician's Tale' is not noticeably different from the romances and the comic tales, whereas the majority of saints' legends and legendary exempla is composed in the 'rhyme-royal' stanza, which is evidently meant to produce an effect of stylization and solemn pathos as well as a sense of meditative detachment from the action. The relationship between narrator and tale is, in most cases, less marked than in the case of the burlesque tales. It is limited to some general appropriateness to the narrator's estate, sufficiently distinct to give each tale its particular flavour and to distinguish it quite clearly from the less edifying performances.

The legend contributed by the Second Nun is a comparatively simple example. The narrator's personality is adequately defined by her 'profession', and the story of Saint Cecilia, no doubt familiar enough to most of Chaucer's audience, is obviously presented as an instance of untroubled piety, not disturbed by any theoretical theological questions, but intent on devout contemplation alone. The narrator's own humble attitude towards her subject is, moreover, meant to induce the hearer to follow her example of unquestioning veneration and imitation. The spirit of the narrative and its homiletic intention almost blur the distinction between the Second Nun's fellow-pilgrims and the reader. It is, of course, possible that Chaucer did not get round to really adapting this legend, which may well have been written much earlier, to the context of the frame: thus the Prologue sounds more like the voice of a conscious artist who deliberately avoids rhetorical embellishment for the sake of a simple moral impact than that of a sociable narrator:

> Yet preye I yow that reden that I write,
> Foryeve me that I do no diligence
> This ilke storie subtilly to endite,
> For bothe have I the wordes and sentence
> Of hym that at the seintes reverence
> The storie wroot, and folwen hire legende,
> And pray yow that ye wole my werk amende.   (VIII.78–84)

On the other hand, it is precisely this disregard of the specific narrative situation that serves to include the reader in the assembly of listeners to whom the legend is addressed and make him share in the true aim of medieval saints' legends, the pious contemplation of the image of saintly steadfastness and its divine validation. There is no effort to invest the events of the story with a realistic animation, and the narrator's own devout absorption in the legend, where each episode is presented as a testimony of the exhilarating strength of truly Christian convictions, is perhaps the most striking feature of the tale.[47] At the same time, as she specifically points out, the work of translation itself was, for her, an act of faith, saving her from the sin of spiritual idleness and proving its true worth in the process of public recitation. There cannot be any clear separation of subject and impact. The meditative and liturgical tone unites narrator and audience into a reverently contemplative congregation. Just as the holy Saint forces everyone who comes face to face with her to commit himself for her or against her, so the legend does not care for neutral and indifferent listeners, but aims to appeal to a community whose faith responds to the manifestation of divine grace. Few Middle English legends express this homiletic urge as powerfully as Chaucer's 'Second Nun's Tale'.

The tale told by the Prioress proceeds from a very similar devotional stance and starts with a prayer-like prologue which is a paraphrase of the eighth psalm; the subject-matter, however, is not taken from the traditional saints' legends, but presents a Christian miracle which does not really invite devout contemplation but rather a kind of wondering satisfaction at the workings of God's power and justice. It seems to disturb or even annoy the modern reader far more distinctly than can have been the case in Chaucer's own time. From all we know about medieval piety, it is clear that such miraculous tales were received by the majority of believers as genuine and perfectly legitimate forms of religious propaganda and that there is no reason for us to doubt the narrator's sincerity or to suspect a satirical intention on Chaucer's part. There are, on the other hand, some significant indications that this story is informed by a somewhat different kind of religious devotion from that found in the 'Second Nun's Tale', and this raises a number of questions, without giving any unmistakable clue as to the author's own position.

It would surely be unjustified to try and discover subversive authorial irony behind each of the Prioress' fervent protestations of faith or to speak of 'ridiculing childish legends'.[48] In this area we simply have to concede a genuine historical change in taste if not in religious convictions: our modern experiences of Christian fanaticism or anti-Semitic cruelty are not particularly relevant for a proper understanding of the text.[49] Nevertheless, Chaucer throws into relief a particular aspect of medieval popular religion with such pointed precision that the contrast to other expressions of Christian devotion within *The Canterbury Tales* alone is enough to make the audience aware of the somewhat limited mentality behind the legend. It is evidently another proof of Chaucer's consummate art of parody (in the widest sense), his remarkable ability to create distinct poses without committing himself to a definitive evaluation by unequivocal satire.

The simple legend thus raises, with particular urgency, the problem of historical or subjective interpretations, and it is perhaps more appropriate to become aware of these difficulties with self-critical modesty than to try and remove them by some theoretical formula.[50] The text and its reception are even less easy to keep separate than in many other cases, because the story appeals so strongly to the critical independence of the reader that a purely historical interpretation, even if it were possible, would suppress the very delicate ambiguity which stimulates the reader's spontaneous involvement and challenges him to take sides. It is this teasing ambiguity that makes Chaucer's narrative art so immediately moving even today and makes it so different from many unproblematic documents of medieval piety.[51] The text simply does not provide any firm basis for pinning down the poet, but it offers a number of provocative simplifications which no learned reminders and definitions of medieval religion will clear away and which, in the modern reader, raise some doubts as to the innocence and the exemplary character of this legend. Such doubts are a perfectly legitimate reaction to Chaucer's suggestive narrative style and they tend to become anachronistic only when they reduce the elusive distance created by the distinct stance of the narrator to a plain and definitive authorial evaluation. The text has a curious power to provoke more questions than it actually contains. It is all very well to try and reconstruct its original meaning, if there is such a thing; but the modern reader will suspect more complex motives behind the pious legend and will not easily be convinced that they are all of his own making.

It is, I think, hardly profitable to associate the story too closely with the portrait of the Prioress in the 'General Prologue'. The worldly vanities of the lady suggested there do not reappear in her tale, nor are there in other ways very striking similarities between Madame Eglentyne and the character of the narrator as it appears from her performance – unless we choose to regard the pronounced and almost suspicious deference shown to her by the poet and the Host as a common feature. To no other pilgrim does the Host show himself so respectful:

> and with that word he sayde,
> As curteisly as it had been a mayde,
> 'My lady Prioresse, by youre leve,
> So that I wiste I sholde yow nat greve,

I wolde demen that ye tellen sholde
A tale next, if so were that ye wolde.
Now wol ye vouche sauf, my lady deere?'   (VII.444–50)

The tale itself, however, seems to impress him less deeply than the other pilgrims:

Whan seyd was al this miracle, every man
As sobre was that wonder was to se,
Til that oure Hooste japen tho bigan,
And thanne at erst he looked upon me.   (VII.691–4)

One is almost tempted to assume that the lack of understanding shown by this coarse-minded master of ceremonies is meant to draw our attention to the dignity of the narrative, as is clearly the case in some other instances, notably after the 'Tale of Melibee'.[52]

However alert we may be to possibly objectionable implications of the Prioress' story, it should not distract us from the plain fact that it is basically a serious and edifying tale which, like the legend of Saint Cecilia, is meant to make us join in the praise of God's power, and whose narrative method is largely subordinated to the homiletic intentions behind it. The theme of innocent, childlike piety which determines the style and the action of the legend is not invalidated by any ambiguity. The concise brevity of the tale, dispensing largely with rhetorical embellishment, didactic digression or realistic detail, alone argues against any undue prominence of less edifying elements. Neither the conventional hatred of the Jews nor the drastic punishment of the murderers is exploited beyond the necessities of the plot, whose real centre is the praise of God and the Holy Virgin out of the mouth of the innocent child, a particularly moving confirmation of the psalm quoted at the outset: 'by the mouth of children thy bountee / Parfourned is' (VII.457–8).[53] The legend does not offer an example of human perfection and virtuous living or make any claims to moral instruction, but aims only to serve the glorification of God, doing so above all by a pronounced simplicity of presentation and by repeated liturgical and biblical associations, as well as by the narrator's devout and by no means sentimental participation. The personal tone, however, is meant to direct the reader's attention not towards the character of the speaker, who puts herself on the same level with the tender child (VII.484–5), but at the tale's continual relevance.

However the reader may respond to the subject of the legend, he will not receive the story as non-committal entertainment, and it is this bid for his personal involvement that all the moral and legendary tales of the collection have in common.

The tales contributed by the two men of learning not actually in the service of the Church are, as befits their narrators' estate, less simply devotional and do not concern saints and martyrs but exemplary women whose fates are, at the same time, remarkably close to romance and miraculous adventure.[54] Both tales belong to a genre which seems to have been particularly popular at the time, half-way between legend and romance, combining moral instruction and exciting entertainment. The 'Man of Law's Tale' is a particularly good example. The moving adventures of Constance, persecuted on account of her faith and exposed to one trial after another, bear many resemblances to other stories of romance: the false accusation, the heroine's exposure on the sea, the repetition of similar episodes, the motif of the painful separation of members of a family reunited after long years of suffering. The heroine's exemplary steadfastness does not end in martyrdom, but in public vindication and a life of untroubled Christian activity. The ending thus combines the worldly happiness which is the reward of the true romance heroine with a triumphant demonstration of divine grace and perfect virtue.

The peculiarly mixed character of the work becomes apparent, for instance, in the narrator's almost bashful attitude towards marriage. Unlike Cecilia and other heroines of homiletic romances, Constance is not introduced as a model of Christian chastity; she is a wife and a mother, and the moving pathos of her exile is heightened by the innocent baby's suffering with her. On the other hand, she is not quite like the faithful lover of the romance tradition either, and the narrator finds it necessary to insert a word of apology for the conception of her son, apparently betraying a certain awareness of the latent contradictions within this kind of tale:

> They goon to bedde, as it was skile and right;
> For thogh that wyves be ful hooly thynges,
> They moste take in pacience at nyght
> Swiche manere necessaries as been plesynges
> To folk that han ywedded hem with rynges,
> And leye a lite hir hoolynesse aside,
> As for the tyme, – it may no bet bitide.   (II.708–14)

The heroine's 'hoolynesse' can, apparently, not be kept up in every situation.

At the same time, she is very active as a worker of miracles and a missionary, and her sufferings are at first directly related to her faith; in the course of the story, however, they mount up to a climax of trials and coincidences which seems no longer explicable in terms of cause and effect and is more characteristic of popular romance. The conviction that behind all this there is a benevolent divine providence working out its harmonious plan arises not so much out of the action itself as from the confident interpretation of the narrator, who uses every turn of the story to remind the listener of the eternal truths he finds confirmed by it. In the Anglo-Norman chronicle where Chaucer found the subject of the tale, the events are related in a rather more simple manner, largely without comment, but the Man of Law seizes every opportunity offered by the action to add homiletic contemplations, spiritual instruction and direct appeals to his audience – suggesting an orthodox and not very critical devotion.[55] More important than the speaker's personal convictions, however, are his urgent efforts to appeal to his listeners' sympathy, to their willingness to receive the Christian message and to meditate on the miraculous events. Such appeals can also heighten the dramatic suspense. Thus the narrator stops before describing the ordeal to reflect on Constance's seemingly hopeless situation:

> Allas! Custance, thou hast no champioun,
> Ne fighte kanstow noght, so weylaway!
> But he that starf for our redempcioun,
> And boond Sathan (and yet lith ther he lay),
> So be thy stronge champion this day!
> For, but if Crist open myracle kithe,
> Withouten gilt thou shalt be slayn as swithe. (II.631–7)

It is in particular the somewhat sensational and rather incredible elements of the story that are turned into homiletic exempla. Any possible objections of the reader to the improbable nature of the events are countered by eager didacticism and rhetorical exuberance. The pose of the pious man of learning is thus clearly emphasized, and this establishes another point of view within the debate described in *The Canterbury Tales*, as well as providing Chaucer with an opportunity of introducing a different narrative genre into his collection.

The 'Clerk's Tale' has a very different effect on the reader and, again, the intensity of our reaction is not provoked so much by the subject-matter as by the deliberately ambiguous presentation of it.

Chaucer's personal additions to the story are, at first sight considerably less significant than in the case of the 'Man of Law's Tale'. The 'Clerk's Tale' is a fairly straightforward and faithful translation of Petrarch's Latin prose, with some gleanings from a French version. Chaucer has turned the prose of his original into elaborate stanzas and this was bound to make the translation less literal, but for long stretches of the story he follows his models with a faithfulness rather unusual for him.[56] There is no point where the action is changed to any noticeable degree, and there are neither drastic cuts nor rhetorical digressions such as often interrupt the Man of Law's narrative. Nevertheless, a great number of minor shifts of emphasis and of brief additions has been noted. Not all of them, perhaps, should be interpreted as conscious modifications of the source, but taken together they suggest that Chaucer was not content with an uncritical reproduction of somebody else's work, but had his own views about the traditional story. It seems very likely that in this tale told by a learned book-lover he wanted to dramatize the rhetorical process of adaptation and critical transmission of traditional story-material, thus offering a more literary and bookish variant of the narrative stances presented in this collection.[57] The Clerk, familiar with French and Latin at least, retells a story he found among the works of a famous author, but he cannot quite conceal his own personal reaction to these events, and he is certainly aware of contradictions and difficulties that might arouse the reader's resentment. Most members of the audience will also notice that the story presents, at the same time, a very pointed challenge to the ideas of female predominance expounded by the Wife of Bath, and this is even made explicit near the end of the tale. Where two stories are so obviously related to each other in subject and theme, the concept of a 'marriage group' seems to be justified, if only in a very limited way.[58]

Here again, however, we should not make too much of the dramatic aspect of the narrative. The Clerk's critical attitude towards his source comes out in only a few places, such as the rather deprecating summary of Petrarch's introduction (IV.53–5); at least it should not prevent the reader from taking the moral and spiritual claims of the story entirely seriously and from resisting the temptation to take exception to incongruities that belong only to the surface of the story, not its ultimate meaning. The tale of Griseldis is, above all, the story of a trial undergone patiently and without protest, a trial explicitly compared to that of Job, the biblical model of all tribulations and ordeals imposed by God on his servants (IV.932). By contrast to the romance of Constance, the improbability here lies not so much in the external events – though these are, on closer examination, miraculous enough – as in the characters themselves, whose behaviour appears neither convincing nor worth imitating when judged by the standards of our daily intercourse. Such considerations have repelled many readers, but these obviously miss the real point of this tale, whose popularity throughout the centuries surely proves that it has always exercised a certain fascination and not just given offence.[59]

Of course, the 'Clerk's Tale' does not give a faithful picture of society in the fourteenth or in any other century, and it is not presented as a comment on the question of equality in marriage, but as an example of Christian humility, patience and unconditional obedience to the will of God. The narrative largely dispenses with any attempt at such realistic credibility as would engage the readers' sympathies for the actors as individuals. The paradigmatic character of the action as a parable of divine care for man's salvation and of our need to acknowledge our imperfect state is underlined by stylization, biblical associations and concentration on the crucial points of the story. Thus the twelve-year separation of the mother and her children is silently passed over, and other improbabilities too are dealt with in such a casual and cavalier manner that most readers will accept the somewhat unrealistic strangeness of the plot from the start. In this way we are prepared for the interpretation proposed by Chaucer, as well as by Petrarch, at the end of the tale; it is, at the same time, a warning not to waste one's time examining the story's surface too closely:

> This storie is seyd, nat for that wyves sholde
> Folwen Grisilde as in humylitee,
> For it were inportable, though they wolde;
> But for that every wight, in his degree,
> Sholde be constant in adversitee
> As was Grisilde; therfore Petrak writeth
> This storie, which with heigh stile he enditeth.   (IV.1142–8)

Just as most of the biblical parables only try to illustrate one particular point and must not be analysed as to their deeper meaning in every detail, so here too the reader is meant to recognize the one aspect of human behaviour with which the tale is really concerned. Griseldis has vowed unconditional obedience to her husband, who has lifted her out of her low estate by an act of grace, just as God chooses for great purposes inconspicuous human beings, regardless of their own particular merit. Griseldis remains faithful to her promise in the face of cruel temptations, and she relinquishes her elevated position as humbly and unquestioningly as she first accepted it. The exemplary nature of the attitude demonstrated by her behaviour is in no way diminished by the questions and objections provoked on the level of the external action. They have the effect of engaging the reader's attention in the first place; the same purpose is served by the more emotional parts of the narrative, as well as by the delicate individualization of Walter, who, as the author of Griseldis' trials, carries out God's plan, but about whose human imperfections the narrator leaves us in no doubt. There is not the slightest attempt to present him as a man to whom we would concede the right to inflict such temptations on his wife.

Many critics have pointed out that, in comparison with his sources, Chaucer has given greater prominence to the paradigmatic as well as to the potentially offensive aspects of the story, thus sharpening our awareness of the irritating contradictions inherent in his material.[60] There is rather less unanimity when it comes to offering an explanation of this tension, by no means unique in Chaucer's work. Whereas Elizabeth Salter finds in the 'Clerk's Tale' a 'confused ordering of values'[61] which Chaucer himself, perhaps, was not aware of, Spearing sees the reason for these discrepancies in the person of the narrator, whose efforts to come to terms with his material, together with criticism of Petrarch's uncritical version of it, are an important part of Chaucer's poem. Thus the Clerk cannot refrain from improving on Petrarch's rather timid reservations by a decided condemnation of the unnecessary temptation which is repeated several times. He makes it clear from the start that Walter's behaviour is by no means justified by the happy outcome:

> He hadde assayed hire ynogh bifore,
> And foond hire evere good; what neded it
> Hire for to tempte, and alwey moore and moore,
> Though som men preise it for a subtil wit?
> But as for me, I seye that yvele it sit
> To assaye a wyf whan that it is no nede,
> And putten hire in angwyssh and in drede. (IV.456–62)

There are other places, too, where it becomes evident that this narrator is not just a detached translator, but a critical reader who reacts spontaneously whenever he encounters injustice, undeserved suffering and contradictions. This decidedly personal response of the narrator provokes the reader into defining his own reaction and, in this way, serves the homiletic effect. At the same time, Chaucer emphasizes the human side of the story by unobtrusive additions which are, perhaps, more important in guiding our sympathies than appears at first sight. Griseldis' pathetic parting from her children, her almost silent grief at the apparent loss of her husband's love, and her touching concern for the fortitude of his future wife create an atmosphere of emotional participation which makes a purely symbolic interpretation of the plot more difficult, but also more rewarding.[62] Griseldis is not just the inanimate embodiment of one particular virtue; she is not quite blind to the fact that it is not God alone who is the author of her trials, but a fallible human being in whose love she had believed, and this makes her tribulations all the more painful for us and, by the same token, her enduring patience all the more admirable.

The surprising epilogue, marked off from the tale by a change of metre and a distinctly frivolous tone, is another indication that Chaucer was well aware of the possible difficulties created by the story. It turns its moral upside down and provides a hilariously outrageous reply to the ideas of the Wife of Bath. The principle of wifely submission to her husband's will, which seems to be stretched almost to the breaking-point in the story of Griseldis, is translated into its opposite, and thus both extremes are reduced to absurdity as far as their practical applicability is concerned. This does not, however, deprive the tale itself of its moral basis. The utterly absurd interpretation can make us all the more receptive to the seriousness and the ethical demands of the story, which is beyond the reach of ordinary commonsense and everyday experience. The burlesque confrontation of the legend with the comic philosophy of the Wife of Bath should make it clear even to the most casual reader that two diametrically opposed modes of expression and areas of moral thinking are contrasted with each other here. At the same time, possible objections by the audience are anticipated and refuted by parody. Thoughtless solemnity is prevented by deliberate frivolousness, and this creates a tension which, to my mind, is anything but a sign of artistic failure, but rather a sophisticated device, very typical of Chaucer and expressive of his pluralistic representation of human society. The Clerk is almost alone among the Canterbury pilgrims in remaining somewhat detached from his own narrative and declining to identify with it. He is prepared to consider the possibility of contradictory interpretations and to allow the listener a margin of personal judgement. In this he seems more akin to his creator than most of the other pilgrims, who treat their stories with uncritical reverence or self-centred enjoyment.

The most original and amusing of all the edifying tales contributed by scholars or clergymen is, without doubt, the 'Nun's Priest's Tale'; in this case, however, the brilliant effect has very little to do with the person of the narrator. The figure of the Nun's Priest, not mentioned at all in the 'General Prologue', is puzzling in more than one way; he seems to have been added to the company of pilgrims at a later stage, and the prologue as well as the epilogue to his story show clearly signs of revision – a favourite starting-point for all kinds of speculative reconstructions and historical or even biographical guesswork.[63] The irresistible, comically instructive effect of the tale does not, however, depend on these background matters, largely obscured by the transmission of the text. It must suffice us to know that the narrator is a priest whose consummate virtuosity as a preacher, popular in the best sense and yet wonderfully learned, is illustrated most impressively by his performance. We are not told anything about his character or his relationship to any of the other pilgrims, so that, in reading the tale, we can hardly help identifying the speaker with Chaucer himself, whose own stylistic bravura seems to be particularly close to this rhetorical showpiece.

Here, again, a rather unassuming story is enriched by stylistic and thematic embroidery to such an extent that the actual plot almost disappears under the weight of digressions and amplifications. This produces, at the same time, an amusing discrepancy between the modest occasion and the rhetorical exhibitionism. The simple animal fable is extended into a rich compendium of nearly all the themes that play a prominent part in *The Canterbury Tales* and even in the rest of Chaucer's poetry. It looks like a demonstration of the experienced preacher's and exegete's faculty of extracting pious edification from even the most trivial detail. What the narrator wants to pass on to the reader as a useful piece of advice for dealing with texts he has already been practising throughout his performance:

> But ye that holden this tale a folye,
> As of a fox, or of a cok and hen,
> Taketh the moralite, goode men.
> For seint Paul seith that al that writen is,
> To oure doctrine it is ywrite, ywis;
> Taketh the fruyt, and lat the chaf be stille.　　　(VII.3438–43)

In this sense, the 'Nun's Priest's Tale' may also be taken as an introduction to the art of reading: for those whose moral perceptions have been sharpened by attending to this kind of instruction, every insignificant episode provides an occasion for a contemplation of fundamental questions relating to our Christian existence. The common cock becomes a mirror of human imperfection and vulnerability. His fall illustrates the capriciousness of Fortune and the disastrous consequences of imprudent self-assurance and pride no less memorably than the Monk's monotonous 'tragedies', whose soporific effect is decried by the Host (VII.2788–802), and his ill-boding dream raises the problem of divine providence with little less dramatic urgency than the sufferings of Troilus after Criseyde's departure. The relationship between the self-complacent Chauntecleer and his loquacious Pertelote adds another variation on the theme of marriage and the role of women, thus continuing the debate sparked off by the Wife of Bath, with some more borrowings from traditional anti-feminist satire. Again and again, the story provides opportunities for conventional rhetorical set-pieces – such as the narrator's indignation at the perfidious fox, who is placed in a line with such classic traitor figures as Sinon, Ganelon and Judas Iscariot; or the lament at Chauntecleer's fall, with an explicit reference to the great theorist of rhetoric, Geoffrey of Vinsauf; or the elaborate description of the cock according to all the rules of the art of rhetoric. The bright combination of colours here has given rise to all kinds of heraldic and symbolic speculations, but the main point is surely the extravagant display of stylistic virtuosity, not any topical allusion.

　　The fact that this tale, more than any other, has tempted readers to search for specific historical references is partly accounted for by the tradition of medieval animal allegories, but even more, perhaps, by the wealth of precise and seemingly gratuitous detail. For the modern reader, however, the tale has significance enough even without such explanations, and there is nothing to suggest that topical allusions, if there are any, were more than additional humorous effects for insiders, relating to the story's surface rather than to its centre, and certainly not essential for understanding its deeper meaning.[64] What is far more important is that the narrative technique keeps the reader on the alert for new and surprising significances at every turn of the plot. He is virtually encouraged to give free rein to his interpretative imagination, but this applies, above all, to the didactic substance of the text, not to any supposed personal references as to which we today can, at best, merely speculate.

Diversity of themes and stylistic variety are the most striking features of this tale. The realism of the introduction creates, at the outset, a lively and unpretentious background for the cock's entrance. The precisely listed details give the impression of a rather modest social milieu, far removed from the luxuries of a courtly life-style, as is suggested by the account of the widow's healthy diet and the ironic reference to 'hire bour and eek hir halle' (VII.2832). Against this background, the ostentatious epic gestures and the high-sounding comparisons used in the description of the cock, with their constant references to the great world outside, strike us as a surprising incongruity of style, as a comic discrepancy between the poetical means and the anything but elevated subject. After such an introduction the reader will find the courtly terminology employed to portray the relationship between Chauntecleer and 'damoysele Pertelote' ridiculously inappropriate, because it is obvious that we are not to expect a courtly love-allegory in the guise of birds, as in *The Parliament of Fowls* or even in the second part of the 'Squire's Tale'. There, from the start, the poet had created an atmosphere of a stylized fairy-tale world, whereas here we are constantly reminded that the story is about a very ordinary farmyard cock within a thoroughly uncourtly environment.[65]

The contrast between the reality of the widow's smallholding and the literary and didactic pretensions of the learned narrator runs through the whole work and hardly calls for a detailed interpretation. One of the highlights of the 'Nun's Priest's Tale' is the domestic dispute about Chauntecleer's nightmarish dream. Whereas Pertelote, with her pragmatic explanation of his symptoms and her household remedies against constipation, recalls the unromantic realities of poultry farming and, at the same time, represents a practical bourgeois scepticism against highfalutin bookish theory, the observations of the well-read cock seem to be on the level of a serious philosophical argument about the authority of foreboding dreams. They sound somewhat amusing, coming from the beak of a domestic cock, but at the same time, they touch on questions that were evidently of genuine interest to Chaucer and were the subject of many scholarly arguments. The three brief stories adduced by the cock to support his conviction of the truth conveyed by such dreams obviously come from the preacher's rich fund of moving exempla and make clear that the whole tale is a skilfully disguised homily using an entertaining animal fable as an excuse for all kinds of instruction and exhortation.[66]

The contrasts clash even more abruptly towards the end of the tale, where the didactic moral, the warning against flatterers and indiscretion, is almost smothered by the furious chase after the deceitful fox and his prey. The abduction of the cock is not only a demonstration of the inconstancy of Fortune, just punishment of imprudent vanity and an occasion for heroic lament; it is also an economic catastrophe within the poor widow's little sphere. The sudden transition from rhetorical declamation to the noisy and dramatic pursuit of the robber is a justly famous instance of Chaucerian stylistic bravura; the reasoning and moralizing mode of discourse is immediately followed by a precise realization of swiftly moving action. The rhetorical flight is suddenly checked in mid-air, and the prosaic reality of the small farm cottage is brought to the fore. The reader's attention is redirected to the surface plot, but this should, at the same time, make him willing to give more thought to the deeper meaning of the fable. It is to this meaning that we are again referred when the cock has cunningly freed himself from the fox's teeth:

> For he that wynketh, whan he sholde see,
> Al wilfully, God lat him nevere thee! (VII.3431-2)

What actually was the cock's undoing – and the fox's, for that matter – was evidently blindness in the widest sense of the word. The concept of blindness can be applied at various levels of the story, from the literal action of the fable to the mental and spiritual 'discrecioun' necessary for every Christian.[67] This universal applicability of the fable to the moral life of every individual – or even, if we like, to the whole Church – naturally raises the question whether Chaucer is indulging in a joke or whether a certain kind of textual exegesis, the search for abstract morals at any price, is meant to be ridiculed by exaggeration.[68] There seems to be no doubt that Chaucer has placed particular emphasis on the preacher's eagerness for a didactic exploitation of every detail; on the other hand, as so often in the work of this poet, we should not immediately think of satire and parody, but should recognize that a very distinct narrative pose is created by the text, differing very clearly from that of the Knight, the Merchant or the Clerk, who all exhibit different attitudes towards their own stories. Even though the relation between the fable and the rhetorical amplifications seems to be comically out of proportion, it is by no means completely absurd, but should help the reader to a clearer view of the difficulties of interpretation and of some fundamental problems of poetical theory which were being discussed throughout the Middle Ages and must trouble everyone who has a true appreciation of literature at heart. What is the use of a fable? How far is a reasonable interpretation allowed to go? Where does ridiculous overinterpretation begin? The problem will probably be different with every new text, and every reader will arrive at a different answer. Chaucer's narrative art, more than that of most other Middle English poets, demonstrates in how many different ways simple stories can be presented and made meaningful, and how unprofitable it would be to devise a systematic set of rules applicable to every kind of literature. The exuberant exegetical imagination of the Nun's Priest is as legitimate as the unobtrusive criticism of the Clerk.

The whole tale is a particularly persuasive illustration of the fact that literary joke, amusing entertainment and solid instruction hardly ever exclude each other in the work of Chaucer, but illumine one another and add up to a most original unity. It is a successful synthesis of 'best sentence' and 'moost solaas', the two conditions laid down by the Host at the outset of the competition (I.798) – a synthesis achieved in other parts of *The Canterbury Tales* only by a juxtaposition of very different narratives. In view of this exhilarating diversity, it is, in the last analysis, not very material to which particular genre we assign the 'Nun's Priest's Tale': it combines elements of the sermon, the moral exemplum, the animal fable, the comic beast epic, and yet it is none of these. In this respect, too, it is particularly representative of the experimental diversity of styles and forms within this collection and of Chaucer's undogmatic narrative art, which above all seeks to enter into a dialogue with the critical reader.

Notes

Abbreviations

Archiv	*Archiv für das Studium der Neueren Sprachen und Literaturen*
CE	*College English*
ChR	*Chaucer Review*
CL	*Comparative Literature*
CQ	*Critical Quarterly*
E&S	*Essays and Studies*
EC	*Essays in Criticism*
EETS, ES, OS	Early English Text Society, Extra Series, Original Series
ELH	*English Literary History*
ESt	*English Studies*
JEGP	*Journal of English and Germanic Philology*
LStE	*Leeds Studies in English*
MÆ	*Medium Ævum*
MLN	*Modern Language Notes*
MLQ	*Modern Language Quarterly*
MLR	*Modern Language Review*
MP	*Modern Philology*
N&Q	*Notes and Queries*
PLL	*Papers on Language and Literature*
PMLA	*Publications of the Modern Language Association of America*
PQ	*Philological Quarterly*
RES	*Review of English Studies*
SAC	*Studies in the Age of Chaucer*
ShJW	*Deutsche Shakespeare-Gesellschaft West. Jahrbuch*
SP	*Studies in Philology*
TSE	*Tulane Studies in English*
UTQ	*University of Toronto Quarterly*
YES	*Yearbook of English Studies*
ZfRP	*Zeitschrift für Romanische Philologie*

1 Chaucer in his time

1 See *Chaucer Life-Records*, ed. Martin M. Crow and Clair C. Olson (Oxford, 1966). See also the stimulating review of scholarship by A. C. Baugh, 'Chaucer the Man', in *Companion to Chaucer Studies*, ed. Beryl Rowland, rev. edn (New

Notes

York; Oxford, 1979), pp. 1–20, with a good bibliography, and the excellent brief survey by F. R. H. Du Boulay, 'The Historical Chaucer', in *Geoffrey Chaucer*, ed. Derek Brewer, Writers and their Background (London, 1974), pp. 33–57. Most general surveys include a biographical chapter. Particularly helpful are the generously illustrated volumes by Derek Brewer: *Chaucer*, 3rd edn (London, 1973) and *Chaucer in His Time* (London, 1963; reissued in paperback, 1973).

2 See *The Works of Geoffrey Chaucer*, ed. F. N. Robinson, 2nd edn (Boston, Mass., 1957), p. xxi.

3 See the valuable survey by Wendy Childs, 'Anglo-Italian Contacts in the Fourteenth Century', in *Chaucer and the Italian Trecento*, ed. Piero Boitani (Cambridge, 1983), pp. 65–87.

4 This is what happens in George Williams, *A New View of Chaucer* (Durham, N. C., 1965); the borderline separating historical research and imaginative fiction is sometimes a little blurred here.

5 See Hazel Allison Stevenson, 'A Possible Relation Between Chaucer's Long Lease and the Date of his Birth', *MLN*, 50 (1935), 318–22, and the doubts expressed by George Williams in *N&Q*, 205 (1960), 168. On Chaucer's 'conversion', see the highly speculative, though in parts very plausible, study by Heiner Gillmeister, *Chaucer's Conversion: Allegorical Thought in Medieval Literature* (Frankfurt, 1984), esp. pp. 120–6.

6 There has been, in recent years, some vigorous rethinking about the poet's status in medieval society and the idea of the 'court poet', both by historians and by literary scholars. See the thorough and original study by Richard Firth Green, *Poets and Princepleasers: Literature and the English Court in the Late Middle Ages* (Toronto, 1980), and *English Court Culture in the Late Middle Ages*, ed. V. J. Scattergood and J. W. Sherborne (London, 1983); see also the chapter 'Conditions and Status' in Elizabeth Salter, *Fourteenth-Century English Poetry: Contexts and Readings* (Oxford, 1983), pp. 19–51.

2 The narrator and his audience

1 One of the most useful surveys of these problems is still Wayne Booth, *The Rhetoric of Fiction* (Chicago, Ill., 1961), with many examples from the whole of English and American literature. See also Robert Scholes and Robert Kellogg, *The Nature of Narrative* (New York, 1966) and the influential book by F. K. Stanzel, *A Theory of Narrative*, trans. Charlotte Goedsche (Cambridge, 1984). There is a useful brief discussion of these questions as related to Chaucer by Donald R. Howard, 'Chaucer the Man', *PMLA*, 80 (1965), 337–43.

2 See 'Chaucer the Pilgrim', *PMLA*, 69 (1954), 928–36, repr. in *Chaucer Criticism, Vol. 1: 'The Canterbury Tales'*, ed. Richard J. Schoeck and Jerome Taylor (Notre Dame, Ind., 1960), pp. 1–13, and in E. Talbot Donaldson, *Speaking of Chaucer* (London, 1970), pp. 1–12. For my own, slightly different, interpretation, see below, chapter 8.

3 There is a good reproduction in both volumes of Patricia Kean's *Chaucer and the Making of English Poetry* (London, 1972). See the highly speculative reconstruction by Margaret Galway, 'The "Troilus" Frontispiece', *MLR*, 44 (1949), 161–77, also with a good reproduction of the original. A more critical account is given by Elizabeth Salter and Derek Pearsall, 'The Troilus Frontispiece and

Chaucer's Audience', *YES*, 7 (1977), 68–74. See also my own more general discussion in 'The Audience of Chaucer's *Troilus and Criseyde*', in *Chaucer and Middle English Studies in Honour of Rossell Hope Robbins*, ed. Beryl Rowland (London, 1974), pp. 173–89, repr. in *Chaucer's Troilus. Essays in Criticism*, ed. Stephen A. Barney (Hamden, Conn., 1980), pp. 211–29.

4 See the general remarks by George Kane, *The Autobiographical Fallacy in Chaucer and Langland Studies*, The Chambers Memorial Lecture (London, 1965), and the fresh approach to the problem in John Burrow, *Autobiographical Poetry in the Middle Ages: The Case of Thomas Hoccleve*, Sir Israel Gollancz Memorial Lecture (British Academy, 1982), and 'The Poet as Petitioner', *SAC*, 3 (1981), 61–75, repr. in John Burrow, *Essays on Medieval Literature* (Oxford, 1984), pp. 161–76.

5 See Bertrand Bronson, 'Chaucer's Art in Relation to its Audience', *Five Studies in Literature*, University of California Publications in English, 8:1 (Berkeley, Calif., 1940), pp. 1–53, esp. pp. 37–42; the whole study is still one of the best accounts of the oral character of Chaucer's poetry. See also Bertrand Bronson, *In Search of Chaucer* (Toronto, 1960), pp. 25–33. Most modern studies acknowledge the general fact, but not all draw the same conclusions from it. See also my 'Chaucer's Audience', *LStE*, n.s., 10 (1978), 58–73.

6 See Arthur K. Moore, '*Sir Thopas* as Criticism of Fourteenth-Century Minstrelsy', *JEGP*, 53 (1954), 532–45. On the 'Tale of Melibee' as part of the whole structure of *The Canterbury Tales*, see Donald R. Howard, *The Idea of the Canterbury Tales* (Berkeley, Calif., 1976), pp. 309–16.

7 See the particularly stimulating essay by Morton W. Bloomfield, 'Authenticating Realism and the Realism of Chaucer', *Thought*, 39 (1964), 335–58, repr. in M. W. Bloomfield, *Essays and Explorations* (Cambridge, Mass., 1970), pp. 175–98.

8 See the excellent study by Robert O. Payne, *The Key of Remembrance: A Study of Chaucer's Poetics* (New Haven, Conn., 1963). The idea that Chaucer's poems are primarily about the function of poetry has become rather fashionable of late. It can easily turn into a meaningless formula, and I would endorse it only in the more concrete and limited sense implied in my discussion.

9 On *The Legend of Good Women* see below, chapter 7, where earlier criticism of the poem is referred to. The most important study in the present context is Lisa J. Kiser, *Telling Classical Tales: Chaucer and the 'Legend of Good Women'* (Ithaca, N.Y., 1983).

10 See the discussion below, chapter. 8. On the historical background of the 'Retraction', see the older essay by J. S. P. Tatlock, 'Chaucer's *Retractions*', *PMLA*, 28 (1913), 521–9.

11 On Chaucer's language, see the excellent introduction by David Burnley, *A Guide to Chaucer's Language* (London, 1983); on the general historical background, see A. C. Baugh and T. Cable, *A History of the English Language*, 3rd edn (London, 1978), and N. F. Blake, *The English Language in Medieval Literature* (London, 1977).

12 See Caroline F. E. Spurgeon, *Five Hundred Years of Chaucer Criticism and Allusion, 1357–1900* (Cambridge, 1925), I, 14 and 58. On Chaucer's immediate impact on fifteenth-century poetry, see Denton Fox, 'Chaucer's Influence on Fifteenth-Century Poetry', in the first edition of *Companion to Chaucer Studies*,

Notes

ed. Rowland (Toronto, 1968), pp. 385–402, unaccountably omitted from the second edition, and Derek Pearsall, 'The English Chaucerians', in *Chaucer and Chaucerians: Critical Studies in Middle English Literature*, ed. D. S. Brewer (London, 1966), pp. 201–39. Chaucer's language and style have not yet been studied in sufficient detail, and the present book is no exception. See the interesting study by Norman E. Eliason, *The Language of Chaucer's Poetry: An Appraisal of the Verse, Style, and Structure*, Anglistica, 17 (Copenhagen, 1972). The book's subtitle indicates the variety of aspects treated. There are some very good chapters on stylistic problems in Burnley's *Guide to Chaucer's Language*. More specific, but extremely helpful and suggestive is J. D. Burnley, *Chaucer's Language and the Philosopher's Tradition* (Cambridge, 1979).

13 See the excellent essay by D. S. Brewer, 'The Relationship of Chaucer to the English and European Traditions', in *Chaucer and Chaucerians*, ed. Brewer, pp. 1–38; on the popular romances, see my *The Middle English Romances of the Thirteenth and Fourteenth Centuries* (London, 1969).

3 Convention and individual style:
The Book of the Duchess

1 D. W. Robertson bases his interpretation on this assumption; see his rather less than impartial review of scholarship in *Companion to Chaucer Studies*, ed. Rowland, pp. 403–13, and his more historically orientated article 'The Historical Setting of Chaucer's *Book of the Duchess*', *Medieval Studies in Honor of Urban Tigner Holmes, Jr.*, ed. John Mahoney and John Esten Keller (Chapel Hill, N.C., 1965), pp. 169–95.

2 One of the best accounts of Chaucer's originality within the conventions taken over from the 'sources' is in Wolfgang Clemen's chapter on the poem in *Chaucer's Early Poetry* (London, 1963), pp. 23–66. A detailed survey of the French antecedents and models of the poem can be found in James Wimsatt, *Chaucer and the French Love-Poets: The Literary Background of the Book of the Duchess* (Chapel Hill, N.C., 1968). See also James I. Wimsatt, 'Chaucer and French Poetry', in *Chaucer*, ed. D. S. Brewer, pp. 109–36.

3 See the very helpful survey by A. C. Spearing, *Medieval Dream-Poetry* (Cambridge, 1976).

4 See R. M. Lumiansky, 'The Bereaved Narrator in Chaucer's *The Book of the Duchess*', TSE, 9 (1959), 5–17. Lumiansky thinks that the narrator is consoled in the course of the poem, just as the black knight is. J. Burke Severs disagrees and denies that Chaucer portrays himself here either as a lover or as a mourner: see 'Chaucer's Self-Portrait in the *Book of the Duchess*', PQ, 43 (1964), 27–39.

5 See Clemen, pp. 29–37. The point is made very briefly in John Livingston Lowes, *Geoffrey Chaucer* (Oxford, 1934), pp. 94–7, and in Charles Muscatine, *Chaucer and the French Tradition: A Study in Style and Meaning* (Berkeley, Calif., 1957), pp. 102–5. The episode is a particularly good example of what Patricia Kean very aptly calls Chaucer's 'urbane manner': see the chapter on *The Book of the Duchess* in her *Chaucer and the Making of English Poetry*, I, 31–66, which is very illuminating on many aspects of the poem.

6 There are some very good interpretations of the poem from this point of view. See Bertrand H. Bronson, '*The Book of the Duchess* Re-Opened', PMLA, 67 (1952),

863–81, repr. in *Chaucer: Modern Essays in Criticism*, ed. Edward Wagenknecht (New York, 1959), pp. 271–94, and John Lawlor, 'The Pattern of Consolation in *The Book of the Duchess*', *Speculum*, 31 (1956), 626–48, repr. in *Chaucer Criticism, Vol. 2: 'Troilus and Criseyde' & The Minor Poems*, ed. Richard J. Schoeck and Jerome Taylor (Notre Dame, Ind., 1961), pp. 232–60. Clemen also discusses this aspect.

7 The ending of the poem, with its fairly obvious allusion to Lancaster's name, strongly suggests some personal reference: 'A long castel with walles white, / Be seynt Johan! on a ryche hil' (1318–19); but one still should be careful not to take this level of meaning too seriously.

8 See Bronson, p. 880: 'sympathy is the only effective kind of help that can be offered directly in the face of bereavement'.

9 There has been a lengthy scholarly debate on this issue: see (to mention only a few interesting contributions) Kemp Malone, *Chapters on Chaucer* (Baltimore, Md, 1951), pp. 19–41; James R. Kreuzer, 'The Dreamer in the *Book of the Duchess*', *PMLA*, 66 (1951), 543–7; Donald C. Baker, 'The Dreamer Again in *The Book of the Duchess*', *PMLA*, 70 (1955), 279–82. There are some very sensible remarks on this point in the essays by Bronson and Lawlor quoted above, n. 6. More recent criticism has had little to add to this.

10 See the excellent essay by Dorothy Bethurum, 'Chaucer's Point of View as Narrator in the Love Poems', *PMLA*, 74 (1959), 511–20, repr. in Schoeck–Taylor, II, 211–31.

11 On the relationship between courtly poetry and the theme of consolation, see the discussion by Phillip C. Boardman, 'Courtly Language and the Strategy of Consolation in the *Book of the Duchess*', *ELH*, 44 (1977), 567–79.

12 Most thoroughly in Bernard F. Huppé and D. W. Robertson, *Fruyt and Chaf: Studies in Chaucer's Allegories* (Princeton, N.J., 1963), pp. 32–100; see the critical reviews by Donald R. Howard in *Speculum*, 39 (1964), 537–41, and Ian Bishop in *MÆ*, 32 (1963), 238–42.

13 See the valuable discussion of these problems by Peter Dronke, *Medieval Latin and the Rise of the European Love Lyric*, 2nd edn (Oxford, 1968), I, pp. 1–56 and viii–ix. The most brilliant account of the older view is C. S. Lewis, *The Allegory of Love* (London, 1936). See also the humorous note by E. Talbot Donaldson, 'The Myth of Courtly Love', *Ventures* (Magazine of the Yale Graduate School), 5 (1965), 16–23, repr. in *Speaking of Chaucer*, pp. 154–63.

14 See John Lawlor's essay, cited above, n. 6, and D. S. Brewer, 'Natural Love in *The Parlement of Foules*', *EC*, 5 (1955), 405–18; see also D. S. Brewer, 'Love and Marriage in Chaucer's Poetry', *MLR*, 49 (1954), 461–4.

15 See the stimulating essay by John M. Steadman, ' "Courtly Love" as a Problem of Style', in *Chaucer und seine Zeit. Symposium für Walter F. Schirmer*, ed. Arno Esch (Tübingen, 1968), pp. 1–33.

16 'Chaucer's Point of View', p. 519.

17 See the essays cited above, n. 1. A very similar interpretation is proposed in Huppé–Robertson.

18 See Ian Bishop, *Pearl in its Setting* (Oxford, 1968), pp. 23–4, where he draws attention to some very slight parallels between the two poems. On the forms of consolation in *Pearl*, see the interpretation by A. C. Spearing in *The Gawain-Poet* (Cambridge, 1970), pp. 96–170.

19 Reproduced in Robertson, 'The Historical Setting' and in the beautifully produced pictorial volume by Roger Sherman Loomis, *A Mirror of Chaucer's World*
(Princeton, N.J., 1965), no. 18. The tomb was destroyed in the great fire of 1666
and only survives in an engraving. On Henry Yevele, see John Harvey, *English
Medieval Architects: A Biographical Dictionary down to 1550* (London, 1954),
pp. 312–20. One scholar has even denied any connection between *The Book of
the Duchess* and the actual death of Blanche and dates the poem years earlier
(Eliason, pp. 57–8). This is only possible because the poem is not a religious elegy
or consolation in any obvious sense: but Eliason's suggestion sounds a little
fanciful and most scholars will not abandon the traditional dating, though it may
serve as a salutary reminder that there is no real proof.

4 Traditional genre and personal message:
The Parliament of Fowls

1 The best and most thorough edition is that by D. S. Brewer, *The Parlement of
Foulys*, Nelson's Medieval and Renaissance Library (London, 1960). Wolfgang
Clemen's chapter on the poem (pp. 122–69) is particularly illuminating, as is
Kean's (I, 67–85). See also the useful survey of criticism by Donald C. Baker in
Companion to Chaucer Studies, ed. Rowland, pp. 428–45.

2 This seems to me a strong argument against such interpretations as that by Huppé
and Robertson (pp. 101–48).

3 This is how Huppé and Robertson evidently understand the phrase (pp. 102–5).
See also Clemen, p. 136, n. 2. In Chaucer's translation of Boethius, I, prose 6 and
12, and V, prose 3, *certayn* is associated with *stabile* and the sense is quite clear.

4 Clemen rightly says that 'these lines could indeed stand as a motto for all the rest
of Chaucer's work' (p. 131).

5 On the *Somnium Scipionis*, see Brewer's edition, pp. 42–3, with some extracts in
an appendix (pp. 133–7). See also the discussion by J. A. W. Bennett, *The
Parlement of Foules: An Interpretation* (Oxford, 1957), pp. 30–57. Bennett's
book is the most thorough interpretation of the poem as far as sources and
parallels are concerned. There are some very helpful remarks on the impact of
Macrobius on the whole poem in Kean, I, 69–77.

6 The exact wording of line 65 is in some doubt; see Brewer's edition, p. 61 and
n. 102.

7 There are some good observations on the stylistic variety and the comic contrasts
in the poem in Robert Worth Frank's 'Structure and Meaning in the Parlement of
Foules', *PMLA*, 71 (1956), 530–9. Its stylistic and thematic 'adventurousness' is
also emphasized by Elizabeth Salter in her stimulating chapter, 'Chaucer and
Medieval English Tradition', in *Fourteenth-Century English Poetry*, pp. 117–40
(on *The Parliament of Fowls*, pp. 127–40).

8 See the excellent discussion by Piero Boitani, 'What Dante Meant to Chaucer', in
Chaucer and the Italian Trecento, ed. Boitani, pp. 115–39, esp. pp. 129–30.
Chaucer's poem has, however, its own kind of universality and turns out to be far
more ambitious than its modest size and subject seem to suggest. See the excellent
essay by Victoria Rothschild, '*The Parliament of Fowls*: Chaucer's Mirror up to
Nature', *RES*, n.s., 35 (1984), 164–84.

9 The brilliant and influential study by C. S. Lewis, *The Allegory of Love*, does not

really give an adequate idea of the diversity of allegorical forms and methods. It should be supplemented at least by Rosemond Tuve's richly documented study, *Allegorical Imagery* (Princeton, N.J., 1966), and the stimulating chapter 'The Allegorical Picture' in Pamela Gradon's *Form and Style in Early English Literature* (London, 1971), pp. 32–92, esp. pp. 77–82. See also the useful survey by John MacQueen, *Allegory*, The Critical Idiom, 14 (London, 1970).

10 On the garden topos, see Bennett, pp. 62–106.

11 See Clemen, pp. 141–2, on the personal tone of the description.

12 See the excellent essay by Dorothy Bethurum, 'The Center of the *Parlement of Foules*', in *Essays in Honor of Walter Clyde Curry* (Nashville, Tenn., 1954), pp. 39–50. The significance of the garden for the whole poem seems to me a little overstated.

13 See Bennett, pp. 107–32; Kean, I, 77–82; and the chapter on Natura in E. R. Curtius, *European Literature and the Latin Middle Ages*, trans. W. R. Trask (New York and London, 1953).

14 See the brief remarks on this poem in Peter Dronke's excellent survey, *The Medieval Lyric*, Hutchinson University Library (London, 1968), p. 189.

15 On these problems, see the stimulating article by D. S. Brewer, 'Class Distinction in Chaucer', *Speculum*, 43 (1968), 290–305, repr. in Brewer's *Tradition and Innovation in Chaucer* (London, 1982); Brewer makes convincingly clear that social criticism is not the central issue here.

16 See Bennett, pp. 162–4; Clemen's interpretation is a little more sceptical (pp. 157–9). Gardiner Stillwell sees chiefly the comical and satirical elements in the wooing competition: see his two essays 'Unity and Comedy in Chaucer's Parlement of Foules', *JEGP*, 49 (1950), 470–95, and 'Chaucer's Eagles and their Choice on February 14', *JEGP*, 53 (1954), 546–61. A similar view is offered by Charles O. McDonald, 'An Interpretation of Chaucer's *Parlement of Foules*', *Speculum*, 30 (1955), 444–57, repr. in Wagenknecht, pp. 309–27, and Schoeck–Taylor, II, 275–93.

17 See Macdonald Emslie, 'Codes of Love and Class Distinctions', *EC*, 5 (1955), 1–17, and the discussion in the same volume, pp. 405–18. Emslie sees 'this social placing of courtly love' (p. 9) as the centre of the poem. See also on this point Bronson, *In Search of Chaucer*, pp. 46–7.

18 See Frank, p. 539. More balanced is the careful interpretation by Dorothy Everett, 'Chaucer's Love Visions, with Particular Reference to the *Parlement of Foules*', in her *Essays on Middle English Literature*, ed. P. Kean (Oxford, 1959), pp. 97–114.

19 See the discussion in *EC*, 5 (1955), 405–18, and Bennett, p. 133. See also B. Bronson, 'The Parlement of Foules Revisited', *ELH*, 15 (1948), 247–60. Bronson finds a certain amount of contradiction within the debate, which suggests a change of Chaucer's original plan.

20 This is suggested in Huppé–Robertson, pp. 141–4; most scholars disagree. See also *EC*, 5 (1955), 405–18.

21 On the role of the poet, see Charles A. Owen, Jr, 'The Role of the Narrator in the Parlement of Foules', *CE*, 14 (1953), 264–9. R. M. Lumiansky also discusses the poetological implications in his essay 'Chaucer's *Parlement of Foules*: A Philosophical Interpretation', *RES*, 24 (1948), 81–9. The wider philosophical issues are also explored in two more recent essays: H. M. Leicester, Jr, 'The Harmony

of Chaucer's *Parlement*: A Dissonant Voice', *ChR*, 9 (1974–5), 15–34, and, in answer to Leicester, David Aers, 'The *Parliament of Fowls*: Authority, the Knower and the Known', *ChR*, 16 (1981–2), 1–17.

5 Tradition and experience:
The House of Fame

1 There are several book-length studies of the poem: J. A. W. Bennett, *Chaucer's Book of Fame* (Oxford, 1968), is very useful on the general background of the poem and its unity; B. G. Koonce, *Chaucer and the Tradition of Fame: Symbolism in the House of Fame* (Princeton, N.J., 1966) is rather more speculative and has to be used with care. The best study is that by Piero Boitani, *Chaucer and the Imaginary World of Fame* (Cambridge, 1984). The book places the poem in a wide European context and is full of new insights and stimulating ideas as well as of useful references.

2 See the chapter 'Venus and Vergil', in Bennett (pp. 1–51), and Clemen, pp. 79–87. For a more philosophical, and to my mind a little too subtle reading, see Charles P. R. Tisdale, '*The House of Fame*: Vergilian Reason and Boethian Wisdom', *CL*, 25 (1973), 247–61. See also Chaucer's own, quite different version of Dido's story in *The Legend of Good Women*: see below, chapter 7.

3 On the character of the narrator in the poem, see David M. Bevington, 'The Obtuse Narrator in Chaucer's *House of Fame*', *Speculum*, 36 (1961), 288–98. Bevington, perhaps, makes a little too much of the narrator's individuality.

4 On the poetological aspect of the poem, see the review by Laurence Shook in *Companion to Chaucer Studies*, ed. Rowland, pp. 414–27, and, with much wider sweep, Boitani's last chapter, 'The Cave and the Labyrinth: Literature and Language', in *Chaucer and the Imaginary World of Fame*, pp. 189–216.

5 On the influence of the *Consolatio Philosophiae*, see Paul G. Ruggiers, 'The Unity of Chaucer's *House of Fame*', *SP*, 50 (1953), 16–29. On Dante's impact, see Boitani, 'What Dante Meant to Chaucer', pp. 117–26.

6 Most eloquently, perhaps, by Clemen, pp. 90–100.

7 This point is made very convincingly by Boitani (see above, n. 5).

8 Many critics comment on the stylistic virtuosity of the poem. Muscatine (p. 108) speaks of the 'playful, exuberant inconstancy that informs the whole', and P. Kean of the 'sheer technical brilliance' (1, 87).

9 See Boitani, *Chaucer and the Imaginary World of Fame*, for a masterly survey of the concept of Fame through the centuries: 'From Homer to the Scholastics', pp. 18–71, and 'The Fourteenth-Century Fame of Fame', pp. 72–158.

10 Boitani, 'What Dante Meant to Chaucer', pp. 124–5, sees a reminiscence of Dante in these lines. Ruggiers in his article, cited above, n. 5, suggests that the 'man of gret auctorite' was to have been Boethius.

11 See the useful survey of earlier criticism in Kay Stevenson, 'The Endings of Chaucer's *House of Fame*, *ESt*, 59 (1978), 10–26. There are good reasons for assuming that the poem was not intentionally left unfinished. See also N. F. Blake, 'Geoffrey Chaucer: the Critics and the Canon', *Archiv*, 221 (1984), 65–79 (on the *House of Fame*, pp. 65–70).

Notes

6 The storyteller and his material:
Troilus and Criseyde

1 See the brief survey of earlier criticism by John P. McCall, *Companion to Chaucer Studies*, pp. 446–63. There is an an excellent up-to-date bibliography in the new edition of the poem by B. A. Windeatt, *Geoffrey Chaucer: 'Troilus and Criseyde'. A New Edition of 'The Book of Troilus'* (London, 1984). This is by far the best and most thorough edition of the poem.

2 See the account in the edition by Robert Kilburn Root, *The Book of Troilus and Criseyde* (Princeton, N.J., 1926), pp. xx–xl; this was the most useful and thorough edition before the appearance of Windeatt's work. Its textual apparatus is now largely out of date; the commentary is still worth consulting. On the Troy-story, see the excellent account by C. D. Benson, *The History of Troy in Middle English Literature* (Cambridge, 1980).

3 There is a useful English translation of Boccaccio's poem as well as the version of Benoît, in *The Story of Troilus*, ed. R. K. Gordon (London, 1934). See also N. E. Griffin and A. B. Myrick, *The Filostrato of Giovanni Boccaccio: A Translation with Parallel Text* (Philadelphia, Pa, 1929). Windeatt's edition gives the Italian text complete, printed in parallel columns with Chaucer's 'translation', so that the reader can see at a glance where Chaucer added material or rearranged the story. Windeatt's commentary, also printed parallel with Chaucer's poem, is invaluable for its detailed comparison between the two versions. Many interpretations discuss the original use Chaucer made of Boccaccio's poem. See the classic study by C. S. Lewis, 'What Chaucer Really Did to *Il Filostrato*', *E&S*, 17 (1931), 56–75, repr. in Schoeck–Taylor, II, 16–33, and in *Chaucer's Troilus: Essays in Criticism*, ed. Barney, pp. 37–54, which gives a very one-sided account. Stylistic differences are very helpfully discussed in Muscatine, pp. 124–65.

4 See Windeatt's note on 1.394. We shall probably never know whether Chaucer really believed Lollius to be a Latin author, whether he used the name as a pseudonym for Boccaccio, or whether he deliberately made it up. This does not, however, materially affect the relationship between the two poems.

5 See *Consolatio Philosophiae*, II, prose 2, in Chaucer's translation and Chaucer's own 'Glose' on *tragedye*: 'Tragedye is to seyn a dite of a prosperite for a tyme, that endeth in wrecchidnesse' (70–2). Many critics have commented on the close relationship between Chaucer's poem and the *Consolatio*. See the interesting, though rather one-sided, article by D. W. Robertson, 'Chaucerian Tragedy', *ELH*, 19 (1952), 1–37, repr. in Schoeck–Taylor, II, 86–121, and T. P. Dunning, 'God and Man in *Troilus and Criseyde*', in *English and Medieval Studies Presented to J. R. R. Tolkien on the Occasion of his Seventieth Birthday*, ed. Norman Davis and C. L. Wrenn (London, 1962), pp. 164–82. John P. McCall first pointed out a structural relationship between the five books of each of the two works: 'Five-Book Structure in Chaucer's *Troilus*', *MLQ*, 23 (1962), 297–308.

6 Windeatt's excellent edition and commentary make such detailed comparison much easier. See also the general remarks in his introduction, pp. 3–11, which are more helpful than many more sweeping critical accounts.

7 Muscatine (see above, n. 3) is very good on the stylistic variations and their

function; there is also a good chapter on *Troilus* in Payne (pp. 171–232), though he sometimes overstates the ironical contrasts. Derek Brewer's masterly essay on the poem in *The Middle Ages*, ed. W. F. Bolton, Sphere History of Literature in the English Language, I (London, 1970), pp. 195–228, is particularly sane and to the point on these and other aspects of the poem.

8 This is suggested, a little too dramatically, by Robertson (see above, n. 5). Many recent interpretations see some kind of ironic commentary in the contrast of the two characters. See the thorough, if sometimes over-subtle, study of irony in the poem by Ida L. Gordon, *The Double Sorrow of Troilus* (Oxford, 1970). See also the discussion of contrasts in Roger Sharrock, 'Second Thoughts: C. S. Lewis on Chaucer's *Troilus*', EC, 8 (1958), 123–37, mainly a criticism of Lewis' rather too neat account.

9 See (apart from C. S. Lewis) especially Alfred David, 'The Hero of the *Troilus*', *Speculum*, 37 (1962), 566–81, and Robert P. apRoberts, 'The Central Episode in Chaucer's *Troilus*', PMLA, 77 (1962), 373–85. A similar tendency can be found in Bertram Joseph, 'Troilus and Criseyde – "a most admirable and inimitable Epicke poeme"', E&S 1954, 42–61, and (a little more cautious and subtle) in Dorothy Everett's excellent essay, '*Troilus and Criseyde*', in her *Essays on Middle English Literature*, pp. 115–38. See also the very sane and balanced interpretation by E. T. Donaldson in his *Chaucer's Poetry: An Anthology for the Modern Reader* (New York, 1958), pp. 965–80, repr. in Burrow, *Geoffrey Chaucer*, pp. 190–206, and the excellent chapter on the poem in Kean, (I.112–78).

10 On the function of comedy in the portrayal of Criseyde, see two illuminating essays: Alfred David, 'Chaucerian Comedy and Criseyde', and Mark Lambert, '*Troilus*, Books I–III: A Criseydan Reading', both in *Essays on Troilus and Criseyde*, ed. Mary Salu (Cambridge, 1979), pp. 90–104 and 105–25. See also my 'Chaucerian Comedy and Shakespearean Tragedy', ShJW, 1984, pp. 111–27.

11 Pandarus' terminology makes clear that for him the situation is very much like a deer-hunt: 'Lo, hold the at thi triste cloos, and I / Shal wel the deer unto thi bowe dryve' (II.1534–5).

12 Pointed out by Dunning (pp. 175–6) and others. I cannot agree with critics who see this passage as a criticism of extra-marital love. Chaucer seems to have kept the question of marriage deliberately out of the poem.

13 See Dunning's article and Peter Dronke, 'The Conclusion of *Troilus and Criseyde*', MÆ, 33 (1964), 47–52, esp. pp. 50–2. A similar view is discussed in Elizabeth Salter, '"Troilus and Criseyde": A Reconsideration', in *Patterns of Love and Courtesy: Essays in Memory of C. S. Lewis*, ed. John Lawlor (London, 1966), pp. 86–106; she finds, however, something like an inconsistency in the poem's attitude. For C. S. Lewis' description of the poem as 'a great poem in praise of love', see *The Allegory of Love*, pp. 176–97; the quotation comes from p. 197.

14 This is rightly pointed out by Dronke. A similar view, based on a discussion of the figure of the poet, is to be found in the excellent interpretation of the poem in Robert M. Durling, *The Figure of the Poet in Renaissance Epic* (Cambridge, Mass., 1965), pp. 44–66. See also Dunning's article for a similar reading.

15 Alfred David talks of 'tragic error' (p. 578); the analogy to Adam's fall is stressed by Robertson, pp. 30 and 36.

Notes

16 The ambiguity of the situation is pointed out by Ida L. Gordon, pp. 114–17. See also Alan T. Gaylord, 'Gentilesse in Chaucer's *Troilus*', *SP*, 61 (1964), 19–34. The critical force of Chaucer's irony is rather overrated there.

17 See the rather strained attempt to exonerate Criseyde in apRoberts, pp. 373–83.

18 See the excellent essay by John Burrow, 'Honour and Shame in *Sir Gawain and the Green Knight*', in his *Essays on Medieval Literature*, pp. 117–31; although dealing with a different poem, this seems to me very relevant here. See also D. S. Brewer, 'Honour in Chaucer', *E&S 1973*, 1–19, repr. in *Tradition and Innovation in Chaucer*. It is worth noting in this connection that Chaucer inserted eight stanzas on the need for secrecy between his translation of two stanzas of Boccaccio: see III, 288–343.

19 This is not to deny that questions of psychologically plausible behaviour play an important part here and that Criseyde is a character within a narrative sequence of events. See Payne, *The Key of Remembrance*, pp. 180–3, and Geoffrey Shepherd, 'Troilus and Criseyde', in *Chaucer and Chaucerians*, ed. Brewer, pp. 65–87, esp. pp. 78–80.

20 On the whole scene, see the excellent essay by Jill Mann, 'Troilus' Swoon', *ChR*, 14 (1979–80), 319–35.

21 See Dronke, 'The Conclusion of *Troilus and Criseyde*', pp. 50–2, and Durling, pp. 53–5, for a refutation of this view.

22 On the debated position of the two stanzas following III.1323, see Windeatt's edition, pp. 47–8.

23 The discussion is well summarized by Hans Käsmann, '"I wolde excuse hire yit for routhe". Chaucers Einstellung zu Criseyde', in *Chaucer und seine Zeit*, ed. Esch, pp. 97–122. His conclusions are, however, different from mine.

24 This is demonstrated by Hans Käsmann by a detailed comparison between Chaucer's poem and his sources, (pp. 100–10). The view, frequently expressed, that Chaucer 'minimizes Criseyde's guilt in every way possible', simplifies what actually happens in the text. The quotation is from S. S. Hussey, *Chaucer: An Introduction*, 2nd edn (London, 1981), p. 74.

25 See Käsmann, p. 110; he denies, *pace* E. Salter, that there is a break or contradiction within the poem and argues that Chaucer has carefully prepared us for Criseyde's betrayal. I am not so sure.

26 See, for instance, Tennyson's *In Memoriam*, VII: 'Dark house, by which once more I stand / Here in the long unlovely street.'

27 See Howard Patch, 'Troilus on Determinism', *Speculum*, 6 (1931), 225–43, repr. in Schoeck–Taylor, II, 71–85. The whole question is discussed within a larger context in the excellent article by Morton Bloomfield, 'Distance and Predestination in *Troilus and Criseyde*', *PMLA*, 72 (1957), 14–26, repr. in Schoeck–Taylor, II, 196–210, and in Bloomfield's *Essays and Explorations*, pp. 201–16.

28 See *Consolatio Philosophiae*, V, prose 4–6.

29 See Bloomfield's discussion; my own conclusions are very similar to his. Chaucer makes Criseyde much more emphatic in her protestations and assurances. This is not, I think, meant to discredit her by deliberate dramatic irony, but rather to underline her complete sincerity at this point. See Windeatt's edition and his commentary on IV.1667–87. See the very helpful interpretation of the parting scene in A. C. Spearing, *Criticism and Medieval Poetry*, 2nd edn (London, 1972),

pp. 147–56. I agree entirely with Spearing's claim that Chaucer 'allowed the great betrayer a final moment of integrity and dignity' (p. 154).

30 See John P. McCall, 'The Trojan Scene in Chaucer's *Troilus*', *ELH*, 29 (1962), 263–75, for a good discussion of the connections between the history of Troy and the fate of the lovers.

31 See Robertson, 'Chaucerian Tragedy', p. 32. A similar reading had been proposed some years previously by James Lyndon Shanley 'The *Troilus* and Christian Love', *ELH*, 6 (1939), 271–81, repr. in Wagenknecht, pp. 385–95, and in Schoeck–Taylor, II, 136–46. See also Alan T. Gaylord, 'The Lesson of the *Troilus*: Chastisement and Correction', in *Essays on Troilus and Criseyde*, ed. Salu, pp. 23–42.

32 See Elizabeth Salter's essay, cited above, n. 13. She overstates, in my opinion, the contradictions between the first part of the poem and its ending, but she is certainly pointing out a real problem when she writes: 'the final answers given by *Troilus* do not match the intelligence and energy of the questions asked, the issues raised' (p. 106). Donaldson's interpretation is similar, but he sees it mainly as a question of narrative technique: see his stimulating essay, 'The Ending of Chaucer's *Troilus*', in *Early English and Norse Studies Presented to Hugh Smith in Honour of his Sixtieth Birthday*, ed. Arthur Brown and Peter Foote (London, 1963), pp. 26–45, repr. in *Speaking of Chaucer*, pp. 84–101.

33 This is shown by Donaldson who, however, over-dramatizes the narrator's dilemma. See also his essay, 'Criseyde and her Narrator', in *Speaking of Chaucer*, pp. 65–83, where he talks about the 'wildly emotional attitude of the narrator' (p. 68). There is a very good discussion of the narrator's attitude in the chapter on Chaucer in Durling, *The Figure of the Poet in Renaissance Epic*. See also Robert M. Jordan, 'The Narrator in Chaucer's *Troilus*', *ELH*, 25 (1958), 237–57, and the chapter on the narrator in I. L. Gordon, *The Double Sorrow of Troilus*, pp. 61–92.

34 See the differing interpretations by Dronke ('The Conclusion of *Troilus and Criseyde*', pp. 47–9) and Käsmann (pp. 120–1). Durling argues convincingly that more important than Troilus' fate is the new perspective opened up by this analogy to the *Somnium Scipionis* (p. 246, n. 20). The 'greatness of Troilus' beatitude' (Dronke, p. 49) is, after all, a little subdued and does not quite outweigh the tragedy. See also the excellent study of the whole tradition behind this ending in John M. Steadman, *Disembodied Laughter: Troilus and the Apotheosis Tradition* (Berkeley, Calif., 1972), and the excellent commentary in Windeatt's edition, p. 559.

35 See Dronke, 'The Conclusion of *Troilus and Criseyde*', pp. 48–9; a different view is proposed by Durling, pp. 64–5, who finds the association in Chaucer's final arrangement of these stanzas unintentional and misplaced. See also Windeatt's commentary on the ending, in his edition of the poem, for much useful material on the background and the transmission.

36 Of the lines V.1748–50, Donaldson very aptly says: 'How true! And how supremely, brilliantly, inadequate!' ('The Ending of Chaucer's *Troilus*', p. 36).

37 See my 'The Audience of Chaucer's *Troilus and Criseyde*', (cited above, chapter 2, n. 3).

Notes

7 The storyteller and his audience:
The Legend of Good Women

1 One of the first and most thorough modern accounts of the collection and its problems is Robert Worth Frank, Jr, *Chaucer and 'The Legend of Good Women'* (Cambridge, Mass., 1972). He sees the *Legend* as an important stage in Chaucer's development as a storyteller between *Troilus* and *The Canterbury Tales*.

2 On the poetological aspects of the collection, see the interesting study by Lisa J. Kiser, *Telling Classical Tales: Chaucer and the 'Legend of Good Women'* (Ithaca, N.Y., 1983).

3 See Boitani, 'What Dante Meant to Chaucer', pp. 125–6.

4 The differences between the two versions of the Prologue are very interesting. See, for instance, D. S. Brewer, *Chaucer*, 3rd edn, pp. 98–102. On the textual situation, see the illuminating article by George Kane, 'The Text of *The Legend of Good Women* in CUL MS Gg. 4. 27', in *Middle English Studies Presented to Norman Davis in Honour of his Seventieth Birthday*, ed. Douglas Gray and E. G. Stanley (Oxford, 1983), pp. 39–58.

5 For a more sophisticated interpretation, see the chapter 'Daisies, the Sun, and Poetry', in Kiser, pp. 28–49.

6 In the F-version, the poet–narrator is himself more personally involved in the service of the Flower and the Leaf and he celebrates the worship of love. The G-version keeps the narrator more in the background, or at least makes it clear that he is not a practitioner of love but of love-poetry. It is more in keeping with the general theme of the Prologue to make most of the poet's experience part of the dream. His life outside the dream is relevant to the reader only insofar as the narrator has produced translations and poetry on the subject of love.

7 See the chapter 'On Misunderstanding Texts', in Kiser, pp. 71–94.

8 See the interesting, if somewhat biased, article by Elaine Tuttle Hansen, 'Irony and the Antifeminist Narrator in Chaucer's *Legend of Good Women*', *JEGP*, 82 (1983), 11–31.

9 The term 'legend' is in itself rather ambiguous, because outside Chaucer it was always restricted to saints' lives, not to unhappy lovers.

10 Kiser's description of the legendary as 'self consciously "bad art"' (p. 97) is, perhaps, a little too extreme, but her reading seems to me more in tune with Chaucer's intention than that of Frank.

11 On this point see Hansen's article, cited above, n. 8.

12 See Peter Godman, 'Chaucer and Boccaccio's Latin Works', in *Chaucer and the Italian Trecento*, ed. Boitani, pp. 269–95 (on Cleopatra, pp. 281–90).

13 See Hansen, pp. 26–7.

14 See the excellent article by V. A. Kolve, 'From Cleopatra to Alceste: An Iconographic Study of *The Legend of Good Women*', in *Signs and Symbols in Chaucer's Poetry*, ed. John P. Hermann and John J. Burke, Jr (University, Ala., 1981), pp. 130–78. Quotations from pp. 146 and 132. Kiser sees the snake pit as an image of hell and points to the remarkable analogies between Cleopatra's legend and hagiographic traditions (pp. 107–9).

15 Frank, pp. 48–53. Kiser offers a more sophisticated reading and sees the 'Legend of Thisbe' as an act of rebellion against the God of Love's demands. Chaucer's

purpose is not very clear; the story is certainly not told as a straightforward parody, but it is more than an uncritical translation.

16 See Gower's *Confessio Amantis*, III.1331–1494.

17 See Kiser, who rightly claims that it is 'unlike Chaucer to approve of any simpleminded moral clarity (such as that which the "good women" are all meant to project)', (p. 94).

18 See Hansen, p. 26. Hansen is more concerned with the content, feminist or anti-feminist, of the stories. Just as important, however, is the literary issue, the questioning of primitively didactic storytelling and stupid moralizing.

19 Frank, p. 84; he thinks the legend a failure (p. 90).

20 The first part of the legend is more elaborate and suggests something of the traditional stature of the characters. The second half returns to the more superficial tone of many of the other legends.

21 See Chaucer's earlier account of Dido's story in *The House of Fame*, and above, chapter 5.

22 Frank, p. 152.

23 *Pace* Frank, p. 155. It is, of course, possible that Chaucer's contemporaries found more genuine tragic pathos in Phyllis' complaint, and readers may well differ as to the degree of subversive irony in Chaucer's account.

24 See N. F. Blake, 'Geoffrey Chaucer: the Critics and the Canon', pp. 71–4.

25 *Ibid.*, p. 73. See also the very sane and balanced discussion by Frank, pp. 189–210 ('The Legend of Chaucer's Boredom'). Frank also quotes the passage from Lydgate.

26 This is not to deny, however, that there are significant differences in style and narrative technique as well as in emphasis and degrees of seriousness, but the task imposed on the narrator makes, almost inevitably, for a certain monotony which Chaucer does not go out of his way to disguise.

27 Kiser is, perhaps, overstating her case when she summarizes: 'Chaucer juxtaposes "good" poetry with "bad" because he wishes to convey to us that he is serving two masters in the *Legend* – both Ovid and the God of Love' (p. 146), but she has certainly put her finger on the central problem.

8 Pilgrims and narrators:
The Canterbury Tales

1 See the description of the manuscripts in the monumental compilation by John M. Manly and Edith Rickert, *The Text of the Canterbury Tales. Studied on the Basis of all Known Manuscripts*, 8 vols. (Chicago, Ill., 1940), esp. vols. I and II. A more radical view of the problems of transmission and arrangement is presented and put into practice in the edition by N. F. Blake, *The Canterbury Tales by Geoffrey Chaucer. Edited from the Hengwrt Manuscript*, York Medieval Texts, second series (London, 1980). See also N. F. Blake, 'The Relationship between the Hengwrt and the Ellesmere Manuscripts of the "Canterbury Tales"', *E&S*, n.s., 32 (1979), 1–18, and 'Critics, Criticism and the Order of the Canterbury Tales', *Archiv*, 218 (1981), 47–58, and his more comprehensive study, *The Textual Tradition of the Canterbury Tales* (London, 1985).

2 See the useful discussion of possible models and parallels in *Sources and Analogues of Chaucer's Canterbury Tales*, ed. W. F. Bryan and G. Dempster

(Chicago, Ill., 1941), pp. 1–81. A very sensible recent treatment of the subject is chapter 1, 'The Genre of the Story-Collection', of Helen Cooper, *The Structure of the Canterbury Tales* (London, 1983), pp. 8–55.

3 See the edition by Karl Brunner, *The Seven Sages of Rome*, EETS, OS, 191 (1933), with a good account of the textual transmission, and Cooper, pp. 23–5.

4 For a recent assessment, see Donald McGrady, 'Chaucer and the *Decameron* Reconsidered', *ChR*, 12 (1977–8), 1–26. McGrady adduces persuasive arguments to support his claim that Chaucer did indeed know the *Decameron* and was influenced by it.

5 See Robinson's textual notes for some details. The compilation by Manly and Rickert presents all the material.

6 There is a useful and sensible assessment by Robert A. Pratt, 'The Order of the *Canterbury Tales*', *PMLA*, 66 (1951), 1141–67. His own solution to the problem does not seem to me entirely convincing. A more realistic view seems to me that of Charles A. Owen, Jr, 'The Alternative Reading of *The Canterbury Tales*: Chaucer's Text and the Early Manuscripts', *PMLA*, 97 (1982), 237–50. See also Owen's more comprehensive treatment in his book *Pilgrimage and Storytelling in the Canterbury Tales: The Dialectic of 'Ernest' and 'Game'* (Norman, Okla., 1977). There is a brief, but particularly clear, account of these and many other problems by Derek Pearsall, '*The Canterbury Tales*', in *The Middle Ages*, ed. W. F. Bolton, Sphere History of Literature in the English Language, I (London, 1970), pp. 163–94.

7 See the hypothetical reconstruction by Charles A. Owen, 'The Plan of the Canterbury Pilgrimage', *PMLA*, 66 (1951), 820–6, and his summary of research on the subject: 'The Design of the *Canterbury Tales*', in *Companion to Chaucer Studies*, ed. Rowland, pp. 221–42, with useful bibliographical references. There is a good brief account in Cooper's chapter 2, 'The Ordering of the *Canterbury Tales*' (pp. 56–71).

8 See Owen's chapter in the *Companion to Chaucer Studies* (cited above, n. 7), and his article, 'The Development of the *Canterbury Tales*', *JEGP*, 57 (1958), 449–76. See the more conventional and, to my mind, more convincing view by R. M. Lumiansky, 'Chaucer's Retraction and the Degree of Completeness of the *Canterbury Tales*', *TSE*, 6 (1956), 5–13.

9 See the stimulating chapter '*The Canterbury Tales*: Concepts of Unity' in Robert M. Jordan, *Chaucer and the Shape of Creation: The Aesthetic Possibilities of Inorganic Structure* (Cambridge, Mass., 1967), pp. 111–31, and his earlier article 'Chaucer's Sense of Illusion: Roadside Drama Reconsidered', *ELH*, 29 (1962), 19–33. Perhaps the most influential among earlier advocates of a 'dramatic' reading of *The Canterbury Tales* are G. L. Kittredge, in his *Chaucer and his Poetry* (Cambridge, Mass., 1915), and J. L. Lowes, *Geoffrey Chaucer* (London, 1934). These two books, still very well worth reading, have been particularly important in giving wide currency to the idea of *The Canterbury Tales* as a 'human comedy'. This interpretation is pursued and, perhaps, a little overstated in R. M. Lumiansky, *Of Sondry Folk: The Dramatic Principle in the Canterbury Tales* (Austin, Tex., 1955). For differing views, see Malone, pp. 144–225, and Lawlor, pp. 109–39, both with persuasive arguments.

10 See Payne, p. 156. Payne's own interpretation is more concerned with the variety of genres (pp. 147–70).

Notes

11 See *The Tale of Beryn*, ed. F. J. Furnivall and W. G. Stone, EETS, ES, 105 (London, 1909).

12 See John Lydgate, *The Siege of Thebes*, ed. Axel Erdmann, EETS, ES, 108 (London, 1911), Prologue, 18–29.

13 See Robinson's note on the passage (pp. 696–7), and Pratt, 'The Order of the *Canterbury Tales*', pp. 1148–57. Blake omits the passage altogether in his edition of *The Canterbury Tales* because it is neither in the Hengwrt nor the Ellesmere manuscript.

14 See the influential interpretation by Ralph Baldwin, *The Unity of the Canterbury Tales*, Anglistica, 5 (Copenhagen, 1955), pp. 19–32, and Arthur W. Hoffman, 'Chaucer's Prologue to the Pilgrimage: The Two Voices', *ELH*, 21 (1954), 1–16, repr. in Wagenknecht, pp. 30–45. Needless to say, almost every account of *The Canterbury Tales* has something to say on this introduction.

15 The manuscript is in the British Library (Add. 18,850). On the whole tradition of seasonal description, see the wonderfully illustrated and most stimulating book by Derek Pearsall and Elizabeth Salter, *Landscapes and Seasons of the Medieval World* (London, 1973), esp. chapter 5, 'The Landscape of the Seasons' (pp. 119–60). On the April date, see Chauncey Wood, 'The April Date as a Structural Device in *The Canterbury Tales*', *MLQ*, 25 (1964), 259–71. A little too much seems to be made of the astrological references here. But see Chauncey Wood's important chapter on 'Chaucer and Astrology' in *Companion to Chaucer Studies*, ed. Rowland, pp. 202–20, with a good bibliography, and his book *Chaucer and the Country of the Stars* (Princeton, N.J., 1970).

16 On the relationship of the 'General Prologue' to the tradition of the dream-allegory, see J. V. Cunningham, 'The Literary Form of the Prologue to the *Canterbury Tales*', *MP*, 49 (1951–2), 172–81, repr. in Burrow, *Geoffrey Chaucer*, pp. 218–32; and M. Hussey, A. C. Spearing and J. Winney, *An Introduction to Chaucer* (Cambridge, 1965), pp. 19–27.

17 On the order of the portraits, see Harold Brooks, *Chaucer's Pilgrims: The Artistic Order of the Portraits in the Prologue* (London, 1962), and J. Swart, 'The Construction of Chaucer's *General Prologue*', *Neophilologus*, 38 (1954), 127–36. A different view is proposed in Jill Mann's excellent study *Chaucer and Medieval Estates Satire: The Literature of Social Classes and the General Prologue to the 'Canterbury Tales'* (Cambridge, 1973).

18 Jill Mann's book supports this with a wealth of material. My own account is heavily indebted to her learned as well as sensitive interpretation of the 'General Prologue'.

19 On the portrait of the Knight, see the interesting article by Charles Mitchell, 'The Worthiness of Chaucer's Knight', *MLR*, 25 (1964), 66–75, and Mann, pp. 106–15. There is a wealth of useful information on the portraits, not all of it equally relevant, in Muriel Bowden, *A Commentary on the General Prologue to the Canterbury Tales*, 2nd edn (New York, 1967). See also Thomas A. Kirby's chapter 'The General Prologue', in *Companion to Chaucer Studies*, ed. Rowland, pp. 243–70. A rather extreme picture of the Knight, to my mind perversely wrong-headed, but certainly challenging, is presented by Terry Jones, *Chaucer's Knight: The Portrait of a Medieval Mercenary* (London, 1980). On the portrait in the 'General Prologue' see pp. 31–140.

20 As Mitchell, Mann and others have shown, words like *worthy*, *gentil*, *good*, and

Notes

curteis seem to be invested with curiously ambiguous meanings by the context. These semantic shifts are an important instrument of Chaucer's satire.

21 See Mann, pp. 128–37. The Prioress has received a great deal of attention, but Mann's account seems to me by far the most sensible.

22 This is pointed out very convincingly by Mann, pp. 121–7. See also J. R. Hulbert, 'Chaucer's Pilgrims', *PMLA*, 64 (1949), 823–8, repr. in Wagenknecht, pp. 23–9.

23 On Langland's influence on Chaucer, see Nevill Coghill, 'Chaucer's Debt to Langland', *MÆ*, 4 (1935), 89–94; J. A. W. Bennett, 'Chaucer's Contemporary', in *Piers Plowman: Critical Approaches*, ed. S. S. Hussey (London, 1969), pp. 310–24; and Mann, pp. 207–11, and *passim*. See also the more general treatment in David Aers, *Chaucer, Langland, and the Creative Imagination* (London, 1980), and the thoughtful essay by George Kane, 'Langland and Chaucer: An Obligatory Conjunction', in *New Perspectives in Chaucer Criticism*, ed. Donald M. Rose (Norman, Okla., 1981), pp. 5–19.

24 See Mann, pp. 168–70, and Haldeen Braddy, 'The Cook's Mormal and its Cure', *MLQ*, 7 (1946), 265–7.

25 On this question, see the final chapter in Mann (pp. 187–202). The whole chapter, including the notes (pp. 289–94), is full of perceptive observations.

26 The most persuasive formulation of this interpretation is E. T. Donaldson's influential essay, 'Chaucer the Pilgrim' (see above, chapter 2, n. 2). See also Rosemary Woolf, 'Chaucer as a Satirist in the General Prologue to the Canterbury Tales', *CQ*, 1 (1959), 150–7, and Cliff Tucker's objections in the same volume, p. 262. Woolf's stimulating essay is reprinted in Burrow, *Geoffrey Chaucer*, pp. 206–14. There is a good discussion of the problem of the narrator in Paul G. Ruggiers, *The Art of the Canterbury Tales* (Madison, Wisc., 1965), pp. 16–41.

27 On the changing point of view in the 'General Prologue', see Baldwin, pp. 67–74. See also Mann, pp. 194–7, and the discussion cited above, chapter 2, n. 2.

28 Mann, p. 198.

29 To these two confessions one might add the intrusion of the Canon's Yeoman and his tale. The whole episode looks like an afterthought, because the Canon's Yeoman is not among the original pilgrims. It shows that the collection could really be extended *ad lib.*, but the relationship between prologue and tale is far less illuminating here than in the case of the Pardoner and the Wife of Bath, and the speaker does not reveal himself in anything like the same original and sophisticated manner. If we look at the intrusion more closely, however, we might well agree with Muscatine who thinks that 'the headlong entry of the Canon and Yeoman cannot be read as Chaucer's afterthought. It seems thoroughly, artistically, premeditated' (p. 220). Muscatine thinks that the two men are really shown to be outside Christian society. Whether an afterthought or not, the whole episode is another dramatic element within the frame, but, again, its main function is to introduce a tale and one whose subject comes as unexpectedly as its narrator.

30 The character of the Pardoner has been a favourite subject of Chaucer criticism. See the stimulating summary by G. G. Sedgewick, 'The Progress of Chaucer's Pardoner, 1880–1940', *MLQ*, 1 (1940), 431–58, repr. in Wagenknecht, pp. 126–58; and Schoeck–Taylor, 1, 190–220. There is also a good article by Alfred Kellogg, 'An Augustinian Interpretation of Chaucer's Pardoner', *Specu-*

lum, 26 (1951), 465–81, though it is a little too theological and far removed from Chaucer's text. More dramatic and, to my mind, a little too fanciful, is the lively treatment of the Pardoner in Donald R. Howard, *The Idea of the Canterbury Tales* (Berkeley and Los Angeles, 1976), pp. 339–71.

31 See Robinson's notes and the excerpts from various 'sources' in Bryan–Dempster, pp. 207–22. Francis Lee Utley's rightly famous compilation, *The Crooked Rib: An Analytical Index to the Argument about Women in English and Scots to the End of the Year 1568* (Columbus, Ohio, 1944), gives a vivid idea of the scope of medieval anti-feminist satire and related literature on this inexhaustible theme.

32 Most of the more recent interpretations of *The Canterbury Tales* assume that there are thematic relationships and that the tales comment on each other. See the sensible treatment by Ruggiers, *The Art of the Canterbury Tales*. Trevor Whittock's *A Reading of the Canterbury Tales* (Cambridge, 1968) has many stimulating ideas but is, on the whole, a little impressionistic and ahistorical. Patricia Kean's discussion of major themes is on far more solid ground: see, *Chaucer and the Making of English Poetry*, II, 110–85, a very thoughtful and rewarding treatment of the whole subject. See also Cooper's chapters, 'An Encyclopaedia of Kinds', and 'Themes and Variations' (pp. 72–90 and 208–39), and the rather more ambitious treatment in Howard, esp. chapter 5, 'The Tales: A Theory of Their Structure' (pp. 210–332).

33 On these two classic debates, see G. L. Kittredge, 'Chaucer's Discussion of Marriage', *MP*, 9 (1911–12), 435–67, repr. in Wagenknecht, pp. 188–215; and Schoeck–Taylor, I, 130–59; and the reply by H. B. Hinckley, 'The Debate on Marriage in the *Canterbury Tales*', *PMLA*, 32 (1917), 292–305, repr. in Wagenknecht, pp. 216–25. The debate is continued in many later discussions of *The Canterbury Tales*. There is a good summary of the whole subject by Donald R. Howard, 'The Conclusion of the Marriage Group: Chaucer and the Human Condition', *MP*, 57 (1959–60), 223–32. On the theme of the Deadly Sins, see Frederick Tupper, 'Chaucer and the Seven Deadly Sins', *PMLA*, 29 (1914), 93–128, and the substantial refutation by John L. Lowes, 'Chaucer and the Seven Deadly Sins', *PMLA*, 30 (1915), 237–371.

34 Ruggiers speaks of 'the metaphor, if you will – of pilgrimage' (p. 247). Chaucer himself, of course, uses the concept of pilgrimage in a metaphorical sense more than once. See especially: 'This world nys but a thurghfare ful of wo, / And we been pilgrymes, passynge to and fro' (I.2847–8). This quotation heads the discussion by Baldwin who has given a particularly persuasive account of this unity. See also Edmund Reiss, 'The Pilgrimage Narrative and the *Canterbury Tales*', *SP*, 67 (1970), 295–305; and the interesting discussion in Eliason, pp. 209–44.

35 See the interpretation of the 'Parson's Tale' by Baldwin, pp. 95–105. Bernard F. Huppé, *A Reading of the Canterbury Tales* (Albany, N.Y., 1964), is rather one-sided. See also the sensible chapter 7, 'Closure II: the Parson's Tale and Chaucer's Retraction', in Traugott Lawler, *The One and the Many in the Canterbury Tales* (Hamden, Conn., 1980), pp. 147–72.

36 See C. S. Lewis's pertinent remark: 'A clear recognition that our own age is quite abnormally sensitive to the funny side of sententiousness, to possible hypocrisy, and to dullness, is absolutely necessary for any one who wishes to understand the past' ('What Chaucer really did to *Il Filostrato*', p. 64). I find it, on the other

hand, difficult to accept without qualification Baldwin's statement: 'Chaucer himself might have claimed it the most meaningful, and in a dialectical sense, the most artistic of the Tales' (p. 98). Chaucer cannot really have been unaware of the fact that the 'Parson's Tale' belongs to a very different kind of literary genre from all the other tales in the collection, not even excepting the 'Tale of Melibee'.

37 See particularly the interpretations by Baldwin, Lawler and Ruggiers and the stimulating account in Jordan, pp. 227–41. I think many critics nowadays would on the whole agree with Ruggiers' general statement: 'in terms of its beginning and end, the structure of the *Canterbury Tales* is complete' (p. 23).

38 See Ruggiers, p. 40: 'the final service which art can perform is to speak ill of itself'. On the 'Retraction', see the important article by Olive Sayce, 'Chaucer's "Retractions": The Conclusion of the Canterbury Tales and its Place in Literary Tradition', *MÆ*, 40 (1971), 230–48, which quotes many parallels and shows the traditional aspects of the 'Retraction' as well as its function in the context of *The Canterbury Tales*.

39 The search for some concept of unity that will give a satisfactory shape and coherence to this fragmentary collection of tales will probably never end. After the thematic schemes imposed on the work we now have more complicated, abstract and, I believe, arbitrary ideas of what binds the whole work together. Howard's elaborately argued concept of the labyrinth is in many ways attractive and illuminating, but it remains an idea and is both too vague and too hypothetical to be really convincing. An even more learned, and at first sight tempting, but, in the last analysis, all too subjective and unsupported, theory of unity is proposed by Judson Boyce Allen and Theresa Anne Moritz, *A Distinction of Stories: The Medieval Unity of Chaucer's Fair Chain of Narratives for Canterbury* (Columbus, Ohio, 1981). The book is full of interesting insights, and the opening chapters on medieval concepts of unity, of story and of structure are admirable; only the systematic application to Chaucer's undogmatic diversity of tales does not work. Lawler's discussion of some themes and concerns uniting *The Canterbury Tales* is rather more modest and, therefore, more helpful.

9 Stories and storytellers:
The Canterbury Tales

1 On this question, see the stimulating essay by Charles Muscatine, '*The Canterbury Tales*: Style of the Man and Style of the Work', in *Chaucer and Chaucerians*, ed. Brewer, pp. 88–113.

2 See Payne, p. 156: 'the tales are a far more perfect cross section of fourteenth-century literature than the frame is of fourteenth-century society', and 'a virtually complete sampler of conventional forms for the shorter narrative in the later middle ages'.

3 Two particularly good interpretations of the tale emphasize the importance of order and balance as elements of the plot, structure, and style: William Frost, 'An Interpretation of Chaucer's Knight's Tale', *RES*, 25 (1949), 289–304, repr. in Schoeck–Taylor, I, 98–116, and Charles Muscatine, 'Form, Texture, and Meaning in Chaucer's *Knight's Tale*', *PMLA*, 65 (1950), 911–29, repr. in Wagenknecht, pp. 60–82, and, with modifications, Muscatine, pp. 175–90.

4 On Chaucer's use of the *Teseida*, see Robert A. Pratt, 'Chaucer's Use of the

Teseida', *PMLA*, 62 (1947), 598–621, and H. S. Wilson, 'The *Knight's Tale* and the *Teseida* Again', *UTQ*, 18 (1948–9), 131–46. The two most important studies are by Piero Boitani, *Chaucer and Boccaccio*, Medium Ævum Monographs, n.s., 8 (Oxford, 1977), and 'Style, Iconography and Narrative: The Lesson of the *Teseida*', in *Chaucer and the Italian Trecento*, ed. Boitani, pp. 185–99. See also J. A. W. Bennett's essay 'Chaucer, Dante and Boccaccio', in the same volume (pp. 89–113), and the excellent interpretation of the 'Knight's Tale' in Kean, II, 1–52, which continually draws on the differences between Chaucer and Boccaccio's poem. See also the new translation of the *Teseida* in *Chaucer's Boccaccio: Sources of 'Troilus' and the Knight's and Franklin's Tales*, ed. N. R. Havely, Chaucer Studies, 3 (Cambridge, 1980), pp. 103–52.

5 Boitani, 'Style, Iconography and Narrative', p. 195.

6 On Theseus' philosophy, see in particular the discussion in Kean, II, 39–48, and Cooper, pp. 103–5. On the philosophical background and the role of the gods, see also Alan T. Gaylord, 'The Role of Saturn in the *Knight's Tale*', *ChR*, 8 (1973–4), 171–90.

7 Recent interpretations often emphasize these discrepancies of style. See A. C. Spearing's interesting introduction to his edition of the 'Knight's Tale' (Cambridge, 1966), and the rather more one-sided accounts by Paull F. Baum, *Chaucer: A Critical Appreciation* (Durham, N. C., 1958), pp. 84–104, and R. Neuse, 'The Knight: The First Mover in Chaucer's Human Comedy', *UTQ*, 31 (1961–2), 299–315. Elizabeth Salter's thorough analysis in *Chaucer: The Knight's Tale and the Clerk's Tale*, Studies in English Literature, 5 (London, 1962), pp. 9–36, is particularly good on the difficulties and complexities of the tale. See also the stimulating article by Ronald B. Herzman, 'The Paradox of Form: "The Knight's Tale" and Chaucerian Aesthetics', *PLL*, 10 (1974), 339–52, repr. in *Geoffrey Chaucer*, ed. Willi Erzgräber, Wege der Forschung, 253 (Darmstadt, 1983). For a very wide-ranging interpretation of the 'Knight's Tale', especially its imagery and its iconographic associations, see the important book by V. A. Kolve, *Chaucer and the Imagery of Narrative: The First Five 'Canterbury Tales'* (London, 1984), pp. 85–157.

8 The fact that Chaucer had evidently written his version of the story before he started on *The Canterbury Tales* in earnest, as seems likely from the reference to it in the Prologue to *The Legend of Good Women* (F, 420–1; G, 408–9), does not really affect this argument. We shall probably never know how far Chaucer changed the style of the story to make it fit into the frame of *The Canterbury Tales*.

9 Terry Jones sees a very close correspondence between the Knight and his story, but I am not convinced by his reading of either of the two. See pp. 141–216, for his rather provocative interpretation of the 'Knight's Tale'.

10 This applies to a number of recent interpretations. See Robert Haller, 'Chaucer's *Squire's Tale* and the Uses of Rhetoric', *MP*, 62 (1964–5), 285–95, and, much more one-sided, Joyce E. Peterson, 'The Finished Fragment: A Reassessment of *The Squire's Tale*', *ChR*, 5 (1970–1), 62–74. For a very balanced view of the question, see the excellent article by Derek Pearsall, 'The Squire as Story-Teller', *UTQ*, 34 (1964–5), 82–92, repr. in *Geoffrey Chaucer*, ed. Erzgräber, pp. 287–99. It is usefully supplemented by K. H. Göller, 'Chaucers "Squire's Tale": "The Knotte of the Tale"', *Chaucer und seine Zeit*, ed. Esch, pp. 163–88.

Notes

11 The view that the Franklin deliberately interrupts the Squire to stop the tale is advanced by Pearsall and Peterson; Haller proposes a somewhat different interpretation.

12 See Göller, pp. 171–4.

13 See Göller, whose reading of the whole episode is largely ironic (pp. 179–87).

14 See the discussion by Haller and by Göller.

15 See (apart from the brief discussion in Haller and in Pearsall) A. C. Spearing's introduction to his very thorough and stimulating edition of the 'Franklin's Tale' (Cambridge, 1966), pp. 5–11. Spearing also believes that the Franklin deliberately cuts the Squire's tale short (p. 7). I am not so sure. On the status of the Franklin in relation to traditional chivalry, see the well-documented study by Roy J. Pearcy, 'Chaucer's Franklin and the Literary Vavasour', ChR, 8 (1973–4), 33–59.

16 See above, chapter 8 and n. 32. Most modern critics use the term 'marriage group' only with reservations.

17 See Spearing's edition.

18 See ibid., pp. 47–50. For a more positive view and a very sane assessment of the whole tale, see Gertrude M. White, 'The Franklin's Tale: Chaucer or the Critics', PMLA, 89 (1974), 454–62.

19 Of course, the nature of the promises is more than a little doubtful and must have been so for Chaucer's audience, too. See Alan T. Gaylord, 'The Promises in "The Franklin's Tale"', ELH, 31 (1964), 331–65, repr. in Geoffrey Chaucer, ed. Erzgräber, pp. 300–35. See, however, for a different approach, Gerald Morgan, 'A Defense of Dorigen's Complaint', MÆ, 46 (1977), 77–97.

20 See the particularly stimulating and original study by Leo Spitzer, 'Marie de France – Dichterin von Problem-Märchen', ZfRP, 1 (1930), 29–67. On the English lays, see my The Middle English Romances of the Thirteenth and Fourteenth Centuries, pp. 40–8. Mortimer O. Donovan, The Breton Lays: A Guide to Varieties (Notre Dame, Ind., 1969), is a useful, though somewhat superficial work of reference. See the important study by Kathryn Hume, 'Why Chaucer Calls the Franklin's Tale a Breton Lai', PQ, 51 (1972), 365–79.

21 See Kemp Malone, 'The Wife of Bath's Tale', MLR, 57 (1962), 481–91, with good observations on the character of the narrator.

22 The differences between the two introductions are pointed out by Gradon, p. 292. On the beginnings of The Canterbury Tales, see also Lowes, pp. 167–72.

23 See The Canterbury Tales, I.2809–14 (the 'Knight's Tale'); the associations between the two passages are pointed out by Whittock (pp. 78–9), among others.

24 These connections between various genres are emphasized by Muscatine: see Chaucer and the French Tradition, pp. 223–30. The 'Miller's Tale' is described as an example of 'mixed style'.

25 See the very stimulating and well-documented summary of research by D. S. Brewer, 'The Fabliaux', in Companion to Chaucer Studies, ed. Rowland, pp. 296–325.

26 See the valuable article by E. T. Donaldson, 'Idiom of Popular Poetry in the Miller's Tale', English Institute Essays, 1950 (New York, 1951), pp. 116–40, repr. in Speaking of Chaucer, pp. 13–29. There are similar observations in Paul E. Beichner, 'Characterization in The Miller's Tale', Schoeck–Taylor, I, 117–29.

27 See the discussion in Gradon, pp. 283–97. The whole chapter on 'Medieval

Notes

Realism' is full of helpful observations on the concept of realism. On the story's background, see the excellent study by J. A. W. Bennett, *Chaucer at Oxford and at Cambridge* (Oxford, 1974), pp. 26–57.

28 See 1.798; 'solas' is also what Alison and Nicholas enjoy in bed together (1.3654).

29 There is a clear allusion to courtly love-poetry in Aleyn's 'Aube', not very elevating in the circumstances (1.4236–9). See R. E. Kaske, 'An Aube in the "Reeve's Tale"', *ELH*, 26 (1959), 295–310. Kaske stresses the parodic elements of the passage and quotes many parallels from French, Provençal and medieval German literature. On the comic aspects of the 'Reeve's Tale', see Glending Olson, 'The Reeve's Tale as a Fabliau', *MLQ*, 35 (1974), 219–30. Murray Copland's article, '*The Reeve's Tale*: Harlotrie or Sermonyng?', *MÆ*, 31 (1962), 14–32, repr. in *Geoffrey Chaucer*, ed. Erzgräber, pp. 357–80, provides a very thorough and convincing interpretation, even though he perhaps over-stresses the narrative situation a little. On the Cambridge and Trumpington background, see Bennett, *Chaucer at Oxford and at Cambridge*, pp. 86–116 and Appendix B, 'Mills and Milling' (pp. 120–3).

30 N. F. Blake, 'Geoffrey Chaucer: The Critics and the Canon', pp. 75–6, expresses some doubt, but offers no alternative.

31 See especially Murray Copland, '*The Shipman's Tale*: Chaucer and Boccaccio', *MÆ*, 35 (1966), 11–28, who comments helpfully on Chaucer's variations of the fabliau and argues persuasively that it was meant for this particular narrator from the start. Even more appreciative are John C. McGalliard, 'Characterization in Chaucer's *Shipman's Tale*', *PQ*, 54 (1975), 1–18; V. J. Scattergood, 'The Originality of *The Shipman's Tale*', *ChR*, 11 (1976–7), 210–31, and Peter Nicholson, '"The Shipman's Tale" and the Fabliaux', *ELH*, 45 (1978), 583–96 (a useful comparison with Chaucer's other fabliaux).

32 On the literary allusions and their significance, as well as on the functions of irony, see the excellent article by J. A. Burrow, 'Irony in the Merchant's Tale', *Anglia*, 75 (1957), 199–208, repr. in J. A. Burrow, *Essays on Medieval Literature* (Oxford, 1984), pp. 49–59.

33 Burrow calls the passage an 'internal monologue'. John C. McGalliard leaves the decision open: see his 'Chaucerian Comedy: The *Merchant's Tale*, Jonson, and Molière', *PQ*, 25 (1946), 343–70, esp. pp. 351–4. Bertrand Bronson argues for a separation between the story and the prologue, absent in several manuscripts and possibly an afterthought: see his 'Afterthoughts on the Merchant's Tale', *SP*, 58 (1961), 583–96. Bronson is quite right in claiming that the story is complete in itself, without any reference to the narrator. In the present (Ellesmere) version, however, it is certainly modified and enriched by the introduction.

34 See, for instance, Robert M. Jordan, 'The Non-Dramatic Disunity of the *Merchant's Tale*', *PMLA*, 78 (1968), 293–9, and in *Chaucer and the Shape of Creation*, pp. 132–51. The majority of recent studies, however, emphasizes the thematic unity of the story. See Burrow, and, with particular emphasis on the concluding episode, Karl P. Wentersdorf, 'Theme and Structure in *The Merchant's Tale*: The Function of the Pluto Episode', *PMLA*, 80 (1965), 522–7.

35 On Chaucer's use of the *Miroir*, see John C. McGalliard, 'Chaucer's *Merchant's Tale* and Deschamps' *Miroir de Mariage*', *PQ*, 25 (1946), 193–220. Important excerpts from Deschamps, as well as other sources and parallels, are given in Bryan–Dempster, pp. 333–56.

Notes

36 On the old knight's blindness, see Paul A. Olson, 'Chaucer's Merchant and January's "Hevene in Erthe Heere"', *ELH*, 28 (1961), 203–14. His blindness is seen as a sign of the sin of avarice, which seems a little one-sided.

37 This aspect is brought out very well in Burrow's essay, cited above, n. 32.

38 See *The Canterbury Tales*, I.1761 (the 'Knight's Tale'), v.479 (the 'Squire's Tale') and *The Legend of Good Women*, F, 503 (G, 491).

39 See Margaret Schlauch, 'Chaucer's *Merchant's Tale* and Courtly Love', *ELH*, 4 (1937), 201–22. She bases her discussion on a rather narrow concept of 'courtly love': C. Hugh Holman, 'Courtly Love in the Merchant's and the Franklin's Tales', *ELH*, 18 (1951), 241–58, also takes a rather too negative view.

40 Most critics of the tale comment on the garden motif. See D. W. Robertson's influential essay, 'The Doctrine of Charity in Mediaeval Literary Gardens: A Topical Approach through Symbolism and Allegory', *Speculum*, 26 (1951), 24–49. The application of his findings to the 'Merchant's Tale', however, is somewhat one-sided. See Alfred L. Kellogg, 'Susannah and the *Merchant's Tale*', *Speculum*, 35 (1960), 275–9, where some parallels between Chaucer's tale and the well-known apocryphal Old Testament story of Susannah in the bath are convincingly pointed out.

41 On the ambiguous function of the allusions to the Song of Songs, see Peter Dronke, *Poetic Individuality in the Middle Ages: New Departures in Poetry 1000–1150* (Oxford, 1970), pp. 198–9. Gertrude M. White, '"Hoolynesse or Dotage": The Merchant's January', *PQ*, 44 (1965), 397–404, argues against any one-sided condemnation of Januarie.

42 This is the view of Whittock (*A Reading*, pp. 280–5). Howard (p. 300) argues that the story is 'a perfect choice for the last tale', but I find some of his observations somewhat far-fetched. See the long footnote by Ruggiers on critical opinions (pp. 247–8), and Cooper, pp. 195–200. On the Manciple's individual style, see the subtle study by V. J. Scattergood, 'The Manciple's Manner of Speaking', *EC*, 24 (1974), 124–46. See also R. D. Fulk, 'Reinterpreting the Manciple's Tale', *JEGP*, 78 (1979), 485–93.

43 The great number of satirical digs against friars has often been pointed out. For references see Brewer's article in *Companion to Chaucer Studies*, ed. Rowland, referred to above, n. 25. On the historical background, see Arnold Williams, 'Chaucer and the Friars', *Speculum*, 28 (1953), 499–513, and Nicholas Havely, 'Chaucer, Boccaccio and the Friars', in *Chaucer and the Italian Trecento*, ed. Boitani, pp. 249–68. See also the lively and still useful study by J. J. Jusserand, *English Wayfaring Life in the Middle Ages* (London, 1889: University Paperbacks, 1961), especially the chapter 'Wandering Preachers and Friars', and G. R. Owst, *Literature and Pulpit in Medieval England*, 2nd edn (Oxford, 1961), pp. 161–3, where a similar homiletic story is quoted.

44 See the interesting and helpful interpretations of the 'Canon's Yeoman's Tale' in Muscatine, pp. 213–21, in Ruggiers, pp. 131–41, and in Howard, pp. 292–8. See also John Gardner, 'The Canon's Yeoman's Prologue and Tale': An Interpretation', *PQ*, 46 (1967), 1–17, and Jackson J. Campbell, 'The Canon's Yeoman as Imperfect Paradigm', *ChR*, 17 (1982–3), 171–81.

45 See Whittock, pp. 179–84. He seems to me to overstate the tale's function within the framework. That there is rather more to the tale than has often been recognized is shown by Anne Middleton in her excellent study, '*The Physician's*

Tale and Love's Martyrs: "Ensamples mo than ten" as a Method in the *Canterbury Tales*', *ChR*, 8 (1973–4), 9–32. Middleton is particularly helpful on the context of the tale and some poetological implications.

46 'The *Physician's Tale* presents ethical complexities evoked by no other version of the story' (Middleton, p. 14). This, as she points out, has a profound effect on our response: 'most of Chaucer's changes in his sources assure that we *will* be uneasy, that we will not be able to suspend our disbelief entirely, and forget a world of wider and more emotionally complex choices than the source tale offers, and the Canterbury narrator advocates' (p. 15). (She applies this to the 'Clerk's Tale' as well as to the 'Physician's Tale'.)

47 There is a thorough interpretation of the tale and its place within the tradition of Middle English legends in Theodor Wolpers, *Die englische Heiligenlegende des Mittelalters*, Buchreihe der Anglia, 10 (Tübingen, 1964), pp. 302–8. On the iconographical background, see the illuminating study by V. A. Kolve, 'Chaucer's *Second Nun's Tale* and the Iconography of Saint Cecilia', in *New Perspectives in Chaucer Criticism*, ed. Rose, pp. 137–74. Chaucer follows his source so closely that it is hard to detect any very personal modifications and additions. For the text, especially the *Legenda Aurea*, see Bryan–Dempster, pp. 664–84. What is, perhaps, noteworthy, is the fact that this is the only true saint's legend included by Chaucer in *The Canterbury Tales*, and it shows a heroine and wife far more spirited and self-assured than most of the ladies in the secular stories. Although she dies as a martyr, she shows none of the passive pathos of love's martyrs in *The Legend of Good Women* or elsewhere. Instead of weeping and lamenting, she laughs at her tormentors and tells the Governor to his face that he is a fool. An original and challenging view of the relationship of Chaucer's version to the tradition of the Cecilia legend is argued by Sherry L. Reames, 'The Cecilia Legend as Chaucer Inherited It and Retold It: The Disappearance of an Augustinian Ideal', *Speculum*, 55 (1980), 38–57. I find it difficult to accept all the wider implications of this study, but it certainly shows that the tale raises more interesting questions than is usually thought. See also the earlier study by the same author, 'The Sources of Chaucer's "Second Nun's Tale"', *MP*, 76 (1978–9), 111–35. Another aspect that has recently been investigated is the relation between the 'Second Nun's Tale' and the 'Canon's Yeoman's Tale'. See Bruce A. Rosenberg, 'The Contrary Tales of the Second Nun and the Canon's Yeoman', *ChR*, 2 (1967–8), 278–91, and Cooper, pp. 188–95.

48 'Verspottung kindischer Legenden' – so A. Brandl a hundred years ago, quoted approvingly by Baum, p. 75. Baum's own interpretation is a little more careful, but tends in the same direction.

49 The popular romance *Havelok*, probably written by a learned clerk or cleric, has some even more gruesome descriptions of 'justice' administered to traitors. (*The Lay of Havelok the Dane*, ed. Walter W. Skeat, 2nd edn rev. K. Sisam (Oxford, 1915), lines 2416–511. R. J. Schoeck gives a rather negative interpretation of the legend in his 'Chaucer's Prioress: Mercy and Tender Heart', in Schoeck–Taylor, I, 245–58. I agree with Derek Pearsall who says of similar interpretations: 'Again, this view is lamentably unhistorical, and totally ignores the nature of the genre, with its sharp distinction of black and white, good and bad, in which the Jews are inevitably cast in the role of villains' ('The Canterbury Tales', p. 179).

Notes

50 See the warning by Ruggiers not 'to read one's own sensibilities into the fictional character' (p. 183, n. 9). His own interpretation is more cautious and rightly states that there is 'an irresoluble residue of ambiguity' with which we have to be content.

51 One might quote here a great deal of recent literary theory, which has taught us that every text has countless gaps to be filled by the reader's own imagination and that the 'meaning' of a text is always a complex product of the words on the page and the active cooperation of the reader's mind. For a less theoretical statement, see E. T. Donaldson's refreshing essay, 'Chaucer and the Elusion of Clarity', *E&S 1972*, 23–44.

52 The Host's interruption may, of course, also be interpreted as a tactful ending of the awed silence induced by the legend, in which he also shared. This is the view of G. H. Russell, who sharply protests against the idea that there is any irony in the tale; see 'Chaucer: *The Prioress' Tale*', in *Medieval Literature and Civilization: Studies in Memory of G. N. Garmonsway*, ed. D. A. Pearsall and R. A. Waldron (London, 1969), pp. 211–27.

53 See Marie Padgett Hamilton, 'Echoes of Childermas in the Tale of the Prioress', *MLR*, 34 (1939), 1–8, repr. (with revisions) in Wagenknecht, pp. 88–97.

54 See the chapter 'Homiletic Romances' in my *The Middle English Romances* (pp. 120–58). *Le Bone Florence of Rome* is a very typical romance of this kind, and there are a number of points in common between the 'Man of Law's Tale' and *Emare*. There is none of Chaucer's stylistic virtuosity and sophistication in these romances.

55 See Bryan–Dempster, pp. 155–206, for the texts of sources and Gower's version.

56 See Bryan–Dempster, pp. 288–331. Most interpretations comment on Chaucer's treatment of his sources. Robinson's edition also notes the most important additions. For a very thorough and perceptive summary, see Robin Kirkpatrick, 'The Griselda Story in Boccaccio, Petrarch and Chaucer', in *Chaucer and the Italian Trecento*, ed. Boitani, pp. 231–48.

57 See the stimulating chapter, 'Chaucer's Clerk's Tale as a Medieval Poem', in A. C. Spearing, *Criticism and Medieval Poetry*, 2nd edn (London, 1972), pp. 76–106. Perhaps Spearing exaggerates the Clerk's independence, but his account is full of interesting observations.

58 See above, chapter 8.

59 The most eloquent defence of the tale against ahistorical criticism is James Sledd, 'The *Clerk's Tale*: The Monsters and the Critics', *MP*, 51 (1953–4), 73–82, repr. in Wagenknecht, pp. 226–39, and in Schoeck–Taylor, 1, 160–74. He passes over the more disturbing aspects of the story a little too lightly, however.

60 See especially Elizabeth Salter, *Chaucer: The Knight's Tale and The Clerk's Tale*, pp. 37–65, where the discrepancies are very well defined, though possibly exaggerated.

61 See p. 65 of her analysis.

62 Salter and Spearing emphasize this aspect. See the often quoted passage where Griseldis looks back on the early stage of their love with a pathetic sense of loss that also seems to imply a thinly veiled reproach:

> O goode God! how gentil and how kynde
> Ye semed by youre speche and youre visage
> The day that maked was oure mariage!

> But sooth is seyd – algate I fynde it trewe,
> For in effect it preeved is on me –
> Love is noght oold as whan that it is newe.   (IV.852–7)

63 This is not to deny that there is a genuine problem here, but I doubt whether the state of the textual tradition will ever make a solution possible.

64 A notorious example of a 'historical' or topical reading is Leslie Hotson, 'Colfox vs. Chauntecleer', *PMLA*, 39 (1924), 762–81, repr. in Wagenknecht, pp. 98–116.

65 The stylistic range of the story is particularly well described in Muscatine, pp. 237–43; he very aptly calls the tale 'above all brilliant, varied, a virtuoso performance' (p. 237).

66 See the excellent essay by Jill Mann, 'The *Speculum Stultorum* and the *Nun's Priest's Tale*', *ChR*, 9 (1974–5), 262–82, with very perceptive comments on Chaucer's use of the animal fable.

67 See Heiner Gillmeister, *Discrecioun. Chaucer und die Via Regia*, Studien zur englischen Literatur, 8 (Bonn, 1972), for some very stimulating and some rather speculative ideas on this point and many other problems in connection with the 'Nun's Priest's Tale'.

68 This is the view of Stephen Manning, 'The Nun's Priest's Morality and the Medieval Attitude Towards Fables', *JEGP*, 59 (1960), 403–16, with a wealth of useful material from medieval discussions of fables. More positive is the account by R. T. Lenaghan, 'The Nun's Priest's Fable', *PMLA*, 78 (1963), 300–7. He aptly calls the tale a 'sophisticated fable' (p. 307) and offers a useful survey of its rhetorical diversity and background. See also A. Paul Schallers, 'The "Nun's Priest's Tale": An Ironic Exemplum', *ELH*, 42 (1975), 319–37.

Further reading

This is a very selective bibliography. It lists only books I have found particularly useful or stimulating and want to recommend to the reader.

Bibliographies

Baird, Lorrayne Y. *A Bibliography of Chaucer, 1964–1973*. Boston, Mass.: G. K. Hall, 1979. (A systematic and complete list of everything published on Chaucer between 1964 and 1973.)

Baugh, Albert C. *Chaucer*, Goldentree Bibliographies. 2nd edn. Arlington Heights, Ill.: AHM Publ. Corp., 1977. (A very useful compact bibliography.)

Crawford, William R. *Bibliography of Chaucer 1954–63*. Seattle: University of Washington Press, 1967. (See Baird.)

Griffith, Dudley David. *Bibliography of Chaucer 1908–53*. Seattle: University of Washington Press, 1955. (See Baird and Crawford.)

Hammond, Eleanor Prescott. *Chaucer: A Bibliographical Manual*. New York: Macmillan, 1908. (A useful guide to early Chaucer criticism.)

Rowland, Beryl, ed. *Companion to Chaucer Studies*. Revised edn. New York: Oxford University Press, 1979. (A particularly helpful survey of scholarship on Chaucer's poetry, with articles by various authors on individual poems and aspects, and with excellent bibliographies.)

An annual Chaucer-bibliography is published in *The Chaucer Review*.

Editions

Baugh, Albert C., ed. *Chaucer's Major Poetry*. New York: Appleton–Century–Crofts, 1963; London: Routledge, 1963. (A very useful commented edition which contains nearly all the poetry.)

Blake, N. F., ed. *The Canterbury Tales by Geoffrey Chaucer. Edited from the Hengwrt Manuscript*, York Medieval Texts, 2nd series. London: Edward Arnold, 1980. (An unusual edition, presenting Chaucer's text in a rather unfamiliar form; useful for comparison with the traditional (Ellesmere) text; with glossarial and explanatory notes.)

Brewer, D. S., ed. *The Parlement of Foulys*, Nelson's Medieval and Renaissance Library. London: Nelson, 1960; 2nd edn Manchester: Manchester University Press, 1972. (By far the best single edition of this poem, with very good commentary.)

Donaldson, E. Talbot, ed. *Chaucer's Poetry: An Anthology for the Modern Reader*.

New York: Ronald Press, 1958. (Contains nearly all the poetry, with particularly helpful and original commentary and useful glosses.)

Fisher, John H., ed. *The Complete Poetry and Prose of Geoffrey Chaucer.* New York: Holt, Rinehart and Winston, 1977. (Another useful edition, with explanatory notes.)

Manly, John M. and Edith Rickert. *The Text of the Canterbury Tales: Studied on the Basis of all Known Manuscripts.* 8 vols. Chicago, Ill.: University of Chicago Press, 1940. (Indispensable for studying the transmission and the textual variants.)

Robinson, F. N., ed. *The Works of Geoffrey Chaucer*, 2nd edn. Boston, Mass.: Houghton Mifflin, 1957; London: Oxford University Press, 1957. (This is the 'standard' edition, with full notes and commentary, a little out of date in bibliographical matters; all quotations in my text come from this edition.)

Root, Robert Kilburn, ed. *The Book of Troilus and Criseyde. By Geoffrey Chaucer. Edited from all the Known Manuscripts.* Princeton, N.J.: Princeton University Press, 1926. (A very full and helpful edition, though largely superseded now by Windeatt's edition.)

Skeat, Walter W., ed. *The Complete Works of Chaucer.* 6 vols. and supplement. Oxford: Clarendon Press, 1894–7. (The fullest edition to date, still useful for textual information.)

Windeatt, B. A., ed. *Geoffrey Chaucer: 'Troilus and Criseyde'. A New Edition of 'The Book of Troilus'.* London: Longman, 1984. (A splendid and indispensable edition, with full textual apparatus, explanatory notes and the complete text of Boccaccio's *Il Filostrato* on the same page.)

Anthologies of criticism

Barney, Stephen A., ed. *Chaucer's Troilus: Essays in Criticism.* Hamden, Conn.: Shoe String Press, 1980. (A useful collection of seventeen essays, three of them printed here for the first time.)

Brewer, Derek, ed. *Chaucer: The Critical Heritage.* 2 vols. London: Routledge, 1978. (An indispensable collection of comment and criticism ranging from 1385 to 1933, with good introductions.)

Burrow, J. A., ed. *Geoffrey Chaucer: A Critical Anthology*, Penguin Critical Anthologies. Harmondsworth: Penguin Books, 1969. (A very informative collection of critical comment from the time of Chaucer: short excerpts rather than full essays.)

Erzgräber, Willi, ed. *Geoffrey Chaucer*, Wege der Forschung, 253. Darmstadt: Wissenschaftliche Buchgesellschaft, 1983. (Twenty essays on various aspects of Chaucer's poetry, sixteen of them in English; with a good bibliography.)

Schoeck, Richard J., and Jerome Taylor, eds. *Chaucer Criticism, Vol. 1: 'The Canterbury Tales'.* Notre Dame, Ind.: University of Notre Dame Press, 1960. (Sixteen essays or excerpts from books.)

Chaucer Criticism, Vol. 2: 'Troilus and Criseyde' and the Minor Poems. Notre Dame, Ind.: University of Notre Dame Press, 1961. (Seventeen essays, all previously published.)

Spurgeon, Caroline F. E., ed. *Five Hundred Years of Chaucer Criticism and Allusion 1357–1900.* 3 vols. Cambridge: Cambridge University Press, 1925. (A valuable collection of material of Chaucer criticism and comment through five centuries.)

Wagenknecht, Edward. *Chaucer: Modern Essays in Criticism*. New York: Oxford University Press, 1959. (Twenty-six essays, previously published.)

General surveys and introductions

Baum, Paull F. *Chaucer: A Critical Appreciation*. Durham, N.C.: Duke University Press, 1958.

Brewer, Derek. *An Introduction to Chaucer*. London: Longman, 1984. (Largely rewritten and augmented version of Brewer's particularly sound and stimulating *Chaucer*, 3rd edn, revised and with additional material. London: Longman, 1973.)

Bronson, Bertrand H. *In Search of Chaucer*. Toronto: University of Toronto Press, 1960. (A very lively and intelligent brief critical survey.)

Burlin, Robert B. *Chaucerian Fiction*. Princeton, N.J.: Princeton University Press, 1977. ('Close reading' of all the major works.)

Coghill, Nevill. *The Poet Chaucer*. 2nd edn. London: Oxford University Press, 1967. (A masterly brief survey.)

Hussey, Maurice, A. C. Spearing, and James Winney. *An Introduction to Chaucer*. Cambridge: Cambridge University Press, 1965. (A brief introduction to the study of Chaucer, on the background rather than on the poems.)

Hussey, S. S. *Chaucer: An Introduction*. 2nd edn. London: Methuen, 1981. (A well-balanced introduction for the student.)

Kane, George. *Chaucer*, Past Masters. Oxford: Oxford University Press, 1984. (A very brief, but concise and useful, survey for the non-specialist; good on the historical and literary background.)

Kean, P. M. *Chaucer and the Making of English Poetry*. 2 vols. Vol. 1: *Love Vision and Debate*; Vol. 2: *The Art of Narrative*. London: Routledge, 1972. (A very thorough and informative survey, particularly good on the literary context.)

Kittredge, George Lyman. *Chaucer and His Poetry*. Cambridge, Mass.: Harvard University Press, 1915. (A classic survey, lively and full of seminal ideas.)

Lawlor, John. *Chaucer*. London: Hutchinson, 1968. (A stimulating critical survey.)

Malone, Kemp. *Chapters on Chaucer*. Baltimore, Md: Johns Hopkins Press, 1951. (Sound essays on various poems and aspects.)

Muscatine, Charles. *Chaucer and the French Tradition: A Study in Style and Meaning*. Berkeley: University of California Press, 1957. (One of the most influential books on Chaucer's style and his relation to European traditions, with excellent analyses of the major works.)

Preston, Raymond. *Chaucer*. London: Sheed & Ward, 1952. (Good general survey.)

Robertson, D. W., Jr. *A Preface to Chaucer: Studies in Medieval Perspectives*. Princeton, N.J.: Princeton University Press, 1962. (A very controversial book, with a heavy emphasis on allegorical and doctrinal aspects; not an introduction, but a very original and learned exposition of the background.)

Shelly, Percy Van Dyke. *The Living Chaucer*. Philadelphia: University of Pennsylvania Press, 1940. (Lively general introduction.)

Speirs, John. *Chaucer the Maker*. 2nd edn. London: Faber, 1951. (Refreshingly undogmatic and original, though a little dated and ahistorical in places.)

Further reading

More specialized studies

Aers, David. *Chaucer, Langland, and the Creative Imagination*. London: Routledge, 1980.

Allen, Judson Boyce, and Theresa Anne Moritz. *A Distinction of Stories: The Medieval Unity of Chaucer's Fair Chain of Narratives for Canterbury*. Columbus: Ohio State University Press, 1981. (A brilliant beginning, on medieval concepts of literary interpretation, but not so convincing in its application to Chaucer's text.)

Baldwin, Ralph. *The Unity of the Canterbury Tales*, Anglistica, 5. Copenhagen: Rosenkilde & Bagger, 1955. (A very influential book on the thematic unity of Chaucer's collection and its frame.)

Bennett, J. A. W. *Chaucer at Oxford and at Cambridge*. Oxford: Clarendon Press, 1974. (A particularly instructive as well as entertaining study, especially on the background of the 'Miller's Tale' and the 'Reeve's Tale'.)

Chaucer's Book of Fame: An Exposition of The House of Fame. Oxford: Clarendon Press, 1968.

The Parlement of Foules: An Interpretation. Oxford: Clarendon Press, 1957. (A thorough and helpful study.)

Blake, N. F. *The Textual Tradition of the Canterbury Tales*. London: Arnold, 1985. (A very useful and informative survey of the problems of transmission, of manuscript tradition and of editorial difficulties.)

Boitani, Piero. *Chaucer and the Imaginary World of Fame*, Chaucer Studies, 10. Cambridge: D. S. Brewer, 1984. (An invaluable and wide-ranging study of *The House of Fame* and its background, especially the tradition of Fame.)

ed. *Chaucer and the Italian Trecento*. Cambridge: Cambridge University Press, 1983. (An indispensable collection of essays by various authors on Chaucer's Italian sources and influences.)

Brewer, D. S., ed. *Chaucer and Chaucerians: Critical Studies in Middle English Literature*. London: Nelson, 1966. (A valuable collection of critical essays on individual poems and various aspects of Chaucer's art.)

ed. *Geoffrey Chaucer*, Writers and their Background. London: G. Bell, 1974. (A very useful collection of essays on many aspects of Chaucer's background, literary, philosophical, and in the arts; with a good survey of scholarship.)

Burnley, J. D. *Chaucer's Language and the Philosopher's Tradition*, Chaucer Studies, 2. Cambridge: D. S. Brewer, 1979. (A stimulating study of various concepts – tyrant, philosopher, reason, gentil man – in Chaucer's poetry and of their meaning.)

Burnley, David. *A Guide to Chaucer's Language*. London: Macmillan, 1983. (A very helpful introduction to many aspects of Chaucer's language.)

Clemen, Wolfgang. *Chaucer's Early Poetry*, trans. C. A. M. Sym. London: Methuen, 1963. (Perhaps still the best guide to the literary art of Chaucer's early poems.)

Cooper, Helen. *The Structure of the Canterbury Tales*. London: Duckworth, 1983. (A very sensible and useful study.)

Curry, Walter Clyde. *Chaucer and the Medieval Sciences*. 2nd edn. London: Allen & Unwin, 1960. (Very useful on Chaucer's 'scientific' background in the widest sense.)

David, Alfred. *The Strumpet Muse: Art and Morals in Chaucer's Poetry*. Bloomington: Indiana University Press, 1977. (An independent and challenging study of the subject of the moral basis of poetry.)

Donaldson, E. Talbot. *Speaking of Chaucer*. London: Athlone Press, 1970. (An important collection of essays, most of them previously published, some of them very influential and all of them well worth reading.)

Eliason, Norman E. *The Language of Chaucer's Poetry: An Appraisal of the Verse, Style, and Structure*, Anglistica, 17. Copenhagen: Rosenkilde & Bagger, 1972. (Not as technical as the title might suggest, with many original observations and interesting ideas.)

Frank, Robert Worth, Jr. *Chaucer and 'The Legend of Good Women'*. Cambridge, Mass.: Harvard University Press, 1972. (The first thorough and sympathetic study of this story-collection.)

Gordon, Ida L. *The Double Sorrow of Troilus: A Study of Ambiguities in Troilus and Criseyde*. Oxford: Clarendon Press, 1970.

Hermann, John P., and John J. Burke, Jr, eds. *Signs and Symbols in Chaucer's Poetry*. University: University of Alabama Press, 1981. (An interesting collection of essays on the 'Robertsonian' approach to Chaucer, by no means uniform in their method.)

Howard, Donald R. *The Idea of the Canterbury Tales*. Berkeley: University of California Press, 1976. (An ambitious and wide-ranging study, perhaps more convincing by its acute observations on the text than by its overall thesis.)

Huppé, Bernard F., and D. W. Robertson, Jr. *Fruyt and Chaf: Studies in Chaucer's Allegories*. Princeton, N.J.: Princeton University Press, 1963. (A rather controversial and one-sided study.)

Jordan, Robert M. *Chaucer and the Shape of Creation: The Aesthetic Possibilities of Inorganic Structure*. Cambridge, Mass.: Harvard University Press, 1967. (A stimulating study, perhaps a little too generalizing.)

Kiser, Lisa J. *Telling Classical Tales: Chaucer and the 'Legend of Good Women'*. Ithaca, N.Y.: Cornell University Press, 1983. (A very thoughtful and interesting study.)

Kolve, V. A. *Chaucer and the Imagery of Narrative: The First Five Canterbury Tales*. London: Arnold, 1984. (A very original and beautifully illustrated book on the iconographic background of Chaucer's narrative art.)

Lawler, Traugott. *The One and the Many in the Canterbury Tales*. Hamden, Conn.: Shoe String Press, 1980. (A stimulating study on the principle of diversity and unity in *The Canterbury Tales*.)

Lawrence, William Witherle. *Chaucer and the Canterbury Tales*. New York: Columbia University Press, 1950. (A sensible and helpful survey.)

Lumiansky, R. M. *Of Sondry Folk: The Dramatic Principle in the Canterbury Tales*. Austin, Tex.: University of Texas Press, 1955.

McCall, John P. *Chaucer among the Gods: The Poetics of Classical Myth*. University Park: Pennsylvania State University Press, 1979. (An important study of an often neglected subject.)

Mann, Jill. *Chaucer and Medieval Estates Satire: The Literature of Social Classes and the General Prologue to the 'Canterbury Tales'*. Cambridge: Cambridge University Press, 1973. (By far the best study of the 'General Prologue' and its literary background.)

Minnis, Alistair. *Chaucer and Pagan Antiquity*, Chaucer Studies, 8. Cambridge: D. S.

Brewer, 1982. (A very original and helpful study of an interesting theme.)

Norton-Smith, John. *Geoffrey Chaucer*, Medieval Authors. London: Routledge, 1974. (Good on the literary background.)

Owen, Charles A., Jr. *Pilgrimage and Storytelling in the Canterbury Tales: The Dialectic of 'Ernest' and 'Game'*. Norman: University of Oklahoma Press, 1977. (Interesting, if sometimes a little hypothetical, on the structure of the collection.)

Payne, Robert O. *The Key of Remembrance: A Study of Chaucer's Poetics*. New Haven, Conn.: Yale University Press, 1963. (A very important study.)

Pearsall, Derek. *The Canterbury Tales*, Unwin Critical Library. London: Allen & Unwin, 1985. (An excellent comprehensive survey of facts and problems, covering most aspects.)

Rose, Donald M., ed. *New Perspectives in Chaucer Criticism*. Norman: University of Oklahoma Press, 1981. (An interesting collection of essays on various aspects of Chaucer's poetry.)

Ruggiers, Paul G. *The Art of the Canterbury Tales*. Madison: University of Wisconsin Press, 1965. (A very sensible and useful study taking full account of earlier scholarship.)

ed. *Editing Chaucer: The Great Tradition*. Norman, Okla.: Pilgrim Books, 1984. (An interesting account of the most distinguished editors and their contribution to our understanding of the text.)

Salu, Mary, ed. *Essays on Troilus and Criseyde*. Chaucer Studies, 3. Cambridge: D. S. Brewer, 1979. (A very interesting collection of original essays by various authors.)

Steadman, John M. *Disembodied Laughter: 'Troilus' and the Apotheosis Tradition. A Reexamination of Narrative and Thematic Contexts*. Berkeley: University of California Press, 1972. (A very learned and helpful study of the ending of *Troilus and Criseyde* and the traditions behind it.)

Whittock, Trevor. *A Reading of the Canterbury Tales*. Cambridge: Cambridge University Press, 1968. (An undogmatic account, taking its standards from modern rather than from medieval poetry.)

Wood, Chauncey. *Chaucer and the Country of the Stars: Poetic Uses of Astrological Imagery*. Princeton, N.J.: Princeton University Press, 1970. (An important book on an interesting subject, perhaps a little speculative in places.)

Background: literary and historical

Bennett, H. S. *Chaucer and the Fifteenth Century*, The Oxford History of English Literature, 2: 1. Oxford: Clarendon Press, 1947. (Useful on the background, though somewhat out of date.)

Bloomfield, Morton W. *Essays and Explorations: Studies in Ideas, Language, and Literature*. Cambridge, Mass.: Harvard University Press, 1970. (Contains some very good essays on Chaucer, previously published.)

Boitani, Piero. *English Medieval Narrative in the Thirteenth and Fourteenth Centuries*, trans. Joan Krakover Hall. Cambridge: Cambridge University Press, 1982. (A very good and original survey; just over half the book is on Chaucer.)

Bolton, W. F., ed. *The Middle Ages* (Vol. 3 of *History of Literature in the English Language*, 12 vols.). London: Sphere Books, 1970. (Some excellent essays on Chaucer.)

Further reading

Brewer, Derek. *Chaucer in His Time*. London: Longman, 1963. (A masterly introduction to life and thought in Chaucer's time, with helpful illustrations.)

Bryan, W. F., and Germaine Dempster. *Sources and Analogues of Chaucer's Canterbury Tales* (1941). New York: Humanities Press, 1958. (An indispensable collection of texts.)

Burrow, J. A. *Essays on Medieval Literature*. Oxford: Clarendon Press, 1984. (A very interesting collection of essays, not all of them previously published; three of them on Chaucer.)

Ricardian Poetry: Chaucer, Gower, Langland and the 'Gawain' Poet. London: Routledge, 1971. (A very original and stimulating study, showing some surprising affinities between these English poets.)

Crow, Martin M., and Clair C. Olson, eds. *Chaucer Life-Records*. Oxford: Clarendon Press, 1966. (An indispensable collection of documents.)

Esch, Arno, ed. *Chaucer und seine Zeit, Symposion für Walter F. Schirmer*, Buchreihe der Anglia, 14. Tübingen: Niemeyer, 1968. (A collection of essays, mostly on Chaucer and his contemporaries, more than half of them in English.)

Everett, Dorothy. *Essays on Middle English Literature*, ed. Patricia Kean. Oxford: Clarendon Press, 1955, repr. 1959. (An important collection of original essays, about half of them on Chaucer.)

Gradon, Pamela. *Form and Style in Early English Literature*. London: Methuen, 1971. (A valuable discussion of some general aspects of medieval literature.)

Green, Richard Firth. *Poets and Princepleasers: Literature and the English Court in the Late Middle Ages*. Toronto: Toronto University Press, 1980. (A very important and useful book.)

Havely, N. R., ed. & trans. *Chaucer's Boccaccio: Sources of 'Troilus' and the 'Knight's' and 'Franklin's Tales'*, Chaucer Studies, 3. Cambridge: D. S. Brewer, 1980. (Very useful source-material.)

Jusserand, J. J. *English Wayfaring Life in the Middle Ages*, trans. Lucy Toulmin Smith (1889). London: Methuen, 1961. (A classic account of roadside life in the English Middle Ages, still instructive and entertaining to read.)

Lewis, C. S. *The Allegory of Love. A Study in Medieval Tradition*. Oxford: Clarendon Press, 1936. (A brilliant and influential account of the allegorical tradition from Prudentius to Spenser, with a lively chapter on Chaucer.)

The Discarded Image: An Introduction to Medieval and Renaissance Literature. Cambridge: Cambridge University Press, 1964. (A very lucid and challenging exposition of some fundamental ideas and authors.)

Loomis, Roger Sherman. *A Mirror of Chaucer's World*. Princeton, N.J.: Princeton University Press, 1965. (A competently and beautifully presented pictorial guide to the age of Chaucer.)

McKisack, May. *The Fourteenth Century, 1307–99*, The Oxford History of England, 5. Oxford: Clarendon Press, 1959. (One of the best historical surveys of the period.)

Medcalf, Stephen, ed. *The Later Middle Ages*, The Context of English Literature. London: Methuen, 1981. (Some good essays on art, society and religion in the later Middle Ages.)

Mehl, Dieter. *The Middle English Romances of the Thirteenth and Fourteenth Centuries*. London: Routledge, 1968. (Discusses many of the narrative texts Chaucer must have read or heard.)

Further reading

Miller, Robert P., ed. *Chaucer: Sources and Backgrounds.* New York: Oxford University Press, 1977. (A very useful collection of texts, often brief excerpts, from a great variety of sources.)

Myers, A. R. *England in the Late Middle Ages*, The Pelican History of England, 4. Harmondsworth: Penguin Books, 1952. (A good brief account, frequently reprinted.)

London in the Age of Chaucer. Norman: University of Oklahoma Press, 1972. (A very helpful background study.)

ed. *English Historical Documents, 1327–1485*, English Historical Documents, 4. London: Oxford University Press, 1969. (A very comprehensive collection of documents of many different kinds.)

Owst, G. R. *Literature and Pulpit in Medieval England: A Neglected Chapter in the History of English Letters & of the English People.* 2nd edn. Oxford: Blackwell, 1961. (A very important book on sermon literature and its impact.)

Pearsall, Derek. *Old English and Middle English Poetry*, The Routledge History of English Poetry, 1. London: Routledge, 1977. (An excellent and stimulating account.)

and Elizabeth Salter. *Landscapes and Seasons of the Medieval World.* London: Elek, 1973. (A very original and beautifully illustrated study of a fascinating subject.)

Rickert, Edith. *Chaucer's World*, ed. Clair C. Olson and Martin M. Crow. New York: Columbia University Press, 1948. (A very useful collection of contemporary materials.)

Rowland, Beryl, ed. *Chaucer and Middle English Studies in Honour of Rossell Hope Robbins.* London: Allen & Unwin, 1974. (Thirty-six essays, the majority on Chaucer.)

Salter, Elizabeth. *Fourteenth-Century English Poetry: Contexts and Readings*, ed. Derek Pearsall and Nicolette Zeeman. Oxford: Clarendon Press, 1983. (Some very interesting and challenging chapters, on literature and society, regional distribution and Chaucer's originality.)

Scattergood, V. J., and J. W. Sherborne, eds. *English Court Culture in the Late Middle Ages.* London: Duckworth, 1983. (An important collection of papers read at a Bristol conference.)

Spearing, A. C. *Criticism and Medieval Poetry.* 2nd edn. London: Arnold, 1972. (An interesting book on the problems of interpreting medieval literature, with two good chapters on Chaucer.)

Medieval Dream Poetry. Cambridge: Cambridge University Press, 1976. (A balanced survey, with a long chapter on Chaucer.)

Windeatt, B. A. *Chaucer's Dream Poetry: Sources and Analogues.* Cambridge: Cambridge University Press, 1982. (A very useful edition of important texts Chaucer must have known well.)

Index

Index

Index

David. A., 214
Davis, N., 213
Dempster, G., 218, 222, 226, 228, 229
Deschamps, E.: *Miroir de Mariage*, 180, 226
Dickens, C.: *Pickwick Papers*, 9
Donaldson, E. T., 10–11, 206, 209, 214, 216, 221, 225, 229
Donovan, M. O., 225
dream–vision, 15, 16, 17–18, 23–4, 26, 27–8, 29, 30, 31–2, 35, 38, 40–1, 53, 54–5, 57, 67, 71, 98–9, 102, 130, 131–2, 141, 208
Dronke, P., 209, 211, 214, 215, 216, 227
Du Boulay, F. R. H., 206
Duke of Ulster, 2
Dunning, T. P., 213, 214
Durling, R. M., 214, 215, 216

Edward III, 2
Eliason, N. E., 208, 210, 222
Emare, 229
Emslie, M., 211
Erdmann, A., 220
Erzgräber, W., 224, 225, 226
Esch, A., 209, 215, 224
estates satire, 50–1, 133, 136–40, 142, 143, 144, 146, 147, 148, 220
Everett, D., 211, 214
exemplum, 26, 38, 86, 95, 106, 118, 148, 158, 184, 187, 188, 189, 190, 191, 196, 203, 204

fabliau, 38, 72, 76, 78, 82, 116, 130, 148, 157, 158, 162, 167, 171, 172–84, 187, 225, 226
Faulkner, W.: *The Sound and the Fury*, 11
Fielding, H., 83, 97
Foote, P., 216
Fox, D., 207
Frank, R. W., Jr, 109–10, 114, 210, 211, 217, 218
Froissart, J., 26
Frost, W., 223
Fulk, R. D., 227
Furnivall, F. J., 220

Galway, M., 206
Gardner, J., 227
Gawain-Poet, 209; *Pearl*, 16, 35, 205; *Sir Gawain and the Green Knight*, 16, 21, 164, 215
Gaylord, A. T., 215, 216, 224, 225
Geoffrey of Monmouth, 61
Geoffrey of Vinsauf, 201
Gillmeister, H., 206, 230
Godman, P., 217

Goedsche, C., 206
Göller, K. H., 224, 225
Goethe, J. W., 3
Gordon, I. L., 214, 215, 216
Gordon, R. K., 213
Gower, J., 112, 190; *Confessio Amantis*, 218, 229
Gradon, P., 211, 225
Gray, D., 217
Green, R. E., 206
Griffin, N. E., 213

Haller, R., 224, 225
Hamilton, M. P., 229
Hansen, E. T., 217, 218
Harvey, J., 210
Havely, N. R., 224, 227
Havelok the Dane, 228
Henry IV, 3
Hermann, J. P., 217
Herzman, R. B., 224
Hinckley, H. B., 222
Hoffman, A. W., 220
Holman, C. H., 227
Homer, 61, 212
Hotson, L., 230
Howard, D. R., 206, 207, 209, 222, 223, 227
Hulbert, J. R., 221
Hume, K., 225
Huppé, B. F., 209, 210, 211, 222
Hussey, M., 220
Hussey, S. S., 215, 221

John of Gaunt (Duke of Lancaster), 3–4, 22, 24, 28–9, 30, 34, 36, 209
Jones, T., 220, 224
Jonson, B., 226
Jordan, R. M., 216, 219, 223, 226
Joseph, B., 214
Josephus, 61
Jusserand, J. J., 227

Käsmann, H., 215, 216
Kane, G., 207, 217, 221
Kaske, R. E., 226
Kean, P., 206, 208, 210, 211, 212, 214, 222, 224
Keller, J. E., 208
Kellogg, A. L., 221, 227
Kellogg, R., 206
Kirby, T., 220
Kirkpatrick, R., 229
Kiser, L. J., 207, 217, 218
Kittredge, G. L., 126, 143, 219, 222

Index

Index